BIOGRAPHICAL SKETCHES

OF EMINENT

MUSICAL COMPOSERS.

ARRANGED IN CHRONOLOGICAL ORDER.

BY

L. B. URBINO.

———•———

BOSTON:
OLIVER DITSON COMPANY.
NEW YORK: CHICAGO: PHILA: BOSTON:
C. H. Ditson & Co. Lyon & Healy. J. E. Ditson & Co. John C. Haynes & Co.

PREFACE.

IN writing these Biographical Sketches which we now present to the public, we have consulted Brockhaus, Clément, Fétis, Schoelcher, Schmidt, Hilgenfeldt, Weber (Max), Lampadius, Jahn. Nissen, and many other valuable works, hoping to make such selections as would interest and instruct those students of music who have little time to read elaborate works on the great masters whom we all admire.

We have introduced the names of several old worthies whose works, though at present almost passed into forgetfulness, were fully appreciated in their day, and served for the foundation on which others have firmly built.

That some sketches are longer than others, is owing to the material from which we selected, rather than our interest in, or the real merits of, the musician.

That this little work may meet the approbation of those interested in art, is the wish of the writer.

L. B. URBINO.

BIOGRAPHICAL SKETCHES

OF

MUSICAL COMPOSERS.

GABRIELI.

1510–1586.

ANDREA GABRIELI, one of the most distinguished composers of the sixteenth century, was born in Venice, 1510. In 1536 he became a singer in the Ducal Chapel, and in 1556 organist at St. Mark's, which position he retained during his life.

Many of Gabrieli's compositions, such as madrigals, organ-music, &c., were published in Nuremburg and Antwerp.

ORLANDO DI LASSO.

1520–1593.

ORLANDO LASSO, or Roland de Lattre, one of the greatest composers of the sixteenth century, is the prince of the Franco-Belgian Pleiades of musicians, who at that time filled Europe with their harmonious productions. Roland de Lattre was born at Mons in 1520. It is said that when, as a choir-boy, he sang in the Church of St. Nicholas, the beauty of his voice attracted the attention of Ferdinado Gonzaga, a general in the service of Char es V., vice-king of Sicily. After much solicitation on the part of the general, the parents of the young Roland consented to place their son under his protection. Ferdinand took him first to St. Dedice, then to Milan and Sicily. At the age of eighteen we find him in Naples with the Marquis of Terza. His reputation must have been well established at this time; for, on going to Rome, he was handsomely received by the cardinal-archbishop of Florence, with whom he remained several months. A still better proof of the high estimation in which his talents were held is, that he was soon after appointed chapelmaster of the Church of St. Latran. It was about this time that he published his first collection of masses.

Hearing that his parents were dangerously ill, he resigned his situation, and hastened to console them by his filial tenderness; but, alas! when he arrived at Mons they were no more.

Whilst our illustrious composer was in Antwerp, he won the friendship and esteem of Duke Albert of Bavaria, one of his ardent admirers.

At the Diet of Spire, the Emperor Maximilian conferred the title of nobility on him and his legitimate descendants. In April, 1571, Pope Gregory decorated him with the order of the Golden Spur. Charles IX., King of France, added to these honors by giving him a grand reception in Paris, and lading him with costly presents. Some time after, this French monarch invited him to direct the Chapel of the Louvre, which he accepted, and was on his way thither when he received the news of the death of the monarch. He then returned to the Duke of Bavaria, whom he had left with reluctance, and was immediately re-instated in his former position with an increase of salary. The favor that Roland enjoyed with the good duke, and which continued unchanged and unclouded during the life of this excellent prince, had no doubt been much enhanced by his marriage with Regina Weckinger, maid of honor to the reigning duchess. The new sovereign of Bavaria, William V., though more reserved and unsocial with Roland, was willing to pay generously for music, which he loved exceedingly. In 1587 he made Roland a present of a garden at Messing, on the route to Fürstenfeld, and fixed an annual pension of one hundred florins upon his wife.

Meanwhile the man of genius, who by his inspirations had held the attention of the musicians of three kingdoms during forty years, felt his strength failing, and begged permission to retire for a while in Messing. Soon, however, he returned to Munich in an alarming state of health. He had injured his brain by overwork to such a degree that death was welcome to him. He died in his seventy-fifth year, leaving six children.

The number of his sacred and profane compositions amount to seven hundred and sixty-five, many of which were published during his lifetime. The greater part of his manuscripts are preserved in the royal library of Munich.

On Corpus-Christi day of 1554, there was a violent storm in Munich. The Duke William, seeing that the procession did not go out of the church, ordered the host to be carried as far as the porch ; but scarcely had Lasso commenced singing the prescribed psalm than the rain suddenly ceased, and the sun shone forth in all its splendor. The people shouted " *A miracle*," and looked upon Di Lasso as a saint.

PALESTRINA.

1524–1594.

PALESTRINA, a small town of the Roman States, gave its name to Giovanni Pierluigi,[1] who was born there in 1524. Very little is known concerning his childhood, only that his parents were poor, and that he learned the elements of literature and music as a child of the choir. Such, in fact, was the ordinary début of many of our most celebrated composers. In 1540 he went to Rome, where he studied sacred music in the famous school founded by Gondimel. Eleven years after, Palestrina was teacher of the choir-children belonging to the chapel Gulia : he was then twenty-seven years old. Three years after, he published his first collection of compositions.

Jules III., the reigning pontiff, accepted the dedication of this collection, and was so much pleased with its author that he placed Palestrina among the choristers of the pontifical chapel, contrary to his own laws, which required examination before admission ; also, that the chapel-singers should be informed of such admission by a special order. They, little dreaming of the lustre which Palestrina was destined to shed upon their company at some future day, received him with coldness, and wrote in the chapel journal, under date of Jan. 13, 1555, that his admission was granted without their consent.

Unfortunately for Palestrina, Pope Jules III. died five weeks after; and his successor Marcel II., also a friend of the composer, held the pontifical power only three and twenty days. The famous mass known as the *Mass of Pope Marcel*[2] was written at this time. It is said that the

---

[1] He was also called Prenestino and Prænestinus, and distinguished by his contemporaries as the prince of music.

[2] "*Missa Papæ Marcelli:*" this wonderful composition is universally admired

pope, dreading the inconveniences which the use of music as an accompaniment to religious worship offered, formed a resolution to banish it from the church; but, when he heard Palestrina's mass, he changed his mind, and gave up an idea which would have been so fatal to one of the most important branches of music.

After the death of Marcel, Cardinal Caraffa, who ascended the pontifical throne under the name of Paul IV., displayed much zeal in his attempts to reform his clergy and his court. He commenced with the pontifical chapel, vigorously executing the article in the church regulations which interdicted the laity from performing the functions of choristers, three of whom, including Palestrina, belonged to the laity and were married. Palestrina had united himself when very young to a woman whose Christian name was Lucretia; and, at the time of which we are speaking, he had four children. Notwithstanding that the choristers were jealous of Palestrina, they pleaded his cause with the pope, proving that he had given up more advantageous positions to fulfil the functions for which he was so well qualified, and which, moreover, had been promised him for life; but Paul IV. was inflexible, and dismissed the three married men. However, he granted them a pension of six crowns a month.

Palestrina, far from expecting such a turn in his affairs, took it so to heart that he became seriously ill. Then it was pleasant to see the devoted attention of his former colleagues, who, with fraternal affection, did every thing in their power to comfort and relieve him.

Meanwhile he received some advantageous offers; and the 1st of October, 1555, two months after his dismissal from the pontifical chapel, he was appointed chapel-master of St. Jean de Latran.

During the five months that Palestrina held this very honorable but not particularly profitable position, he devoted his leisure to the composition of several remarkable works, among which are those celebrated religious pieces for service during Holy Week.[1]

In 1569 he published the second book of his masses, and in 1570 the third, both of which he dedicated to Philip II., King of Spain. From this time his works rapidly succeeded each other, and obtained brilliant success. In March, 1571, he was appointed chapel-master of the Vatican.

When Pope Gregory XIII. undertook to reform sacred music, he gave special charge of it to Palestrina, who it seems was in no particular hurry to do the work, for we find at his death only a choir-book completed. Hygin, son of Palestrina, continued the collection commenced by his father, and sold it as his father's work; but he was accused of fraud, his contract broken, and the manuscript put in a place of safety.

Palestrina's wife died July 21, 1580. The loss of the companion, whom he so tenderly cherished, not only made him sick, but otherwise affected him so sensibly that he became discouraged, marks of which are found in a passage of the dedication to Pope Sixtus V. Again he complained of his poverty, because he had not the means to publish his works.

---

[1] His "Improperia" and "Lamentation" are performed yearly at fixed periods in the pontifical chapel. The ceremony which accompanies the execution of this music greatly increases its effect. The altar and walls of the chapel are despoiled of their ornaments; the pictures are covered; the cardinals are dressed in serge; there is no incense, there are no candles: every thing pictures trouble and desolation. One sees the cross before which the faithful, who come two by two to worship, prostrate themselves: meanwhile the sad music reverberates through the arches of the chapel. Who can imagine the effect which this wondrous composition produced upon the hearers in Palestrina's time, accustomed as they then were only to a plain monotonous chant?

The last years of Palestrina's life were very sad. The disease which attacked him soon after the death of his wife was making such rapid progress, that he plainly saw his end was approaching. Having called his youngest son, he recommended that he should send his unpublished works to press at once.[1] He died Feb. 2, 1594.

All the musicians of Rome united in rendering homage to the memory of Palestrina. He was buried in the Vatican ; but another monument left to celebrate the great reformer of sacred music is the complete edition of a portion of his works, and his biography written by the Abbé Baini.

Notwithstanding his exquisite taste and his profound piety, Palestrina slid into the path of the musicians of the sixteenth century, in trying to treat of popular themes ; and he even composed a mass for five voices upon the famous song of the "The Armed Man." But afterwards his genius became independent and creative.

The music of Palestrina, so pure, chaste, and tranquillizing, is one of the most astonishing productions of the human mind.

MONTEVERDE.

1568–1643.

CLAUDE MONTEVERDE was born at Cremona in 1568. He belonged to a very poor family, and entered the service of the Duke of Mantua as a violin-player when he was quite a youth. All the glory that he afterwards acquired is due solely to his genius. Although there are errors in his works, yet they are filled with such beauties as only a richly endowed nature can produce.

[1] Palestrina left an enormous number of compositions, only a part of which have been published, though all glow with the fire of genius.

He went to Rome about the year 1600. In 1630 he brought out his opera, " Proserpina Rapita," with a pomp and splendor until then unknown.

Monteverde deserves to be considered as one of the most active propagators of the lyric art.

ALLEGRI.

1580–1652.

GREGORIO ALLEGRI descended from a family who had become illustrious by having given to the world a Correggio. Gregorio Allegri was born in Rome in the year 1580. After having studied music with Nanini and other good masters, he took sacred orders, and obtained a benefice in the cathedral of Fermo. About the same time he began to publish his concertos, hymns, and other sacred music. His compositions attracted the attention of Pope Urban VIII., who appointed him singing-chaplain of the papal chapel. This position he retained until his death, which took place Feb. 18, 1652. Allegri was a very pious priest ; and he was as charitable a musician as he was a scientific one. Interested in poor prisoners, his benevolence was especially exercised in their behalf.

The most celebrated work of Allegri is his " Miserere " for two choirs, one for four voices, the other for five, which is sung in the Sistine Chapel during Holy Week. The Roman court so highly prized the exclusive possession of this famous composition, which they considered in a certain sense holy, that they threatened any one who should take or give away a copy of it with ecclesiastical penalties. Mozart eluded the prohibition, and dared to disobey. The courageous child, in his admiration of the wonderful music, listened so attentively that he was able to write it out at home; and, when he went to hear it again, he put his manuscript in his hat, where he made such corrections as were necessary. Since that time the " Miserere " has been published in London and elsewhere.

The Emperor Leopold I., who was an amateur musician, begged the pope, through his ambassador at Rome, for a copy of the " Miserere," to be used at the Imperial Chapel. The favor was granted, a copy made, and sent to the emperor. It so happened that many very distinguished singers, who were at the time in Vienna, took part in the execution of the music, notwithstanding which it was a failure. The emperor thought that the chapel-master at Rome had sent some other than Allegri's " Miserere," and complained to the pope, who, in his turn, remonstrated with the director of the chapel. He excused himself by explaining to his Holiness, that the manner of singing it in his chapel could not possibly be explained by notes, or transmitted otherwise than by example. The holy father could not understand it, but the musical emperor did, and all were satisfied.

Many " Misereres " have been sung in the Sistine Chapel; but none can compare with that of Allegri. Notwithstanding its apparent simplicity, it is very difficult to execute. The arrangement of the voice parts is excellent: the conformity of the musical expression with the sense of the text is perfect; and the air of sadness which pervades the whole excites the devotional feelings of the listener.

Whoever wishes to appreciate its beauties must quietly listen to it in a church, or, better still, in the Vatican, where the time most suitable for hearing this masterpiece is Holy Week.

FRESCOBALDI.

1587-1654.

IT was not enough that the sixteenth century should have produced Palestrina, Monteverdi, Allegri : instrumental music had also to figure in the march of progress.

Girolamo Frescobaldi, the skilful harpsichord-player, was born at Ferrara in 1587. As a boy, his voice was so extremely beautiful, that crowds followed him as he wandered from town to town singing.

At twenty years of age he was an organist of considerable notoriety. At about this time he went to live in the Netherlands ; and here, in 1608, he began to publish his compositions. In 1614 he was invited to Rome, as organist of St. Peter's. The day he took possession of the organ, thirty thousand people, attracted by his fame, came to listen to his performance. Such was the enthusiasm for the fine arts felt in Italy at that time.

From the little that history tells us of Frescobaldi, we have reason to suppose that he led a quiet life at Rome, entirely devoted to his musical studies and compositions. He was one of the first inventors of the fugue, and wrote much valuable sacred music.

CAMBERT.

1628-1677.

IT may be interesting to the lovers of dramatic art, to know that theatrical amusements were introduced into France by the clergy. Cardinal Mazarin invited the Italian virtuosi to bring the opera to Paris. Cardinal Rovera suggested the idea of writing a French opera ; and the Abbé Perrin composed the first French libretto. Thus the princes of the church encouraged the noblest of our pleasures.

The glory of competing with the Abbé Perrin in the creation of the French lyric art, due to Cambert, has unjustly been attributed to Lulli.

Cambert was born at Paris, 1628. He studied the harpsichord under Chambonnières, became organist of one of the principal colleges, and afterwards superintendent of Anne of Austria's music.

By the advice of Cardinal Rovera, the Abbé Perrin wrote a pastoral in five acts, for which Cambert composed the score. The novelty of the enterprise, and the real merits of the music, secured its success, although the words were little worth.

It was performed at Issy, April, 1659, in a low hall of the castle, without ballet, machinery, or any thing to give it effect but the simple interpretation of the amateurs. So much was said of this pastoral, that the king ordered it to be given in presence of the court at Vincennes. Encouraged by this their first enterprise, Perrin and Cambert conjointly wrote a new work, under the title of "Ariane." This work was in course of rehearsal when Mazarin died, which prevented its representation. "Adonis," another opera, met with a similar fate.

However, the indefatigable Abbé Perrin was not to be discouraged. He persevered, in spite of all obstacles, and finally succeeded in gaining his object. June 28, 1669, Louis XIV. granted him the privilege "of establishing musical academies in Paris and other cities, for the purpose of singing theatrical pieces in public." This was the commencement of national dramatic music in France.

Although the privilege of which we have spoken was granted to Perrin, he never forgot his co-laborer Cambert, to whom he was indebted for his success.

Perrin and Cambert united with the Marquis de Sourdéac for machinery, and Champeron for finances, thus forming a society.

On the 19th of March, 1671, they brought out " Pomone," a pastoral in five acts, with a prologue, which must be considered as the first regular French opera. The singers were few, the drama badly constructed, the dancing executed by young men dressed in women's clothes. Notwithstanding the imperfections attendant upon this infancy of art, " Pomone " had a run of eight months, by which Perrin gained thirty thousand livres as his share of the profits. Meanwhile Cambert was steadily improving; but, unfortunately for him, there was in Versailles a man who by his ability and talent had risen from Mlle. Montpensier's kitchens to the office of superintendent of the royal music. This man was Lulli, who, in the double quality of Italian and rival, had at first derided Cambert's works; but, when he learned to know their worth, he tacked about, and determined to rival them. Taking advantage of a dispute that had arisen among the four associates, and the withdrawal of the Marquis of Sourdéac, he, countenanced by the credit of Mlle. Montespan, worked to have the privilege of the Royal Academy of Music taken from Perrin, and given to himself, just as they were on the point of bringing out their opera of "Ariane," which had been postponed on account of the death of Mazarin.

Such gross injustice deeply affected Cambert, who was its chief victim. He went to London in 1673, and brought out his work in presence of Charles II. This prince immediately recognized his merit, and gave him a high position ; but the favors of the English monarch could not console the fugitive. Worn out by grief, he died in 1677, aged forty-nine years. It has been said that the creator of the French opera experienced the fate reserved to almost all inventors in that France who has so often shown herself as ungrateful towards her most illustrious children, as anxious to advance those whom she has adopted.

LULLI.

1633–1687.

THE career of music is more changeable than that of other arts. We admire, and shall always admire, paintings, sculpture, and the literary works of great masters; whilst but few among us, and those mostly amateurs, know any thing, at the present time, of the lyric works of Lulli, whose compositions, distinguished for their grace, elegance, and refined taste, were declared to be inimitable at the time they appeared. But, if there are but few immortal productions in music, still there are lasting names among composers; and posterity will never forget the man who took the French opera from the hands of Cambert, infused his spirit into it, and made it all his own.

Jean Baptiste Lulli was born at Florence in 1633. It seems that his parents were not in easy circumstances, for his father did not hesitate to give him to the Chevalier de Guise,[1] as a present to Mlle. de Montpensier. The boy was about thirteen years of age, and very intelligent. His sudden flashes of wit enabled him to perform the part for which the chevalier destined him in an admirable manner. His duty was that of amusing the Grande Mademoiselle in her leisure moments, while waiting for the distractions which the politics of the day afforded her.

At first the princess was very much pleased with the

---

[1] "The Chevalier de Guise had been requested by Mlle. de Montpensier to bring her a pretty little Italian boy for a page."

young Italian, whose wit and dialect, a mixture of Tuscan and broken French, afforded her great amusement. But, if the position was agreeable to the boy, it was of short duration; for, as soon as he learned enough of French to express himself like other people, he was no longer attractive to the princess, and had the mortification of being placed with the servants, who employed him in the palace-kitchens. At intervals he amused himself with playing the violin, to the great delight of the other servants, who were but too glad to have so good a musician among them. One day while thus occupied, he chanced to be overheard by Count Nogent, who, surprised by his talent, recommended him to Mlle. Montpensier, insisting upon her placing him under the instruction of some able teacher. She did so; and the young Lulli advanced so rapidly that he was soon accepted among the musicians of the court, and brought out his own compositions. But he had the imprudence to set a satirical song, against his benefactress, to music, which cost him his dismissal. Having already acquired a reputation, he received a place among the twenty-four violins, or *Grand Band*, the orchestra of Louis XIV. The king appreciated his qualities as a composer, and in 1652 made him the leader of a new music troop [1] organized expressly for himself, and called the "*Petits Violins*," in distinction from the *Grande Bande*. Lulli drilled his band thoroughly, wrote pleasant pieces for them, and succeeded in making them the best performers in France. Many manuscript overtures which Lulli composed for their use are still preserved. [2] At the

[1] "At this time not half the musicians in France could read music at sight."

[2] "Lulli did much for the improvement of French music. In his overtures he introduced fugues, and was the first to make use of side and kettle drums in the choruses. He is also said to be the inventor of that species of composition called the overture."

same time he turned his attention to the composition of music for ballets and masquerades, in which the king, his courtiers, also he himself, took part ; for, in addition to his musical talents, he was a good actor and dancer.

In 1664 he associated himself with Molière, writing the music to several of his texts ; and he even did not hesitate to appear as clown at Molière's theatre.

Lulli had already composed a great number of pieces for the king's private apartments and the chapel, when, taking advantage of the increasing favors he was receiving, he desired that the privileges of the Academy of Music might be taken from Cambert, and bestowed upon himself. Louis XIV., who would scarcely listen to any other music than Lulli's, granted his request, at the same time charging him with the general direction of all the music at court, besides paying him great prices for his compositions.

In 1672 he obtained permission to erect an opera-house (Academie Royale de Musique), an enterprise which gave France a national opera, and made the name of Lulli important in the history of art. About this time he wrote a pastoral in three acts, which was much enjoyed by the king and his court.

He was not only a composer, but he also created his orchestra, trained his artists in acting and singing, was a machinist as well as ballet-master and musical director.

He wrote a great number of operas, among which we will mention " Atys," considered his *chef d'œuvre :* it remained upon the French stage over a century. His church-music was also highly appreciated in France.[1]

---

[1] "Atys" was called the king's opera, and "Isis," that of the musicians. The sub-ect of this latter opera, represented Jan. 5, 1677, is the adventure of the nymph Io, among celestial deities known as Isis, whom the love of Jupiter exposed to the jeal-

Meanwhile Lulli had recourse to Corneille, Boileau, and La Fontaine; but these authors, in spite of all their talents, were unable to write lyric verses.

The artist required them to recommence their dramatic work, scene by scene; and he was often dissatisfied upon a second trial. One may easily imagine that such authors would be irritated at being subject to the caprices of a foreign musician, and he formerly a stage-dancer. At length they became violent and unpitying. Unhappily, the hatred of a literary people is not limited to a generation; and the memory of Lulli comes to us only through calumniators. Nearly all his biographers have accepted injurious interpretations without examination, and without considering that the violence of the writers renders them suspicious in the eye of a judicious critic.

The year 1681 is memorable in the history of the art of dancing; for in this year Lulli gave "*Il Trionfo dell'Amore*," an opera-ballet in which women danced upon the stage for the first time. Previous to this the art was practised by men dressed in women's clothes. Lulli had the good sense to perceive the absurdity of such a custom, and to replace it by an innovation which proved successful.

He brought out "Armida," one of his best works, in 1686. It is said, that, on the occasion of the first representation of this work, some unforeseen circumstance interfered with the punctuality of its performance, and the king, becoming impatient at the delay, sent an officer of the guards to Lulli to express his dissatisfaction. The words, "The king is waiting," provoked an answer from

ousy of Juno. Mlle. Montespan, being pointed at jokingly as the Juno of the opera, became so angry that she refused to be pacified until Quinault, the innocent author of the libretto, was banished from the theatre.

the artist, as sharp as it was disrespectful. "The king may well wait," he replied : "he is master here, and no one has a right to prevent his waiting as long as he pleases." The courtiers thought he would be punished for his impertinence ; and when the opera was at length given, fearing to compromise themselves by applauding, they received it coldly. But at a second performance, seeing the king manifest much pleasure, they no longer hesitated to applaud. Some time before the performance of "Armida," Lulli was very sick. His confessor refused to give him absolution unless he would throw the score of the opera into the fire, which he did. The same day the Prince of Condé came to see the sick man ; and, hearing that the score was burned, he expressed his regrets at the loss of such a fine work. "Peace, my lord," said Lulli ; "I knew what I was about : I have a copy of it."

The last dramatic production of this artist is "Acis e Galatea." He had composed much sacred music, among which was a "Te Deum." During the performance of this last work, at the celebration of the recovery of Louis XIV. from a severe illness, he accidentally struck his toe with his baton, while leading. At first the wound seemed insignificant, and he paid little or no attention to it, until it became a malignant ulcer, spreading rapidly over the foot and leg. Amputation might have saved him ; but Lulli, dreading the operation, preferred putting himself into the hands of an empiric whose experiments were powerless to combat the evil ; and our unfortunate composer died at Paris, March 22, 1687.

Lulli was excessively quick-tempered ; and one day he broke a violin over the head of a musician of his orchestra. Without wishing to justify such a hasty act, let us only remark that the mildest of men, whose ear is very sensitive, become excited by false notes. We must also remember in what condition the operatic theatre was at the time; how difficult it was to educate for the orchestra men who were generally not musicians, and whom it was necessary to call from the bar-room just at the moment of performance. Much credit is due Lulli for having formed a good troop of lyric actors in a country accustomed to send to Italy for its virtuosi. To do all that he did, required much perseverance and force of character. He triumphed over obstacles, cabals, and pamphlets at the same time. Racine and Molière kept themselves free from the spleen of literary men because *they* understood and loved music better than all the other poets of the glorious Pleiades of Louis XIV.'s time.

STRADELLA.

1645–1687.

ALESSANDRO STRADELLA, a celebrated composer and singer, was born at Naples, 1645. Very little is known of his youth and education. He went to Venice in 1677, where he was engaged to write operas. Meanwhile he gave lessons in singing to a member of the powerful Contarini family; this was no other than a mistress of Contarini himself. The teacher fell in love with his pupil; and, fearing the jealousy of the nobleman, they fled to Turin, where the artist soon won the favor of the duchess regent. But the fugitives did not long remain in undisturbed quiet; for Contarini at the head of forty servants came to claim his lady-love. The duchess, who had promised her protection to the musician, and temporary security in a convent for his companion, was not to be intimidated by the threatening troops. Disappointed in this attempt, Contarini engaged two *bravi* to follow and molest Stradella in every possible manner. They arrived in Rome just as the artist was performing his oratorio of "St. John the Baptist;" to which they listened, and were so much affected by the divine harmony, that they lost all courage to strike at its author, declaring that they never could murder such a brilliant genius.

Stradella was afterwards attacked in the street, and wounded by other emissaries of the Contarini, who had followed him to Turin. However, he recovered from his wounds, and married his beloved, with whom he went to Genoa to perform his opera "La Forza dell' Amore Paterno." Again the revengeful Contarini sent *bravi*, who broke into Stradella's dwelling, and murdered both him and his wife.

Stradella was an excellent musician, and enjoyed a brilliant renown during his lifetime; he was also a good Latin poet, and wrote the texts of most of his religious compositions. "He has been called Italy's most excellent musician of his time."

SCARLATTI.
1649–1725.

ALEXANDER SCARLATTI at an early age displayed extraordinary talents. Able to overcome all the difficulties of counterpoint, which in his time was the only form allowed to musical art, he made rapid progress in instrumental music, and particularly on the harpsichord : therefore he may well be considered the precursor of Rameau, of Händel, and of Bach.

Scarlatti was born at Trapani (Sicily), in 1647. He was carefully educated in music, and studied the masterpieces of the Roman school. When he went to Naples he was remarkable as a singer, a harp and harpsichord player. Biographical information respecting this master is wanting until 1680, when he brought out his opera " L'Onestà nell' Amore," in the palace of Christina, ex-queen of Sweden, in Rome. After this opera, there is another biographical void in the life of our artist, which extends to the year 1693, when the oratorio "I Dolori di Maria" was performed, and the opera of "Tendora" also.

Among other novelties, Scarlatti introduced the " Da Capo " in this opera. The recitative, which had previously been sustained without interruption by the bass, was now for the first time accompanied by the orchestra.

After the death of Christina, which took place 1688, Scarlatti was appointed master of the Royal Chapel of Naples. By order of the viceroy, he revised some of the airs of " L'Odoacre " by Legrenzi.

The score which he revised and restored, so to say, was performed in 1694.

Scarlatti, as strictly conscientious as modest, thus addresses himself to the reader of the text: " The airs which I have composed are marked by an asterisk, in order that my faults may not be prejudicial to the reputation of Legrenzi, whose immortal glory is for me the object of unlimited respect."

A number of works which appeared soon after brought the Sicilian artist into great repute ; and with celebrity came appointments and honors. The charge of Cardinal Ottoboni's music was given him ; the pope decorated him with the golden spur ; and finally, after the conquest of the two Sicilies by the Imperials, he returned to Naples with new titles.

Scarlatti wrote at least a hundred and fifteen operas, but

many of them have not come down to us; for at that time the custom of engraving scores was little known in Italy. There are operas enough, however, to show Scarlatti's vast knowledge, rich imagination, and bold and well-written modulations for the voice.

Independently of his dramatic productions, our musician composed a dozen oratorios, some two hundred masses, and an incalculable number of pieces, such as duos, sere-nades, madrigals, &c. Scarlatti rendered his name im-mortal by the great public service he did in teaching music in the schools.[1]

His death, Oct. 25, 1725, was a loss to the country of which he was one of its most illustrious citizens.[2]

LALANDE.

1657–1726.

LALANDE, the fifteenth child of a poor tailor, was born in Paris. While yet a child, his voice was so charming, that Chaperon, teacher of singing, placed him in the choir of the Church of St. Germain l' Auxerrois. So zealous was the boy to improve his advantages, that he devoted the greater part of every night to study; and in this way learned to play the violin, the harpsichord, bass-viol, and some other instruments, almost without assistance. At fifteen years of age, when the change in his voice pre-vented his singing in the choir, his brother-in-law took him home, and arranged weekly concerts at his house, that the boy might have an opportunity to practise his music. At

---

[1] He labored gratuitously as music-master in a large charity-school known under the name of "Jesus Christ's Poor of Loretto." He was much beloved and universally respected by the Neapolitans.

[2] Scarlatti, who was much in advance of the period in which he lived, may be considered a true reformer in musical art.

this period, Lalande played the violin better than any other instrument; however, upon Lulli's refusing to admit him into his orchestra, the youth was so much vexed that he broke his violin, and turned his whole attention for a while, to the organ. Soon he became such a proficient that his services were required in four different churches; it being customary in his time to engage an organist for three months only. He was likewise employed by Father Fleureau to compose the music for several tragedies that the Society of Jesus was in the habit of performing in its colleges. The religious nature of Lalande well fitted him for such compositions, and he succeeded admirably.

Some time after, Lalande competed for the situation of organist to the king; and Lulli, who was to judge of the merits of the candidates, declared, that, if the place was to be given to the most able, it certainly belonged to Lalande, though, unfortunately, he was too young for so responsible a situation. If the young aspirant lost the situation he desired, he gained the favorable vote of the severe Lulli.

Marshal Noailles, whose daughter took lessons of La-lande, recommended him to Louis XIV., who engaged him as teacher to the royal princesses. Once admitted to court, the character of the master was as much esteemed as his music was admired. He soon became a great favorite with the king, who brought about a marriage between him and Anna Rebel, the best singer of the royal chamber, on whom he bestowed a handsome marriage-portion.

Lalande died June 18, 1726, after having passed forty-five years in the service of the court.

The ability to direct the music, as well as compose for such an assemblage as that of the Royal Chapel of Louis XIV., is a sufficient proof of the talents of the master.

PURCELL.

1658–1695.

HENRY PURCELL was born in London, 1658. Of his early instruction in music, little is known ; but, as he was appointed organist of Westminster Abbey at eighteen years of age, he must have learned the elements of music when a mere child. At twenty-four he was promoted to one of the three places of organist of the Chapel Royal. After this he became famed throughout the kingdom for his many excellent compositions for the church and chapel of which he was organist. It was not long before he was solicited to compose for the stage and chamber, in both of which he succeeded admirably. His songs delighted the hearer for nearly thirty years after his death, when they gave way only to the favorite opera songs of Händel.

Many of Purcell's compositions for the church are still retained in the cathedrals and in the King's Chapel. The "Te Deum" and "Jubilate" of Purcell were intended for the opening of the new Church of St. Paul.

In the year 1713 Händel's "Te Deum" for the peace of Utrecht was produced by command of Queen Anne, and alternately performed with that of Purcell for a number of years. Since 1743, however, Händel's superior knowledge of instruments and more polished melody have taken possession of the national favor; and Purcell's "Te Deum" is only occasionally performed.

The merits of Purcell as a musician have been summed up thus : "His beauties in composition were entirely his own, while his occasional barbarisms may be considered as unavoidable compliances with the false taste of the age in which he lived."

ABELL.

1660–1724.

JOHN ABELL, an English musician, possessed a very fine tenor voice, and was attached to the chapel of Charles II., King of England. This prince had an idea of sending him to Venice to show the Italians what a fine voice England could produce. In the Revolution of 1688, Abell was banished from England as a Papist. Then he went from place to place giving concerts, and met with good success in Holland and Hamburg. He earned much money and received magnificent presents; but he squandered all he had, and was finally obliged to travel on foot with his lute on his back. When he arrived at Warsaw, the King of Poland, who had heard of his wonderful playing and singing, sent for him; but Abell excused himself from appearing in the royal presence, saying he had a very bad cold. The king then ordered that he should be brought to court. He was taken into a large hall with a gallery around it, in which were seated the king and his suite. Abell was placed in an armchair, which was hoisted by means of a pulley; after which several bears were let into the hall, and Abell was told to take his choice between being eaten by the bears, and singing. He chose the latter, and his cold was instantly cured. Some years after, he obtained permission to return to England. He manifested his gratitude by dedicating a collection of songs in different languages to King William. This work was published in London, 1701. One of his songs bears the title, "Pills to Purge Melancholy." Abell lived to a good old age, and died in Cambridge, Eng., in 1724.

KEISER.

1673-1739.

REINHARD KEISER, an illustrious composer of the German school, was born in 1673 in a village situated between Weissenfels and Leipzig. His father, a distinguished musician,[1] taught him the elements of music before he entered St. Thomas's School in Leipzig, where he prepared himself for the university.

At the age of nineteen he was engaged to write the music to a pastoral called "Ismène." This period, 1692, was the dawn of German opera, which hitherto had had no style of its own independent of that of Italy and France. In his compositions Keiser displayed that original genius which was destined to rid itself in some degree from imitation. The success of the pastoral opened the way for "Basilius," which was so much admired that Keiser determined to put it upon the stage in Hamburg, where the national opera was the most flourishing in all Germany.

The music of this opera was so different from what the opera-goers of Hamburg had been accustomed to hear, and its superiority so indisputable, that they wished to hear Keiser's works in preference to any other. However, owing to the intrigues of rival artists jealous of his talents, three years passed before he could bring out "Irène" and "Janus." Then followed the pastoral of "Ismène," a fresh and charming composition, which was heard with pleasure for a very long time. During forty years Keiser was the most active [2] and the most beloved

---

[1] He left much excellent sacred music in manuscript.

[2] During this period he composed no less than one hundred and sixteen operas besides many oratorios and other sacred music.

of all the composers for the theatre in Hamburg. In 1700 Keiser commenced a series of the most brilliant concerts that had ever been given. He chose the best music, the best orchestra possible, the most renowned singers, the most distinguished virtuosi, that could be found. And these were not the only attractions; for in the concert-hall, where elegance reigned, abundance of exquisite viands and costly wines gratified the taste of pleasure-seekers. Keiser himself always appeared in the most splendid attire. Matheson, who often directed the orchestra, declared that these concerts were given in regal style, and that he never saw more magnificence or good taste at court.

After a time Keiser gave up the concerts, and associated himself with an Englishman named Drusike, to establish an opera. The enterprise at first seemed prosperous, but soon failed through mismanagement and foolish expense. Our composer, persecuted by his creditors, was obliged to conceal himself; but soon he took courage, and began to work. In an incredibly short space of time he composed eight operas, considered his best, which sold at a good price, and thus enabled him to satisfy his creditors. Afterward, he married the daughter of a rich musician. She was a fine singer, and her musical talent added new charms to the productions of our artist.

Keiser removed to Copenhagen by invitation of the King of Denmark. When he returned to Hamburg, he devoted his time to the composition of sacred music. In 1734 he wrote the opera of "Circé." This was his last work. He died Sept. 12, 1739, at the age of sixty-six years. The most celebrated artists, the most distinguished musicians, all agree in their high estimation of Keiser's works. Matheson and Schiebe do not hesitate to give him the

first place among the dramatic composers who had preceded them. They assure us that Händel and Hasse
owed much to the information they obtained through the
study of Keiser's works. Telemann is of the same opinion. Hasse is reported to have said that "he considered
Keiser the first musician in the world in his kind; that,
notwithstanding the many changes made in music in the
course of fifty years, one could perceive little difference
between his compositions and those of later writers."
Like most writers of his school, his harmony is strong and
penetrating; but there is a certain something in his compositions which belongs to him alone. Like J. S. Bach,
his instrumentation is instinctive, and not wholly conformable to rules. In his opera of "Frédegonde," he has a
great number of airs, of which the effect is pleasing and
peculiar.

There were so few copies of Keiser's operas, that they
are now a great rarity. Mr. Burney had some original
MSS. of the operas "Héraclius," "Cloris," "Janus,"
"Ariane," and of the oratorio "Nabuchodnosor." The
value of these precious relics was so little appreciated in
England, that, when the library of Mr. Burney was sold,
they went off for six or eight francs each, whilst a collection of old English madrigals brought six hundred francs.

Several of Keiser's operas and other works were in the
palace in Copenhagen when it was burnt, 1794.

MARCELLO.

1680–1739.

BENEDETTO MARCELLO was born in Venice, of a noble
family, in the year 1680. He was eminent as a poet and
a musician. A serenata composed by him, and performed

in Vienna 1716, at the celebration in honor of the birth of the first son of the Emperor Charles VI., was greatly applauded. His two cantatas, " Il Timoteo " and " La Cassandra," are much esteemed. He also composed a mass, and set the " Lamentations of Jeremiah " to music.

" In the year 1724, were brought out the first four volumes of the ' Paraphrase of the Psalms, by Giustiniani, in Italian, set to music for one, two, and three voices, by Benedetto Marcello ; ' and, in the two subsequent years, four more, including the whole first fifty of the Psalms."

ASTORGA.

1681–1736.

EMANUEL D' ASTORGA, well known not only by his misfortunes, but also by his church-music, was born Dec. 11, 1681, at Palermo. He was the son of a distinguished baron, who was surrendered by his mercenaries in a fight against the union of the island with Spain, and was decapitated in 1701. Forced to be present with his mother at the shameful execution, he became unconscious, whilst she died from terror.

By the intercession of the Princess Ursini, he was brought into a convent at Astorga, in Leon, for which city he was afterwards named. He studied music under Scarlatti and Caldara, and in 1704 went from the convent to the court of the Duke of Parma, by whom he was highly esteemed on account of his musical talent. However, the duke soon dismissed him for a supposed relation with his daughter ; but he recommended him to the Emperor Leopold.

After Leopold's death, Astorga, supported by the Spanish court, travelled through all civilized Europe. Finally we find him in Prague. It is supposed that he entered a convent in Bohemia, and there died, Aug. 21, 1736. His masterpiece is a " Stabat Mater," the original of which is preserved in Oxford. He composed many excellent cantatas, and an opera " Daphne," which was represented in Prague in 1726. He also wrote a requiem.

MATHESON.

1681–1764.

JOHANN MATHESON was born in Hamburg, 1681. When seven years of age, he studied under different masters, making good progress in the rudiments of learning and the principles of music. At the age of nine years he was able to sing his own compositions. At eighteen he composed an opera, and performed the principal part himself. In 1704 he visited Holland : the situation of organist in Haarlem was offered him, with a salary of fifteen hundred florins ; but he chose rather to return to his own country.[1] He composed a serenata upon the accession of King George I. to the crown of England. 1715 he was chapel-master in the cathedral of Hamburg.

Notwithstanding the multiplicity of business in which he was engaged, Matheson found time to continue his musical studies. He composed for the church and the theatre, and was generally present at the performance of his own music.

Matheson was well acquainted with Händel. Händel approved so highly of Matheson's compositions, that he often played them for his private amusement ; and Matheson had so much regard for Händel, that he seriously thought of writing his life. Matheson died at Hamburg, 1764.

[1] He became secretary to Sir Cyril Wych, resident at Hamburg for the English court.

RAMEAU.

1683-1764.

RAMEAU, the greatest French musician of the eighteenth century, far exceeded his compeers as a theorist and an artist.

John Philip Rameau was born at Dijon, September, 1683. He evinced great fondness for music when a little child ; and his parents, both musical amateurs, took pleasure in teaching him. The fostering care of a tender mother had great influence in developing his wonderful genius. At the age of seven he could read and execute any piece of music at sight ; an excellent initiation for a great artist, but a poor foundation for the magistracy to which his parents had destined him. The boy's natural taste was far from being modified by the instruction of the fathers at the Jesuits' College ; instead of attending to the studies they gave him, he amused himself with scribbling solfeggios and fragments of sonatas over his papers and books. Besides his despite of the rudiments of classical learning, he was violent and indocile ; in fact, too much of a spoiled child to yield to school discipline. The fathers soon became tired of him, and sent him home to his parents before he had finished his half-year's course of study.

The boy joyfully returned to his infantile occupations. He studied the mechanism of the harpsichord, organ, and violin ; learned the elements of counterpoint from his father and other musicians : in short, he began to draw largely upon the meagre resources offered by Dijon for his musical education. He was so entirely devoted to music, that he seldom opened a book treating on any other subject ; consequently he was not only ignorant of Greek and

Latin, but also of the rudiments of his mother-tongue. Yet he manifested no anxiety to improve, until he wished to correspond with a young widow ; then the necessity of correct grammar and orthography by which to express the sentiments of his heart, and make a favorable impression upon the lady, forced him to study. His father, disturbed by the course he was pursuing, determined to send him to Italy, hoping thereby to wean him from the object of his passion, and carry him back to his first love, music. But the ear of the youth, now eighteen years of age, was formed for French music : therefore the melodies of Scar-latti, Lotti, and others, made but slight impression on him. Perhaps, if he had gone farther south than he did, it might have been different. After remaining a short time in Milan, and in order to obtain the means of returning to his native city, he engaged himself as first violinist to a director of a strolling theatrical company, about forming an orchestra. In this way he visited the principal cities in the South of France, and commenced his reputation as harpsichord player. After an absence of several years, Rameau re-turned to his paternal home ; but he was too ambitious to accept the situation of organist in the St. Chapelle, and determined to seek glory in Paris. He was now thirty-five years old. When he arrived in that city in 1717, Marchand, he who competed with Bach, was creat-ing a great furore in the Church of the Grands-Cordoliers. Every time he played the organ, immense crowds came to hear him. Rameau became one of his most attentive and admiring listeners, and found means to introduce himself to the great organist. Marchand gave him a few lessons ; but, fearing future rivalry from one possessed of so much talent, he did not encourage his pupil. On the contrary, he used his influence to prevent Rameau's obtaining the situation of organist at St. Paul.

Necessity obliged Rameau to accept the offer of an organ in St. Etienne, Lille, from whence he went to Clare-mont, where "he devoted much time to the study of the theory of music, and became the author of several important works on the subject, one of which, 'Demonstration of the Principle of Theory,' has been so highly valued by his countrymen, that they have assigned to Rameau the place of the Newton of music."

This work Rameau wished to bring before the musical critics of Paris; but the term of his engagement with the church was not completed, and neither bishop nor laity were willing to lose the services of so valuable an organist.

Finding that he could not get away by fair means, Rameau had recourse to stratagem. "If they will not release me," he thought, "I will make them drive me away." From the moment he had formed this resolution until his dismissal, his fingers brought forth such barbarous sounds as made the ears of the hearers tingle; and they were at length glad to release him. After he was dismissed, however, he played once more, and in his most brilliant style; for he would not leave without compensating, as it were, for the very bad music he had given them.

His publications attracted much attention. Students were anxious to learn of so excellent an artist. Finally the situation of organist placed him in easy circumstances. Among Rameau's pupils was the wife of Gen. la Pope-linière. This was a great help to the artist, who became a friend of his pupil's husband. The general, who was immensely rich, placed an excellent orchestra at the disposition of Rameau. He loved art; and his greatest pleasure was to have the music of the best artists performed either at his hotel in Paris, or at his country-house in Passy.

Protected by such a friend, Rameau, though fifty years of age, applied himself to composition, and wrote in pleasant security ; for, if his music was not immediately brought before the public, he was sure of performing it to a choice company of connoisseurs.

The first lyric work of this composer was " Samson," a sacred opera, the text of which was written by Voltaire, at the request of Mme. Popelinière. But it was not until " Castor and Pollux," a tragedy in five acts, with a prologue, was brought out, that ample justice was done to the talented artist. Thirty years after, Grimm, in speaking of this admirable composition, said, " It is the pivot on which the glory of French music turns."

Although Rameau began to compose so late in life, he left thirty-six dramatic works. The last, " The Paladino," he wrote when seventy-seven years of age. This energetic vitality, so well preserved in a delicate and apparently feeble body, was doubtless owing to his simple, regular, and temperate habits of living.

It is said, that, when Louis XIV. offered him the title of nobility, he answered, " My nobility is here and here," touching his forehead and his heart.

Notwithstanding that in the course of nineteen years nine hundred and seventy-eight thousand francs were brought into the treasury of the opera through his works, he received but twenty-two thousand ; so that he was actually obliged to give lessons and sell music to meet his current expenses, and enable him to open his purse to the unfortunate.

Rameau died at the ripe age of eighty, respected and beloved by all who knew him.

DURANTE.

1684–1755.

FRANCIS DURANTE, a man of science, with severe taste and strong attachment to formulas, could not be other than he was, viz., a distinguished professor, and an able composer of church music. His genius inclining him to sacred music only, he did justice to himself in not attempting to write for the theatre, where his want of originality and his scholastic rigidity would have prevented him from succeeding.

This musician was born March 15, 1684, in Frattamaggiore, in the kingdom of Naples. As his parents could not afford to pay for his instruction, he was sent to the " Conservatory for the Poor," where, under the direction of Gaetano Greco, he became a proficient upon the harpsichord. The conservatory being suppressed, Durante was placed under the care of Alexander Scarlatti, professor at " Sant' Anofrio." There was such an extreme difference of temperament between master and scholar, that the former exerted but little influence upon the latter; for, while Scarlatti was free and original, Durante clung to the strict formality of rules. It has been said that Durante perfected his musical education at Rome ; however, it is still a question, though it is certain that he paid great attention to the Roman masters. The new character given to the Neapolitan school by his instruction was owing to his rigid accuracy in harmony ; and it is but just to give him the credit of being the most able among all the professors of music in the conservatory of Naples. However, he was no more of a theorist than any of his predecessors. Durante is historically noted as an incomparable professor.

He succeeded Porpora as master of the conservatory of Loretto in the month of January, 1742. In this situation, where he acquired a lasting and brilliant renown, he was paid only forty francs a month; but it was not difficult for him to accommodate himself to this meagre salary. More than negligent in his simple dress, penurious in living, peevish in conversation, and when he tried to be amiable making one think of La Fontaine's ass, he could well dispense with many of the so-called necessities of society. Such is the picture given of the exterior of the master. To complete this portrait, let us add that he was married three times, and that neither of his wives was able to smooth down the asperities of his character. However, he was an excellent man, of good heart, and full of devotion and self-sacrifice. His sincere and active piety redeemed all his exterior defects. We mentioned above how niggardly he was paid; yet, with all that, by strict economy he succeeded in building a chapel in his native village.

This excellent musician and brave man died Aug. 13, 1755. He left a great number of masses, psalms, motets, and hymns, admired for the majesty of style in which they are written, and the perfect arrangement of the parts for the voice. His " Alma Redemptoris " is of the first order ; but his most beautiful works, undoubtedly, are the pupils he formed, among whom we will mention Jomelli, Piccinni, Sacchini, and Paisiello. What a crown of glory for this humble being, who so constantly devoted himself to the accomplishment of the arduous duty of teaching![1]

[1] Durante composed almost entirely for the church. His works are distinguished for elevation and purity of style. A full collection is to be found in the library of the conservatory of Paris.

BACH.

1685–1750.

THE musician destined to render the family name of Bach immortal was Johann Sebastian, who opened his eyes to the light on the 21st of March, 1685, at Eisenach, where his father was a musician of the court and the city.[1] Left an orphan at ten years of age, he was placed under the care of his eldest brother, Johann Christoph, an organist at Ordoff, who gave him some instruction on the clavichord. The child, through inclination and capacity for music, promptly learned its elements; and, precocious as he was, he did not hesitate to undertake the interpretation of the most celebrated masters of the time. One would think that the less gifted elder brother was jealous of the child's brilliant powers; for he refused to allow him the use of a music-book containing several pieces of the masters. However, the young Sebastian contrived to get by stealth the precious book, for which he had in vain plead so earnestly, and set himself to copy it from beginning to end. To do this without awaking the distrust of his brother, he was obliged to work by moonlight, and it took him full six months. Such patience and perseverance surely deserved to be rewarded. Was his brother capable

---

[1] Sebastian Bach descended from a race of musicians. The family name Bach, in his day, dated back to Veit Bach, a Hungarian. This man, a miller by trade, was so fond of music that he took his cithern to mill with him; and, while the corn was grinding, he played a melodic accompaniment to the uniform rhythm of the mill.

The cithern, an instrument of different sizes, with four, five, or six metallic strings, was much used in the sixteenth century.

The successors of Veit Bach, all musicians, held family-gatherings yearly at Eisenach, Arnstadt, or Erfurt. Their festivities always commenced with a choral song, and were continued with mirth and jollity interspersed with humorous music, some of which was improvised for the occasion.

of appreciating the child's zeal? We think not; for, when he found Sebastian secretly studying, he took the copy which had cost so much labor away from him, and the boy did not see it again till after Christoph's death.

The youth, thrown upon his own resources, went to Luneburg, where he obtained a situation as singer in the choir of the Church of St. Michel; there he learned practically what sacred music is. He could not easily have chosen a more favorable place than Luneburg, at whose excellent gymnasium he studied. Besides, its proximity to Hamburg and Zelle enabled him to make frequent visits to those cities so renowned for their schools for singing, organ, and orchestra.

As a youth of eighteen, Bach returned home, a well-instructed, richly gifted disciple of art. In 1703 we find him as court musician at Weimar, 1704 as organist at Ahnstadt, 1707 in the same capacity at Muhlhausen, 1708 court organist at Weimar, and 1714 director of concerts also.

In the meantime he wrote two great church cantatas, both masterpieces; also " Gott ist mein König," and " Ich hatte viel Bekummernitz." Indeed, the love for art, that sacred flame which creates the great artist, was never for a moment extinguished in his heart.

One day in 1705 or 1706, Bach left his pleasant home in Ahnstadt, and directed his steps to the North. The object of his longing was Lubec, where he studied the organ for three months with the celebrated Buxtehudde. Bach was not sufficiently forehanded to take very long journeys : *he* never saw the skies of Italy ; yet he became better acquainted with, and learned to appreciate the celebrated masters of Italy, more than most of those who make pilgrimages thither. He worked assiduously, copied a number of the works of Palestrina, Lotti, and others ; edited and transposed music, that of Vivaldi, for example.[1]

The name of Bach was becoming generally known, and his presence desired at several of the German Courts. What the Italy of the Renaissance was for art, that was Germany in the time of Bach. There was no capital or free city in this feudal and municipal country, which had not a focus of artistic rays more or less intense. A sort of emulation, useful to general progress, animated all the smaller German princes.

The ardor of Bach for study increased with his success, and his persevering efforts were fully appreciated.[2]

Augustus II., Elector of Saxony and King of Poland, who had been conquered by Charles XII., and re-established by Peter the Great, was one of the most magnificent sovereigns of Europe. As if this prince wished to indemnify himself during the second part of his reign for the humiliations and misfortunes suffered in the first part, he neglected nothing to make the little court of Dresden the asylum of joy and pleasure. Artists were his chosen guests ; and when Louis Marchand came as an exile from Paris, to seek refuge in Dresden, the king, delighted by the lightness and brilliancy of his performance, offered him a considerable salary if he would settle at his court. Marchand, a distinguished virtuoso, challenged a competitor. Volumier, the Saxon concert-master, sent for Bach ; and it was agreed that each should improvise upon a theme proposed by the other. The day for trial came, but the French organist did not appear. On inquiring, it was found that he had left the city, thus acknowledging the superiority of his opponent.

[1] And thus made himself master of French and Italian music, that he might judge of the best they contained, though he was no imitator of either.

[2] About this time he married Maria Barbara, youngest daughter of John Michel Bach, an able composer. By his wife he had two daughters and five sons.

The king ordered a hundred louis d'or to be presented to Bach; but the officer to whom the order was given thought best to appropriate the money, and let the honor suffice for the artist.

Whilst Bach held the directorship of Prince Leopold d'Anhalt-Coeten's chapel, he had much leisure, which he employed in study. The old Reincke, who had inspired him with enthusiasm since his early youth, was then living at Hamburg. In 1722 Bach went, as on a pilgrimage, to see this venerable man, now nearly a hundred years old; and improvised, at his request, on the choral, "Upon the Rivers of Babylon." The old athlete, about to disappear from the world's theatre, was still interested in the fate of music. He tenderly embraced his young successor; and, shedding tears of joy, he said, "I did think that this art would die with me; but I see that you will keep it alive."

Frederic II. was one of the great admirers of Bach. The passion of this conqueror of Rossbach for music, a passion which had nearly cost him his life while his father lived, is well known to us. No sooner was he the king, however, than he remained faithful in his devotion to music. Every evening one of the halls of the palace of Potsdam was turned into a concert-hall; and the king, an able flutist, did not disdain to take a part in his select orchestra. He wrote to Bach several times, inviting him to his court; finally the master accepted, and went thither[1] accompanied by his oldest son. When Frederic read his name among the arrivals at Potsdam, he turned to those about him, saying, "Gentlemen, Bach is here!" and ordered him to be sent for immediately. So impatient was he, that he would not wait for the artist to attire himself in court dress. Grateful for the kind hospitality which he received from

[1] In 1747.

the Prussian monarch, Bach wrote a fugue in three parts, and dedicated it to the king, under the title of " A Musical Offering." He also wrote some canons, and a trio for flute, violin, and base.

But the joy of father and son was soon turned to sadness ; for on their return home they found the devoted wife and tender mother sleeping her long sleep in the quiet churchyard.

She was his second wife, an excellent soprano singer, the daughter of a court musician. She became the mother of six sons and seven daughters. All the sons of Sebastian Bach, like their male predecessors for a hundred and fifty years, displayed more or less musical talent. Even the unfortunate David, though incapable of learning to read or write, played with so much tenderness and expression, that those who listened to him could scarcely refrain from weeping. David died before attaining the age of manhood.

Bach may be said to have educated[1] a large class of excellent composers, organ and piano players, which spread over the North of Germany. K. Ph. Em. Bach, Cramer, Clementi, Hummel, and others, — these all, though they may differ in some details, have in their general system not been able to say any thing new ; for their knowledge is all based upon Sebastian Bach's instruction. Although there is no doubt that the influence of Bach was a decided and long-continued one in the theory and practice of music, and that he deserves the title of " father of modern music," yet his compositions, as rich treasures of music,

[1] Bach was not satisfied to tell a pupil *what* was to be done : he always showed his pupils *how*. He would play the lesson over a few times, saying, " That is the way it must be done."

" Whoever thoroughly understands me," said J. Haydn, " knows that I owe much to Sebastian Bach, that I have studied him thoroughly and well, and that I acknowledge him only as my model."

secure for him the grateful souvenirs of posterity, without reference to their influence on contemporaries and descendants.

Bach lived but three years after the ovation which he received in Potsdam. Blindness, brought on by too great labor, saddened his last days. An English oculist operated on his eyes at two different times, to the detriment of his health, which had previously been very vigorous. He languished for some time, and died July 30, 1750, at the age of 65.[1] The inflammatory fever which finally carried him off had been preceded by a sudden recovery of sight, which singular phenomeon led his friends to hope for his recovery. But ten days after, Germany and the musical world had to mourn the loss of one of the greatest geniuses which had honored both.

He was a good husband, a good father, and a good friend. Twice married, the father of twenty children, he did not flag under the heavy burden which the education of such a large family imposed. He was never known to make use of the favors of the rich for his own pecuniary interest. If he had done what many others do, he might have been rich;[2] but he was content with a sufficiency, and in truth he was well satisfied with a comfortable living. Conscious of his genius, he was very modest; and, when any one asked what was the secret of his great power, he

---

[1] He was buried in St. John's churchyard, Leipzig.

[2] It has been said by some writers, that this great musical genius was obliged to be satisfied with the position of organist, which scarcely brought seventy thalers (about fifty dollars) a year; and that, with his large family, he had not sufficient means for their livelihood. However it may be, we find Bach enjoying a quiet happy life, surrounded by his family and friends, and devoting himself unremittingly to music. He was an able performer on various stringed instruments, with which he at times amused himself. He is said to have preferred the clavichord to the piano; and his method for the former instrument laid the foundation of that for piano, as used in our times.

invariably answered that he owed all that he was to industry. We cannot judge absolutely of the temper of Bach
in the ordinary commerce of life by the austere and grand
character of his music. Like many kind people, he willingly yielded to an occasion, and was always ready for a
pun. For example, in a play of words upon his own name,
Bach, which in German means " brook," and the name of
a favorite pupil, Krebs, which means " crab," he used to
say, " I have never taken but one crab in my brook."
When he joked it was always with delicacy, and his playfulness never wounded the feelings of any one.

Despite his great reputation while living,[1] it may be
said that the glory of Bach is in a measure posthumous.
Generally speaking, his contemporaries saw in him only the
skilful organist, the wonderful improviser, the learned
musician. Probably Bach's extreme simplicity and aversion for vain popularity were more or less injurious as to
the bringing out of his works in a proper light during his
lifetime.

The " Matthæus Passion " for two choruses and two
orchestras, one of the greatest masterpieces in music,
waited nearly a century before it was brought out ; condemned, as it were, from its birth, by the modesty of its
author. Mozart had the glory of promoting the grand
movement in favor of our great master towards the end
of the eighteenth century ; and he continued a persevering
research of his unpublished works. Whilst Mozart was
at mass in Leipzig, 1788, he heard one of Bach's hymns,
which produced such an effect upon his ear, that he cried
out, " Thank God, there is something new now ! I learn

---

[1] As an organist, Sebastian Bach stands alone, for he has never been equalled. No
other artist has been able to master this giant instrument, and make it subservient to
his purposes and intentions, as he did.

something." This something new dated back some seventy years; but the admiration of Mozart was sufficient to bring it out from obscurity.

Among the numerous compositions of Bach, we must mention his fugues and preludes, the "Oratorio of the Nativity of Jesus Christ," that of "The Passion," of which we have already spoken, his grand masses, and series of compositions. Speaking of his merit as a composer is not saying all. Bach in the judgment of contemporaries was extraordinarily gifted with the qualities of a virtuoso,[1] — qualities of which posterity cannot judge. The invention, or rather the constant and systematic application of fingering, applied to organ music, is due to him. He was well versed in the construction of organs.

The sons of our immortal artist never attained the paternal glory, though some among them were well-skilled musicians. The eldest, William Friedmann, who was unfortunate, and who was little appreciated during his lifetime, wrote sonatas, fugues, and concertos, displaying sufficient talent to give him a reputation as a musician, if he had not been a Bach.[2]

[1] Bach once observed to a friend in Weimar, that he believed he could play any piece of music at sight. A few days after, he breakfasted with this friend, who laid a piece of music, that at a mere glance seemed nothing difficult, upon the piano. While waiting, Bach, as was his custom, went to the piano, and began to run over the notes he found lying there. Meanwhile his friend went into the next room to see about breakfast. Finally Bach came to the piece above mentioned, and began to play it through; but he stopped and began again and again, to the great amusement of his friend, who was laughing to himself when he heard it. " No, no! " exclaimed the artist, as he entered the breakfast-room, "to play *every thing* at sight is not possible."

[2] Bach was a great worker, even in manhood, often going over, correcting, and revising at night what he had written during the day.

He wrote his recitatives completely as he wished to have them sung, and considered good declamation necessary to a good harmonic basis. He was a very severe critic of his own compositions; indeed, he corrected so carefully, and revised so often, that it was no wonder that the second publication of a work made it seem almost like something new.

At the end of his autobiography, Bach says, " I have taken the trouble to compose

Emanuel, the creator of the modern sonata, had the fate of many precursors. The kind which he invented having been carried to a high degree of perfection by Haydn and Mozart, very little gratitude has been shown him for opening the way which others illustrated after him. It becomes the duty of the historian to protest against the injustice of posterity. We should mention two other sons of Bach, — Johann Christoph, distinguished in counter-point, and Johann Christian, who was the first of the family to write dramatic music. He wrote many operas, some of which became very celebrated.

HÄNDEL.

1685–1759.

HÄNDEL, one of Germany's greatest composers, excelled in oratorio. It is not without reason that the English, his compatriots by adoption, have styled him the Milton of music. That which Palestrina did for the church in the sixteenth century, Händel has done for the temple in the eighteenth. He was born at Halle, in Saxony, Feb. 23, 1685 ; and in his early childhood he manifested astonishing proofs of a musical gift and great strength of will. His father, a barber and surgeon, destined his son to the law ; and, that he might have no opportunity to cultivate his natural taste for music, he banished all musical instruments from the house.[1] The child of seven years, though opposed, was not disheartened. The art-instinct rebelled

---

singing music for the piano, for I think that music ought to touch the heart. The piano-player who merely thrums and drums, with no regard to feeling, cannot succeed in this, according to my ideas." Let our present pianists take this great master's words to heart.

[1] " Music," he said, " is an elegant art and fine amusement, but as an occupation it hath little dignity, having for its object nothing better than mere entertainment and pleasure."

against paternal orders. A servant [1] aided him in getting a small dumb spinet [2] into an upper chamber, and during the night while the family were sleeping he practised upon his instrument, assiduously teaching himself, so that, without the aid of a master, he succeeded in learning to play remarkably well.

When he was about eight years old, his father having occasion to go to the court of the Duke of Saxe-Weissenfels, in whose palace a relative had some domestic employment, took the boy with him. The child, left to wander about the apartments of the palace at will, did not fail to make use of the chapel-organ every time he was left alone where it stood. One day the attention of the prince, attracted to the harmonious sounds drawn from this instrument, asked what virtuoso was giving this unexpected concert. Surprised at learning that it was only a child of eight years, he begged the father of our future composer no longer to oppose the child's natural inclination, but, on the contrary, to use all possible means to develop such a wonderful talent.

The advice of the prince was followed, and the boy confided to the care of F. W. Zachau, organist at the Market Church in Halle. Zachau gave him lessons in counterpoint and the fugue during two years. The pupil made such good progress, that at the age of ten years he composed some charming motets, which were sung in the principal churches of Halle. At thirteen years of age he visited Berlin for a short time. When he returned to Halle, his father was no more. Soon after, he went to Hamburg, where by playing the second violin [3] in the orchestra of

---

[1] His mother or nurse, we are told.

[2] The strings were banded with strips of cloth, to deaden the sound. They were much used in the cells of nunneries.

[3] The violin was not his instrument; he played badly, and was sneered at by the

the theatre, and giving some music lessons, he earned his living. Little is known of his doings from this time until he was invited to Lubec in company with his friend Mattheson to compete for a situation as organist : it was a question of replacing Buxtehude. Händel excelled his rivals ; but the old organist refused to resign unless in favor of a relative. "Take my daughter," he said, "and you shall have the situation ;" but neither Händel nor his friend cared for such a speculation, and, deriving no other benefit by their stay in Lubec than the opportunity to make themselves known, they went again to Hamburg.

Händel, who never seemed able to moderate the violence of his irascible temper, came near losing the friendship of Mattheson, by giving way to a paroxsym of rage. On the 5th of December, 1704, "Cleopatra," an opera of Mattheson's, was performed ; and he, Mattheson, who took the part of Antony, not having to appear in the last act, wished to take his place at the harpsichord, and direct the orchestra, according to Italian custom. But Händel, who was leading at the time, pretended that it was a direct insult to him, and refused to yield the harpsichord to the *maestro*. Impatient and excited almost to fury, he waited till the performance was over, and then had recourse to a duel to wash out the supposed affront. The two friends, suddenly become bitter enemies, drew their swords, and fought like old soldiers in the midst of a great crowd of spectators who made a circle about them. Mattheson rushed with impetuosity upon Händel ; but that kind Providence which watched over our young composer permitted the sword of his opponent to strike against a metal button, and break, which, thanks to the interference of a counsellor of Ham-

band; but one day when he took the place of the harpsichordist, who was absent, they changed their tune, and broke into loud applause.

burg, put an end to the shameful affray. However, the friends were soon reconciled. On the 30th of the following December, Mattheson received Händel at his table; and thereafter no cloud was permitted to shadow their reciprocal friendship. Although Händel devoted himself to teaching, and had a great number of pupils, he wrote much music, both instrumental and dramatic. In 1704 he wrote his first opera, "Almira," which was well received. Soon after he wrote "Nero" and "Florinda," which were not represented till 1708.

Having acquired a reputation, he desired to see Italy,[1] whither he went in 1706; first to Florence,[2] where he brought out his Italian opera, "Rodrigo." Then he went to Venice,[3] where he brought out "Agrippina," an opera which had twenty-six consecutive representations, a rare circumstance in those times. Whilst the celebrated Corelli was performing the overture of this work, Händel, who thought the violinist made a mistake, roughly snatched the violin from his hand, pretending to show him how the music ought to be executed. Instead of becoming excited by such rudeness, Corelli mildly answered, "But, my dear Saxon, this music is in French style, which I do not understand."

While in Rome,[4] he wrote the oratorio of the "Resure-

---

[1] The Prince Gaston de Medici had previously offered to furnish the means for a visit to Italy, which Händel refused, preferring to earn the money for that purpose.

[2] "He was but twenty-one years old when he went to Florence."

[3] Here he met Scarlatti, the great harpsichord-player of Italy. One night Scarlatti, entering a room in which Händel was playing, was so struck with the brilliancy of the performance, that he cried out, "It is either the Devil or the Saxon." Händel and Scarlatti were ever after good friends. "Händel always spoke of Scarlatti with admiration; and Scarlatti, whenever he was complimented on his own playing, used to pronounce Händel's name, and cross himself."

[4] Cardinal Ottoboni treated Händel with great kindness. The cardinal was the people's friend, and provided them with public entertainments, such as comedies, puppet-shows, operas, and the like, whilst he liberally patronized men of science and art.

zione," and the following year the " Pastorale " in Naples ;
then " Acis and Galatea," " Polifemo," and several other
pieces, among which were the allegory " Il Trionfo del
Tempo," and several cantatas. It was in Italy that Händel ripened into the great universal artist, full of inexhaustible resources, which were continually displaying
themselves through all the stages of his long life. He
brought his taste for vocalization to such a degree of
perfection that he could compete with the best Italian
vocalizers. This great vocal accomplishment contributed
not a little to the natural freshness and power of his deep,
full, streaming, and clear melodies.

The Elector of Hanover had offered Händel the situation of chapelmaster, with a salary of fifteen hundred
crowns ; he did even more : when he found that Händel
hesitated to accept this offer, because he wished to visit
England, he gave him leave of absence, stipulating that
his salary should continue the while. Such advantageous
conditions permitted the *maestro* to realize his project ; but
he did not wish to go away without first visiting his mother,
who had become blind. While in Hanover in 1710 as
musical director, he wrote for the Princess Caroline, among
other things, most of his Italian drawing-room duets. In
the same year he took a vacation, and went to London,
where he gained all hearts by his opera " Rinaldo," a good
part of which was arranged for the harpsichord : it was
given at the Haymarket Theatre on the 24th of February,
1711, after which he was *fêted* as the Apollo of his day.
" Rinaldo " was performed but four times, though the
score sold well. The editor Walsh gained fifteen hundred
pounds sterling by its publication. " My dear sir," said
Händel pleasantly to the editor, on hearing of his profits,
" every thing should be equal between us : you shall compose the next opera, and I will sell it."

At the expiration of his furlough he returned to Hanover laden with presents from Queen Anne, who expressed a desire to see him again in London. After a brief sojourn with the prince, he took another vacation, and again went to the hospitable shores of the Thames. This time he composed " Il Pastor Fido " and " Tesso." He was appointed to compose the " Te Deum " and " Jubilate," destined to celebrate the peace of Utrecht. These pieces were played July 7, 1713, with a full band and organ, to the great astonishment of the people, who never had heard sacred music with such an accompaniment. " A representation of ' Tesso ' was advertised May 16, 1713, for the benefit of Mr. Händel, with an entertainment on the harpsichord." " He played also at the house of Thomas Britton, a man who deserves particular mention.

"Thomas Britton belonged to that class of men whom persons of limited views are accustomed to term the lower orders of society; for he gained his bread by crying small coal, which he carried about the streets in a sack upon his shoulders. He lived near Clerkenwell Green, which he made illustrious. How he learned to play upon the *viola da gamba*, is not known ; but he played so well that he grouped around him a number of amateurs, as well as some of the most distinguished persons of the town. Britton was the tenant of a stable, which he divided horizontally by a floor ; on the ground floor was his coal-shop. It was in the upper story, a low room, in which it was hardly possible to stand upright, that the first meetings in the nature of private concerts took place in England, and instrumental music was regularly performed. Here it was that from 1678 to 1714, the period of his death, the itinerant small-coal merchant weekly entertained the intelligent world of London at his musical *soirées*, always gratuitously."

But the chapelmaster neglected to return at the time fixed, and by this, as well as by his composition of a "Te Deum" which was seen in an unfavorable light by all Protestant princes, he fell into disgrace with the Elector George, who became King of England in 1714. Händel brought out his new opera "Amadigi" in 1715. But he was not reconciled with the king till 1717, when, the latter expressing his delight with Händel's instrumental music performed at a water-party on the Thames, the Baron Kilmanseck procured for the artist an interview with the king, and Händel expressed his regret for having offended him. This procedure secured his pardon ; and, to prove its sincerity, the monarch doubled the salary which the deceased queen had given him. From this time Händel was the object of the most flattering attentions of the English nobility. The Count Burlingame even visited him at his lodgings.

In 1718 he became master of the Duke of Chandos' chapel, and removed to Cannon Castle, the residence of that lord.[1] It was in this castle that he composed the sublime oratorio of "Esther," being the first oratorio in the English language ; also the beautiful pastoral, "Acis and Galatea," poetized by Pope, Arbuthnot, and Gay.

One piece of Händel's which has been published many, many times under the name of "The Harmonious Blacksmith," was composed under the following circumstances : —

One day as the chapelmaster was going to Cannons, he was overtaken in Edgeware by a shower, and took shelter in the shop of a blacksmith named Powell. After the

[1] The Duke of Chandos had built for himself a palace, at a cost of two hundred and thirty thousand pounds. "On week-days the duke and duchess entertained all the wits and grandees in town ; and on Sundays the road was thronged with the gay equipages of those who went to worship at the ducal chapel to hear Mr. Händel play on the organ."

usual salutations, Powell continued his work at the forge, singing an old song the while. The hammer, striking in time, drew from the anvil two harmonic sounds, which, according with the melody, made a sort of continuous bass. Händel, struck by the incident, listened, remembered the air, and when he returned home composed for the harpsichord the much-admired " Harmonious Blacksmith."

A change took place in the life of Händel in 1720. A royal academy of music was founded in London,[1] and he, with Bononcini and others, were engaged. This enterprise, for which he wrote the " Radamisto "[2] and thirteen other operas, " Otto " being considered the best, lasted till 1728. All the works were represented in the Italian language, and in quality and performance they formed the most brilliant point of the Italian opera in Europe. Naturally Händel had many things to contend with, and his violent and overbearing temper nearly ruined him. The artists and managers of the theatre were opposed to the irascible Saxon, in consequence of which quarrels arose, so that a separation took place in 1728. Some of the proprietors organized a new theatre, and Händel felt obliged to take the burden of the Haymarket Theatre on his own responsibility. He went to Italy, and brought out several eminent artists, among whom was the celebrated singer Stradella. No greater proof of the fecundity of his genius can be given, than the great number of operas which he wrote and brought out under his own direction at this time.

This constant strain and anxiety had a bad influence on his health. He became momentarily insane; but, thanks to

[1] Several noblemen had subscribed fifty thousand pounds; but Händel found to his cost, that they were more ready to subscribe than to pay.

[2] " When Händel was composing, it was his custom always to speak Italian to himself; and, out of ten memoranda on his manuscripts, nine are written in that language."

his good constitution and strong will-power, as well as the baths of Aix-la-Chapelle, his mind was soon restored, also his right arm, which had been paralyzed. As to his fortune, that had all been spent, and he was in debt, and several times on the point of bankruptcy. Under these painful circumstances, the *maestro* did not belie the accustomed firmness of his character.[1] He bargained with the Covent Garden Theatre for the representation of his " Alceste," the score of which he had adapted, in part, to Dryden's ode, " La Festa d'Alessandro," and which was performed Feb. 10, 1736.

However, it was in vain that Händel brought out several operas : he did not succeed. By this time he felt sure that he could no longer calculate upon dramatic success. Then some of his friends thought of publishing a collection of his works for his benefit ; but the subscription hardly covered the expense of publication.[2] The Count of Middlesex, one of his admirers, came forward at this juncture, and took two works, " Pharamond " and " Alessandreo Severo," for which he paid one thousand pounds sterling. Händel wound up his dramatic career with three operas.

The artist was grieved at what appeared to him the indifference of the English [3] for his last scenic compositions. The thirty-eight operas which he had written are really dramatic in respect to truth and energy of expression, and

[1] " Händel was one of those few men who defend their honor to the death. He did not know what it was to retreat, and would have sacrificed every thing rather than submit to a humiliation."

[2] " True originality has usually the same battle to fight with conventional tastes, stupidity, or ignorance."

Händel's ordinary orchestra was much stronger than it is commonly supposed to have been.

[3] " With certain exceptions, the English aristocracy at that time had no great inclination for Händel."

in action, so far as it was possible for the Italian opera at that time. The fulness of the music, and the beauty of the solos in Händel's operas, have never been surpassed. "There is little doubt that Händel wrote many of his finest airs for particular voices."

Our illustrious musician was now forced, as it were, into the path where his genius met a lasting glory. Many of his operas have been forgotten long since, whilst his sacred music is yearly performed, not only in England, but in Germany and America. Although he had written "Deborah," "Esther," "Israel in Egypt," and "Athalia," he had occupied himself but incidentally with oratorios. But, on leaving the stage, he made a specialty of this sort of music, which afforded him the means of displaying his ability in the figurative style. By the introduction of organ solos in his oratorios, he made an innovation worthy of the composer of Halle. His admirable talent for execution was a powerful element of success to his works. As an organist, he had no rival in Europe at this time, if we except Johann Sebastian Bach.

He wrote a mourning hymn for Queen Caroline in 1737. "The score of this really sublime work, which does not occupy less than eighty pages of printing, was written in less than five days." Now it was that the enthusiasm of the Londoners for the German master, whom they had momentarily forsaken, was more than ever excited, and manifested itself by fabulous receipts. Moderately estimated, the product of the oratorio of "Saul," performed March 28, 1738, amounted to eight hundred pounds sterling. His "Israel in Egypt," given about the same time, acquired the admiration of the connoisseur, but not the general favor of the public. "About this time Mr. Tyers placed a statue of Händel in Vauxhall Gardens. This is said to be the only instance of a statue being erected in honor of an artist during his lifetime." In 1739, he gave the "Ode for St. Cecilia's Day," some compositions for instrumental music, and "L' Allegro ed il Pensieroso."

Being requested to compose something for the dedication of a concert-hall in Dublin, in 1741, he wrote the "Messiah" within four and twenty days, from the 22d of August to the 14th of September; but it was not performed until 1742, when it obtained immense and merited applause. This magnificent oratorio, Händel's masterpiece, has remained so popular in London, that there are at all times more than four thousand singers and instrumental performers capable of executing it from memory and without notes. He brought out "Samson" in 1743. This may be considered as introducing the real period of oratorios.

Now followed in rapid succession, "Joseph," "Semele," "Beelzebub," "Hercules" (with smaller works, as, for example, that for the celebration of the victory of Culloden), "Judas Maccabæus" in 1746; "Alexander Balus" and "Joshua" in 1747; "Solomon" and "Susanna" in 1748; "Theodora" in 1749; "Choice of Hercules" in 1750; "Jephtha" in 1751; at last, in 1757, "The Triumph of Time and Truth," a transformation of "Il Trionfo del Tempo," which he wrote in Rome, 1709. While composing "Jephtha"[1] in 1751, his eyes became diseased, and were operated on for cataract; but the skill of Dr. Sharp was powerless to restore. He lost his sight: yet, resigning himself courageously to his misfortune, he gave as before his twelve oratorical concerts yearly, at the Lental season, playing the organ himself. Eight days before his death, the "Messiah" was given: this oratorio

[1] "The last of his works. It was the song of the swan."

was the last in which he took an active part. He died April 4, 1759, at the age of seventy-four, and was buried in Westminster Abbey. He left six hundred pounds for his monument, which was erected by Roubiliac : this he did to prevent a public collection for that purpose. He left considerable property to charitable institutions and relatives in Germany.

Great in all the branches of his art, Händel is the real creator and perfector of oratorio. Händel's rapidity in composition and creative power have seldom been reached, never surpassed, although every one of his grand oratorios shows an individual formation and collective characteristic, which seems to have required most careful consideration.

Händel was of a noble and commanding appearance : his face was handsome, and wore an expression of tranquillity and mildness which strongly contrasted with that extreme violence of his character of which we have already made mention. One day when the singer Cuzzoni refused to sing an air of the opera "Othon," Händel seized her by the arm, dragged her to a window, and threatened to throw her into the street, if she obstinately refused to sing what he required. The poor terrified woman uttered cries of despair, and promised to sing whatever he desired.

Librettists who presumed to make changes in the text, without the master's consent, were treated in the same rough manner as the interpreters of his music. Aside from this defect, and some inclination for strong drink, the life of Händel is one of the purest that can be cited as an example to artists. While the extraordinary number of compositions with which he enriched the church and the theatre is without doubt the sign of a wonderful facility in composition, it is also a striking proof of a

regular and well-ordered life. Such a continuation of
labor is incompatible with habits of dissipation and disorder. Händel considered his art a sort of priesthood:
therefore, that he might devote himself to it unreservedly,
he remained single. His intimates were three particular
friends, — a painter named Goupy, a pupil named Smith,
and a dyer by the name of Hunter ; besides these, he
received few visitors. He kept aloof from social gather-
ings with as much care as most artists seek them. Certain people of London, finding that he sedulously refused
all invitations to visit, used to say of him, "He is a
bear." Be that as it may, this bear has left us masterpieces, which he would in all probability not have done, if
he had sacrificed his time to the frivolous amusements of
social life.

Händel left seven manuscript volumes to his secretary.
These manuscripts fell into the hands of a bookseller in
Bristol, who sold them to a Frenchman, M. Victor Schœl-
cher, the esteemed author of a life of Händel.

The "Messiah," though written in London, was intended
especially for Dublin, where it was performed April 13,
1742, to a large and enthusiastic audience. The proceeds,
amounting to four hundred pounds, were give to the poor.

One Sunday Händel asked the organist of a country
church where he had attended divine worship, to permit
him to play the people out, to which he readily consented.
But the people were so attracted by his music, that, instead
of vacating their seats, they remained until the organist,
losing his patience, told Händel that he never could play
them *out*, for they would stay *in* as long as he played.

"In the year 1738 only, Händel produced 'Saul,'
'Israel,' Dryden's 'Ode,' and the 'Twelve Grand Concertos,' works of different character, and each of which
was enough to establish the glory of a composer."

"While in Chester, on his way to Ireland, Händel was detained by contrary winds. Wishing to employ this delay in trying his new music, he sought for some one who could read music at sight. A house-painter named Janson was pointed out as the best the town afforded. Poor Janson made such a bungle of it, that the composer, purple with rage, cried out, 'You schountrel! tit you not tell me dat you could sing at soite?' — 'Yes, sir,' replied the astonished Janson, 'but not at *first sight.*' Upon this Händel burst out laughing, and the rehearsal proceeded no further."

"When Händel's 'Messiah' was first performed, the audience was much affected by the music; but when the chorus struck up, 'For the Lord God omnipotent,' in the Alleluia, they were so transported, that they all, even the king, who was present, started up and remained till the chorus ended."

"The 'Messiah' alone brought into the funds of the Foundling Hospital, London, no less than £10,299."

We are told that Händel set more value on the oratorio of "Theodora" than any of his other works. Burney says, "In 1749 his 'Theodora' was so unfortunately neglected, that he was glad to give orders for admission to any professors who did not perform. Two of these gentlemen having afterwards applied to Händel for an order to hear the 'Messiah,' he cried out, 'Oh, your sarvant, mein herren, you are tamnaple tainty! you would not co to "Teodora:" der was room enough to tance dere when dat was perform.'" This dear "Theodora" remained mistress of his heart, although she never brought him any thing but an empty house.

When a friend regretted that the house was so poor, Händel said, "Nevre moind: de music vil sount de petter."

One evening Mr. Fountayne and Händel were walking together in Marylebone Gardens, while the orchestra was playing. "Come, Mr. Fountayne," said Händel, "let us sit down and listen to this piece : I want to know your opinion of it." They sat down, and after a while, Mr. Fountayne turning to his companion said, "It is not worth listening to ; it's very poor stuff." — "You are right," said Händel quietly : "I thought so myself when I had finished it."

Dr. Quin says, "No man ever told a story with more effect ; but it was requisite for the hearer to have a knowledge of French, German, Italian, and English, all which languages he used in his narratives. Had he been as great a master of English as Swift, his *bon mots* would have been as frequent."

It is stated that an old manager of a London theatre, seeing at a rehearsal that the horn-players were quiet, asked them why they did not play. On their answering that they were counting their "*rests*," the indignant manager exclaimed, "Rests, indeed ! I pay you to *play*, not to *rest :* so either play up, or go away."

When the diploma of a Doctor of Music was offered to Händel, he refused it. On being asked why he did not take his degree, he replied, "Vat de dyfil I trow my money away for dat wich de blockhead wish ? I no want."

In his will Händel bequeathed all his manuscripts, his harpsichord and organ, to Christopher Smith, one of his pupils. Smith afterwards became attached to the household of George the Third, who granted him a pension from his own privy purse, presenting it with his own hands to Smith, who was then growing old. Smith, touched by the king's kindness, offered a present which was more than royal : he gave to George III. all Händel's manuscripts, the harpsichord, and the marble bust made by Roubiliac. Such is the origin of the Handelian collection at Buckingham Palace."

Händel's oratorios, properly so called, amount to seventeen. They commenced with "Esther," composed in 1720; "Deborah," in 1733, the period when he was becoming involved in difficulties; "Athalia," 1733; "Saul," 1738; "Israel in Egypt," 1738; "Messiah," 1741, with which he visited Ireland. After his return from Ireland, he wrote "Samson," 1743; "Joseph," 1743; "Belshazzar," 1745; "Occasional Oratorio," 1745; "Judas Maccabæus," 1746; "Alexander Balus," 1747; "Joshua," 1747; "Solomon," 1748; "Susanna," 1748; "Theodora," 1750; "Jephtha," 1752.

HASSE.

1699–1783.

John Adolphus Hasse, a renowned German composer, was born March 25, 1699, at Bergedorf, near Hamburg. He commenced his career as a tenor-singer in the Hamburg theatre, where Kaiser's compositions strengthened his desire for improvement, and determined him to make a thorough study of counterpoint. In 1722 he became court and theatre singer in Braunschweig, which position he gave up in 1724 to go to Italy. Whilst in Naples he studied with Porpora and Scarlatti. An opera which he composed gained for him universal sympathy, and the endearing title of *il caro Sassone*. In 1727 he was engaged as chapelmaster in a conservatory in Venice. It was there that he met with the celebrated singer Faustina Bordoni, whom he afterwards married.

The high reputation of both occasioned their being

called to Dresden, where he took the place of first chapel-master, with a salary of twelve thousand thalers. However, he did not settle permanently in Dresden until 1740, after his return from London. Through the bombardment of Dresden in 1760, he lost his books and his manuscript music which was fully prepared for an edition of his works. Hasse gave up his position in 1763; however, he received a suitable pension. Then he went to Vienna, and in 1770 took his family to Venice, where he died Dec. 23, 1783. Hasse was indisputably the most intelligent composer of his times. Only a few years before his death, he had composed a " Requiem," intending it for his own funeral service, which shows that he had retained his powers for composition to an advanced age.

GRAUN.

1701–1759.

CHARLES HENRY GRAUN, a German composer, was born at Wahrenbrück in Saxony. At the age of twelve he was sent to the Kreuzschule in Dresden, where he studied vocal music with Cantor Grundig, and the piano with the organist Pezold. He took lessons in composition of Chapel-master Schmidt, and cultivated his taste by careful study and hearing good operas, so that when he left the school, in 1720, he began to compose for the church. In 1725 he was appointed tenorist, and soon after vice-chapel-master in Braunschweig.

In 1735 the Crown Prince of Prussia, afterwards King Frederick II., gave him a position in his chapel at Rheinsberg; while there, he wrote many cantatas. When the prince ascended the throne in 1740, he made Graun his Chapel-master, and sent him to Italy to engage the necessary male and female singers for his new opera.[1] After his return he was constantly occupied with compositions for the same. He died in Berlin, Aug. 8, 1759. As a singer, he was distinguished in the execution of the *adagio*, as well as for his refined and good taste. His first compositions were motets for the school in Dresden. Then he wrote church pieces for the Cantor Reinholdt. The number of pieces which he composed in Braunschweig, Rheinsberg, and Berlin, is very great; among them are thirty operas. His music for Ramler's passion-oratorio, " Der Tod Jesu," is considered a masterpiece, particularly on account of the recitative and chorus.

W. F. BACH.

1710–1784.

WILHELM FRIEDEMANN, the eldest, was perhaps the most gifted, but certainly the most unfortunate, of all the sons of the immortal Bach. Wilhelm Friedemann was born in Weimar, 1710. He was an organist first in Dresden, then in Halle. He lived in Leipzig, Braunschweig, Göttingen, and Berlin, where he ended his sad life, July 1, 1784. Much has been extravagantly related of his peevishness, ill-humor, distracted and disorderly conduct, which cannot be verified.

PERGOLESE.

1710–1736.

GIOVANNI BAPTISTA PERGOLESE was born at Jesi in the Roman States, Jan. 8, 1710. He entered the " Conservatory for the Poor " at Naples, where he learned to play the violin, when he was about thirteen. His aptitude for

---

[1] Whilst Graun was in Italy, the king constructed one of the most complete and one of the most magnificent theatres of Europe.

music, and his natural intelligence, helped him through the
greatest difficulties with little or no assistance.   One day
his teacher asked him where he had learned what he was
playing : the young virtuoso answered ingenuously, that
he was simply playing what came to his mind, and that he
did not know if it was good or bad.   Matteis, his professor, desired him to write on paper what he had been
playing.   The next morning Pergolese handed him a
sonata in which he had clearly expressed his ideas by
means of the most happy combinations.   Matteis, more
and more surprised, carried the composition to the head
master of the conservatory, who conceived a great liking
for Pergolese, and took upon himself the direction of his
studies in composition.

Pergolese was still a pupil at the conservatory, when, in
the summer of 1731, he gave his first great work, a sacred
drama, which was performed at the Cloister of St. Agnes.
Through this work he obtained the patronage of the *élite*
of Neapolitan society in a trice.   Soon after he gave two
operas, both of which were so unsuccessful that he wrote
no more theatrical music for several years.   He then composed thirty trios for two violins and a bass.   This he did
expressly for Prince Stigliano-Colonna, his protector.

Meanwhile there was an earthquake which brought consternation to the inhabitants of Naples.   The magistrates
wished to conjure away the danger by a religious ceremony
in the Church of Santa Maria : therefore they requested
Pergolese to compose music suitable for the occasion.
It was then that he wrote his magnificent mass for ten
voices, two choruses, and two orchestras ; also a *mag-
nificat* (psalm) for vespers.   These compositions excited
universal admiration.

After this he again turned his attention to dramatic

writings, and brought out his famous interlude, "La Serva Padrona," which had the most brilliant success. Although there are in the piece only two singing-actors and a mute person, the interest does not flag for an instant, thanks to the truth of the musical expression as well as to the elegance and vivacity of the dialogue. A simple quartet of instruments accompanies the duet.

Pergolese went to Rome in 1734, where he, unfortunately for himself, wrote "L'Olimpiade." Though filled with gems of rare beauty, it had too many details for the ability of the Roman public of that time, and was not well received.

Greatly disappointed, our composer again turned his attention to religious music, which had never betrayed him, and composed the celebrated "Salva Regina," the same year he composed the much-admired cantata, "L'Orphea." Some time before he went to Rome, he had commenced his "Stabat Mater," which had been ordered by a brotherhood to replace that of Scarlatti, sung every Friday through Lent, and for which he had been paid forty francs in advance.

Pergolese was fast wearing away; his lungs were badly affected, and he went to reside in Pozzuoli for the benefit of the sea-air. While there he composed his last song. Although wasting away by fever and phthisic, he worked with incredible ardor. In vain his teacher and friend Feo, who was visiting him, endeavored to persuade him to take some rest. Pergolese heeded not his intercessions. "Oh, my dear master," he said, "I have no time to lose. I *must* finish this work for which I have been paid ten ducats, and which is not worth ten biocchi." When Feo visited him again, the "Stabat" was finished and sent away; but he, the writer, was lying at the point of death.

He died March 16, 1736, at the age of twenty-six. He
was buried a few days after, with little or no ceremony,
in the church of Pozzuoli. Hardly were his eyes closed
when his contemporaries were sensible of having lost a
great artist, and set about bringing his name before the
public, to effect which they raised a report of his having
been poisoned; but this was soon found to be false.
Then they caused his operas to be performed in all the
theatres. Rome called for his "Olimpiade," which they
received with wild applause : the poor defunct had become
the man of the day. For many years his compositions
were continually heard in the churches; and in 1749, thirteen years after his death, a middling-class troop of Italian
singers introduced "La Serva Padrona," and "Il Maestro
di Musica" into France, together with the name of Pergolese, whose talent excited great admiration. His works
were translated into French, and everywhere performed
with success. Naturally it was the same with his "Stabat
Mater," which was introduced into religious concerts, and
of which many editions were published. Finally a monument was erected to his memory in the church of Pozzuoli.

The "Stabat" of Pergolese is one of the masterpieces
of sacred music. In it there is depth of feeling, and an
expression of tenderness, compassion, and love, sustained
throughout.

ARNE.

1710–1778.

Thomas Augustine Arne, one of the best-known
English composers, was born in London, 1710. He was
the son of a paper-hanger, and educated at Eton. His
father destined him for the profession of law; but his

inclination for music prevented his complying with his father's wishes. He gave himself up to the study of the violin, piano, and composition. His first essay was a farce entitled " Tom Thumb," which was performed at the Haymarket Theatre in 1733. His " Comus," which soon followed, was considered an excellent production.

In 1740 he married Cecilia Young, pupil of Gemeniani, a distinguished singer of the Drury Lane Theatre. Both were favorably received in Ireland, where they remained two years. On their return to London, Arne was composer for, and his wife singer at, Drury Lane. In 1759 the title of Doctor of Music was conferred on him at Oxford. His operas were very successful. He also composed some oratorios, which, of course, could not compare with those of the immortal Händel. Of his twenty-five operas, we will only mention " Zara," " Don Saverio," "King Arthur," and "The Guardian Outwitted." His oratorios are " Alfred," " Judith," and " Trip to Portsmouth." Besides the above, he composed many songs, among which is the well-known " Rule Britannia." Madame Arne died about 1765 ; her husband followed her in 1778.

JOMELLI.
1714–1774.

It cannot be disputed that Jomelli was the most brilliant composer of the Neapolitan school, which during half a century produced some fifty musical celebrities. The strict discipline of the conservatories, together with the laborious lives to which the pupils were subjected, contributed to this result. Young artists did not leave these establishments until they were well skilled in the exercises of writing and composing. But as Jomelli proposed to write for the church, and the schools of Naples prepared their pupils for dramatic composers, there was little prospect of his meeting with success until he had studied in Rome, whither he went, favored by the Cardinal of York.

However, in 1741 he obtained permission to perform "L'Ezio" in Bologna. Whilst in that city, he paid a visit to P. Martini, introducing himself as a pupil desirous to take lessons. The good Martini was much astonished at the facility with which the so-called pupil performed the fugue he gave him to try. "Who are you?" he exclaimed: "do you come here to make fun of me? It is I who ought to take lessons of you." — "My name is Jomelli," replied the composer. "I am the person who is to write the opera for the theatre of this city." — "It is of great advantage to the theatre to have a philosophical musician like you," answered Martini; "but allow me to pity you, who will find yourself in the midst of a crowd of ignoramuses, who only corrupt music."

If the learned abbé was wanting in genius, he possessed a profound knowledge of art, which Jomelli was pleased to recognize.

Successful in Bologna and Rome, Jomelli returned to Naples, and put "Eumeneo" upon the stage. In 1749, thanks to the intervention of Cardinal Albani, Jomelli secured a position at St. Peter's, which he filled satisfactorily until May, 1754, when he left for the more advantageous one of Chapel-master to the Duke of Würtemburg.

This was one of the most munificent of the German princes, to whom honor is due for the encouragement he gave to art and artists.

Whilst poor Mozart was miserably paid, and treated like a servant, by the haughty Archbishop of Salzburg, Jomelli was luxuriating at Stuttgard on a salary of four thousand florins, with servants and horses at his command. And, besides a house in Stuttgard, he had a country-seat at Ludwigsburg. Honored by the duke, it was easy for him to do as he pleased with the musicians, in regard to the execution of his own works.

As an Italian, it was natural that he should be prejudiced in favor of Italian artists ; and it was some time before he had faith in the ability of the young Mozart. However, when at length convinced, the good Father Leopold could find no fault with the reception which Jomelli gave to Wolfgang.

Jomelli's long residence in Germany, and association with German musicians, tended greatly to improve his instrumentation, in so far that his countrymen called him the " Gluck dell'Italia." Having gained a handsome fortune, the artist returned to his native city, Aversa. The failure of some of his operas preyed upon his mind, and saddened his last days ; he died in Naples at the age of sixty. The compositions of Jomelli are distinguished by their ease, elevated ideas, and dramatic expression. One cannot help feeling that every phrase tells : inspiration is never wanting. His last production, a " Miserere," is a masterpiece.

C. P. E. BACH.

1714–1788.

CARL PHILIP EMANUEL BACH was born in Weimar, March 14, 1714. He studied law in Leipzig, then went to Frankfort and Berlin. In 1740 he became court musician, and accompanist to Frederick the Great in flute-playing In 1767 he was director of music in Hamburg, where he died. His chief merit consists in the influence he exercised upon pianoforte-playing, through his " Essay on the True Art of Piano-playing," as well as by his masterly compositions, the originality and freshness of which render them truly valuable. His oratorio " Die Israeliten in der Wuste," and other sacred compositions, are much renowned.

GLUCK.

1714–1787.

CHRISTOPHER WILLIBALD GLUCK, one of the most celebrated of German composers, was born on the 2d of July, 1714, at Weidenwang by Newmarket in the Upper Palatinate. His father, a forester,[1] took him to Bohemia, at the age of thirteen, where he attended different schools at Eisenberg, Kommatan, Kamnitz, and Prague,[2] to learn the elements of science and music. He made good progress in singing, playing the violin, pianoforte, and organ. After singing for some time with the choir of St. Ignatius Church, he went to Vienna in 1736 to complete his musical education. There is no doubt that the time was well chosen ; for there were then many artists of renown in that city.

For a time he earned his living by teaching and playing the violin in different villages, where he sometimes took his pay in eggs, which he exchanged for bread when opportunity offered.

Whilst he was in Prince Lobkowitz' house, Prince Melzi of Milan heard him sing, and play the violoncello. The prince became so much interested in the young man, that

---

[1] " His father, a rough and severe man, obliged him and his brother Anton to go barefooted with him through the forest in midwinter, to toughen them, as he said."

[2] Father Czernohorsky, an excellent musician, taught Gluck to play the violoncello and otherwise assisted him.

he took him to Milan, and placed him under the instruction of Giovanni Battista Sammartini, a distinguished composer and organist. Gluck's first opera, " Artarsersi," in 1741, was soon followed by many others for different Italian theatres, so that in 1744 the young artist had already given eight operas with good success ; and now he received a commission to compose an opera for London. He went there in 1745, and the following year brought out "La Caduta de'Giganti," an opera, which, however, did not please the public. "Artamene," which had already been performed in Italy, and which he brought out with some alterations, pleased better. Some writers affirm that Händel pronounced both these operas detestable. This severe judgment of the author of " The Messiah " may be easily explained, when we consider that Gluck had not yet commenced those compositions which have placed him in the rank of immortal musicians.

His engagements in England finished, Gluck returned to the Continent, where he obtained a situation in the royal chapel at Dresden. Shortly after, the death of his father obliged him to return to his native town to attend to the paternal estate. In 1748 he went to Vienna, where he settled himself permanently, only travelling from time to time to transact such business as his music required.

The first of his operas put upon the stage in Vienna was " Semiramide riconosciuta," in 1748. "Telemaco" and "La Clemenza di Tito," with various other works, were performed in Vienna, Rome, and Naples. In 1755 " Il Trionfo di Camillo" and "Antigono" were brought out in Rome, in consequence of which he received from the pope the order of the Golden Spur, and signed himself Chevalier de Gluck. From this time till 1762 he wrote several operas for Vienna and Italian cities, the last of which, "Il Trionfo di Clelia," was performed at Bologna.[1]

Gluck never worked in the afternoon. Dinner over, he made calls, took a walk, or went to a coffee-house, where he remained till supper-time.

Meanwhile he had come to the conclusion that much superior effects could be obtained by a difference in the arrangements and quality of the Italian text-books which had been in use since the time of Metastasio, and by taking into consideration the dramatical as well as the lyrical part.[2] These reflections he communicated to his friend, the poetically gifted Raniero von Calzabigi, who warmly entered into the views of the composer, and placed the text of the opera "Orfeo ed Euridice," which he had prepared in the newly accepted form, in the hands of the artist, who composed the music for it. This opera was performed in 1762 for the first time, at Vienna. His next opera was "Alceste," in 1769; then followed "Paride ed Elena," in 1772, likewise written in the new method by Calzabigi. The three reform operas with their simple airs, carefully declaimed recitatives, and deeper characterization, were not generally successful in the beginning, to the disappointment of both poet and composer; and Gluck found it impossible to confine himself exclusively to the new system. Besides the three above-mentioned operas, he was obliged to compose some in the old form, for example, "Ezio," "La Corona," "Aristeo." Perhaps he would have entirely suspended his reformatory exertions, since they appeared to find no favor, had not Rollet, who was at that time with the French embassy in Vienna,

---

[1] In this city Gluck made the acquaintance of the celebrated Father Martini.

[2] It is worthy of remark, that the author had been writing twenty-odd years for the theatre before he thought of reform.

directed the attention of Gluck to Paris, where the chances of a successful realization of his views were much greater. Rollet complied with the request of Gluck to arrange Racine's "Iphigénie en Aulide" into a text for an opera. Then Rollet made the necessary arrangements with the director of the Grand Opera in Paris, whither Gluck went in the autumn of 1773 ; and, after overcoming many difficulties, he succeeded in bringing out his "Iphigénie" Feb. 14, 1774. The success of this opera was not perceptible until after its second representation.

Marie Antoinette, then dauphine, had somewhat aided Gluck by attempting to overcome the repugnance of the French musicians to Gluck's music ; still there were two parties, viz., the friends of Lulli's and Rameau's schools, which still ruled at the Grand Opera, as well as the representatives of the Italian method. The Abbé Arnault placed himself at the head of Gluck's defenders in opposing the repeated attacks made upon him in the journals of the day. Gluck, determined to conquer, hastily rearranged "Orfeo ed Euridice," [1] which had already been given in Vienna. It was performed Aug. 2, 1774. The enthusiasm with which this work was received may be conceived by the forty-nine consecutive representations given that summer. Indeed, the second act is one of the most astonishing productions of the human mind. This masterpiece was followed, with less success, by "L'Arbre Enchantée," and "La Cythère assiégée" in 1775. Soon after, he put upon the stage his newly adapted tragic opera, "Alceste," the text of which Rollet had carefully prepared.

---

[1] In this opera, written when Gluck was forty-eight years of age, he displayed his powers as a great composer, and heralded a new era in music. He is said to be "the founder of the German opera."

Gluck was now the man of the day. People were anxious to get a sight of him; and many begged, as a great favor, to be permitted to be present at the general rehearsals, that they might see him direct the performance of his work in his nightcap and negligée. During the first performance of this opera, some one among the spectators cried out, "The piece has fallen." — "Fallen from heaven," replied the imperturbable Abbé Arnauld, who created a name for himself by his devoted attachment to the cause of Gluck. Whilst Mlle. Levasseur was singing, —

"Il me déchire et m'arrache le cœur," —

a voice was heard to say, "Ah, miss, you tear out my ears!" which was immediately answered by, "How fortunate, if it is to give you others!" Such was the war of words continually going on between the friends and enemies of the German musician.

Gluck returned to Vienna, and was busied in writing the music to "Roland" and "Armida," when he heard that the amateurs of Italian music in Paris, who thought that his works were wanting in melody, had raised up a rival in the person of Piccini, whom they had called to Paris with a commission to write an opera having Roland for the hero.

Gluck, very much excited, wrote a letter to his friend Du Rollet, complaining bitterly of the manner in which he was treated, not sparing Piccini in his haughty and scornful manner. This letter was published in the "Année litteraire" of 1776, and was the signal for a heated literary engagement.

Gluck hastened to Paris; the opera-hall became the field of battle. The champions of Gluck, at whose head stood the Abbé Arnauld and Suard, took their place beside the king's box, whilst Piccini's friends, headed by Marmontel, Laharpe, and Ginguené, ranged themselves by the queen's box. This gave rise to the name " war of the corners," given to this quarrel. Gluck was ill-treated by Laharpe ; and, without leaving to others the care of defending him, he immediately wrote an overpowering letter to his detractor, who responded in verse, which brought forth an answer from Gluck also in verse. The strife between the two musical parties called forth many newspaper articles, pamphlets, and epigrams, and lasted several years. Every new work that Gluck, or his opponent Piccini, brought out, caused a renewal of the fight.

In 1776 Gluck's " Armida " was performed, and had a cool reception, though fully appreciated afterwards. In 1778 Piccini brought out his " Roland " triumphantly : Gluck had laid his aside. On the 18th of May, 1779, Gluck gained a decisive victory with his " Iphigénie en Tauride." All Paris was enraptured with this masterpiece, which proved the superiority of Gluck's genius. Many are of the same mind as the Abbé Arnauld, who found only one beautiful part in it, and that was the whole. Previous to this time, music had not fully rendered the sentiments of the personages. Whilst Orestes is singing, " My heart is calm," the orchestra continues to paint the agitation of his thoughts. When, during the rehearsal, the musicians who did not understand it stopped, the artist cried out with vehemence, " Go on, go on ! he lies : he has killed his mother." Another saying of his is still more significant. One day when he was praising Rameau's chorus of " Castor and Pollux," one of his admirers said to him by way of flattery, " But what a difference between this chorus and that of your ' Iphigénie ' ! " — " Yet it is very well done," replied Gluck: "one is only a religious ceremony, the other is a real funeral." He had the habit of saying, before setting an opera to music, "I try to forget that I am a musician." [1]

Gluck was unsuccessful with "Echo and Narcisse," an opera in three acts, which was performed Sept. 24, 1779. He had now come to the time of life when rest is required. Feeling hurt by the failure of his opera, he left France, and returned to Vienna, much against the will of Marie Antoinette, who did all in her power to detain him in Paris. His dramatic career was now terminated, and he could peacefully enjoy the fortune which he had made at the theatre.

Gluck was excessively proud.[2] His dedicatory epistles, though remarkable for the clearness of the dramatic theories therein set forth, betray his self-love. There is no doubt that all superior men are conscious of their own merit, and that the greater part of them do not conceal this consciousness. But that which is more to be blamed in Gluck than his lack of modesty is, that his egotism led him to try to injure his rivals. It is said in Vienna, that he used all means to crush the growing reputation of Mozart.[3] At Paris he was known to intrigue against Piccini.[4]

---

[1] Gluck has been accused of vanity. If so, " it is the vanity of the eagle as he wheels above the horde of small birds, and rejoices to be alone with the sun."

[2] His pride was genius conscious of its own immortality.

[3] This is doubtful, inasmuch as he extolled Mozart's music, and invited him and his wife to dinner ; and Mozart speaks of him with reverence and affection.

[4] Other authors say that " Gluck was a single-minded man, devoted to music, and generous to other musicians.

" If he loved money, his purse-strings were often loosed for the needy, and many of his detractors were fed at his hospitable board."

" His house was ever open to the lovers of art; and no stranger missed seeing him, if it were possible."

Salieri consulted Gluck, whose advice he highly esteemed, about his cantata of

His manners were pure; but he was unfortunately very avaricious, and somewhat addicted to drink. He himself declared that he loved money better than any thing; wine next; and, after these, glory. "There can be nothing more logical," he said, by way of explaining this gradation of his tastes. "With the money I buy wine, the wine inspires me, and the inspiration brings me glory."

The reasoning was not so bad; but the composer forgot to add that he liked something stronger than wine. His wife, who knew his weakness, also knew how prejudicial strong drinks were to his health, and kept a careful watch over him. But one day, when a friend came to dine with Gluck, coffee and liquors were served after the repast. The master, who had been deprived of such things for a long time, took advantage of a moment when his wife turned her back, seized a decanter of brandy, and swallowed the contents at once. This imprudence was immediately followed by a fit of apoplexy, which carried off the illustrious musician, Nov. 25, 1787.

ABEL.

1725-1787.

CHARLES FREDERIC ABEL, a celebrated musician, and the most skilful performer on the "viola da gamba" of his time, was born at Coethen, 1725, and learned music under Sebastian Bach. He was employed for ten years at the Royal Chapel of Dresden, when the misfortunes of war obliged the court to reduce its expenses. Abel left in 1758, and travelled through Germany, thence to England, where the Duke of York procured a situation for him, with

"The Last Judgment." Neither being able to decide upon the key in which the Saviour should speak, Gluck said, "In a short time I can tell you for a certainty from the other world." Four days after, he was no longer among the livin,.

a salary of two hundred pounds sterling. Soon after, he was made director of the Chapel of the Princess. He remained in London until 1783, then went to Berlin, where, although sixty-four years old, he excited general admiration by his fine, expressive performances.

Although his temper was quick, and his manners unrefined, he was well received in society. He died June 27, 1787, of a lethargy which lasted three days.

He wrote some seventeen works, which were published in London, Paris, and Berlin. Abel wrote for the English operas, "Love in a Village," and "Berenice."

TRAETTA.
1727-1779.

TRAETTA of Bitonto, in the kingdom of Naples, was educated by Durante at the Conservatory of Loretto, where he studied seven years, after which he taught singing, and wrote music for the churches and convents of Naples. Such was the success of his first opera, performed at St. Carlo, that the manager of that theatre engaged six others, to be performed as fast as composed; a rare piece of good fortune for a young beginner. We are told that Venice, Milan, Rome, and Turin contended for the productions of his pen. The Duke of Parma invited him to his court, made him chapel-master, and teacher of the princesses of his family. Traetta, to prove himself worthy of the high trusts reposed in him, wrote the opera "Ippolito and Aracia" for the celebration of the marriage of the *infante* of Parma with the prince royal of Spain; which was so gratifying to the Court of Spain, that they granted the author a pension.

After the death of Don Philip, Traetta left Parma, and

went to Venice, to direct the conservatory. Two years had scarcely elapsed, when Catherine II. of Russia, hearing his fame, tempted him to come to her court by the most brilliant offers, which he accepted. He composed several operas in a short space of time; but the climate of Russia completely discouraged him. His health was beginning to fail; and what were the accumulation of wealth, and the favors of princes, in comparison to that inestimable gift of health? He must breathe the air of his native country. Permission to go was reluctantly granted by the empress. But it was in vain that he sought to re-establish his health: he languished only a few years.

Like most of the great artists, Traetta was fully conscious of his own merits, and often betrayed the good opinion he had of his works in the most *naïve* manner. It is said of him, that whilst at the harpsichord, directing his opera, he would turn to the public, and say, "Now, ladies and gentlemen, just listen to this."

RICHTER.

1728–1809.

CARL GOTTLIEB RICHTER, born at Berlin, 1728, was considered one of the first German organists, and performers on the harpsichord. Few of his works were published. Among them, however, were, "Six Trios for the Flute," "Two Concertos for the Harpsichord" published in 1772, and "Nine Concertos for the Harpsichord" published in 1775. Richter was master of the celebrated Reichardt.

PICCINI.

1728–1800.

THE name of Piccini recalls the memorable quarrels in which the destiny of the opera was for a time involved. Piccini was forced to yield the palm to Gluck in the unequal contest; for genius will always have the advantage of talent, however great this latter may be.

But it was none the less a great honor for the author of "Didon" to have been chosen as the champion of Italian music. Piccini deserved this honor on account of the multiplicity of his ideas, his capability in the arrangement of dramatic scenes, and also for the ardent conviction which never ceased to animate him.

Nicholas Piccini was born at Bari, in the kingdom of Naples, 1728. His father, a musician, destined him to the ministry, and the child studied to enter holy orders, but nature had made him an artist. If he heard an operatic air, he was sure to remember it ; and his greatest pleasure was to reproduce it upon the piano when he was not observed. One day, in the house of the Bishop of Bari, he took the advantage of being alone in a room where there was a piano ; and, seating himself at it, he played to his heart's content. The prelate, happening to be in an adjoining room, was astonished at the correctness and precision of the performance. "Send the boy, by all means, to a conservatory of music, and not to a theological seminary," he said to the elder Piccini. "If the vocation for the priesthood brings trials and sacrifices, a musical career is not less beset with obstacles. Music demands great perseverance and incessant labor. It exposes one to many chagrins." All this Piccini well knew by experience.

However, he followed the sage advice of the prelate, and placed his son at the school of St. Onofrio when he was fourteen years old. At first he did not study in a manner to confirm the high opinions raised by his natural taste and ability.

The tutor whose duty it was to inculcate the elements of music was wanting in the faculty of making study a pleasure; and our young pupil, disgusted with his lessons, neglected them, and set about writing psalms, hymns, cantatas, and oratorios, under the guidance of his precocious inspiration. He already passed for a prodigy in the eyes of his fellow-students, when an entire mass composed by him came to the notice of the director Leo, who, after examining it carefully, required the boy to perform it. All the professors complimented the gifted composer; but the excellent Leo, more judicious, added serious words to his praise, reproving Piccini for his neglect of application to study, when, with such rich natural faculties, he had every prospect of success. Piccini made such excuses as he could for the little instruction that he had previously received; and Leo kindly promised to take charge of his musical education himself. Leo died soon after, and was succeeded by Durante, one of the best-informed composers of Italy, who said of Piccini, "He is my son : the others are my pupils."

In 1754 Piccini appeared as a dramatic composer. He was then twenty-four years old. His first opera, "La Donna dispettosa," had pretty good success; but he gained much celebrity in the following year, when he brought out "Le Gelosie." This opera brought him to the notice of the managers of San Carlo, who engaged him to write "Zenobia," a serious opera, in which he succeeded as well as in the bouffe style.

Stimulated by success, Piccini wrote a number of operas, both comic and serious, which gained him a reputation throughout Italy. In 1758 the composer was called to Rome, and there gave "Allessandro nell' Indie." The brilliant success of this composition was only surpassed by that of "La Buona Figlia," performed about two years after ; the text is from Goldoni. Piccini now became the favorite of the Italians, particularly those of Rome and Naples ; indeed, no other composer could compete with him.

Piccini had great facility in composing ; it is said that it took him only about eighteen days to compose his *chef-d'œuvre*. In 1761 he composed no less than six operas, all of which were well received. Not only was he happy as an artist, but he enjoyed the delights of a pleasant home. His wife, a pupil named Vicenza Sibilla, was an excellent woman, distinguished for her beauty, the purity of her singing, and the charms of her mind.

Piccini's government over the stage, and feelings of the people, continued until 1773, when he experienced his first defeat in Rome, where a coterie of enemies and envious people intrigued against him. Grieved by the failure of his opera, Piccini became seriously ill. Meanwhile Gluck was revolutionizing the French lyric stage ; and his opponents determined to bring forward a rival in the person of the composer whose name was famous throughout Italy. In 1775[1] they offered Piccini the sum of six thousand

---

[1] In 1775 a member of the family of the Duke of Brunswick visited Piccini, whom he found rocking the cradle of his youngest child, whilst the next older was pulling him by the coat to make him play with her. The mother, seeing a stranger of distinction at the door, ran away, for she was *en dishabille*. The young prince excused himself for entering unannounced, and added, "I am delighted to see so great a man living in such simplicity, and that the author of 'La Bonne Fille' is such a good father."

francs indemnity for whatever losses he might sustain by leaving Italy, and a dwelling in the hotel of the ambassador.

The health of Piccini being re-established, he accepted the proffered terms, and went to Paris, where he commenced a new chapter in his active life. He was kindly received by the Marquis von Carracciolo ; but his house was small, and his apartments not prepared for guests. Piccini was therefore lodged in the garret of a *hôtel garni*, near the Palais Royal. The poet Marmontel, who lived opposite, immediately befriended him : he taught him the French language, and arranged the lyric tragedies of Quinault for his use. Piccini passed his time in the bosom of his family, assiduously studying the language, in which he made rapid progress, and composing.

The engagement of Piccini had been kept secret. Rollet, however, discovered it, and wrote to Gluck, who became much irritated. Aside from the question of talent, Gluck had every advantage over his rival ; for, besides being a favorite of the queen, he was protected by the musicians whom he had instructed in the new forms of his own style.

Piccini, whose disposition was mild and timid, was frightened by the storm which arose at the rehearsal of "Roland," the opera with which he commenced ; and, in truth, he was more dead than alive when the day came for its public performance ; but, notwithstanding his fears and the management of the Gluckists, his success was complete.

The contest of these two great rivals was called the " war of the corners," because the friends of the German master ranged themselves on the side of the king's box, whilst those of his adversary were on that of the queen.

Whilst the Piccinists attacked even the person of Gluck, who was sufficiently versed in French to answer by fresh disputes, the Gluckists spared Piccini, who knew only French enough to understand the poems which were submitted to him, though they often came down upon his partisans.

In the mean time the Italian composer was enjoying more honorable than productive favors. He was giving singing-lessons to the queen at Versailles, who was so much pleased with his instruction that she did not even think of paying his travelling-expenses to Versailles. He also performed the opera of "Phaon" before the court at Choisy. Though greatly admired, this opera was never put upon the stage of Paris. Unfortunately, all idea of remuneration was out of the question; and he lost the magnificent volumes of his score, which were distributed among the members of the royal family. His correspondence shows how greatly he was annoyed by such carelessness and neglect. His distress for means of living contrasted singularly with the royal favors he was said to be enjoying.[1]

In 1778 Piccini was appointed to direct an Italian troupe in Paris, and his situation was thus somewhat improved. He took advantage of his position in bringing out several of his old scores. Just when the contest between the Gluckists and Piccinists seemed to be subsiding, the director of the opera suddenly revived it, by giving the libretto of the same subject, viz., "Iphigénie en Tauride," to the two different parties; one was sent to Gluck, the

---

[1] An order for a march from a Russian colonel greatly relieved his pressing wants. It pleased so much, that the colonel paid him liberally. Piccini in sport declared that he would immediately go to Russia, get an appointment through the colonel, and make his fortune at once.

other to Piccini.[1] The opera of Gluck was performed in
1779, with a success which almost crushed his rival, who,
under such circumstances, ought to have given up his
work ; but some imprudent friends advised him to complete his score, notwithstanding that they were aware of
the inferiority of his libretto. Piccini waited two years,
and then ventured to perform it,[2] thus exposing himself to
certain defeat. Afterwards he brought out "Adèle de
Ponthieu," a weak production, which did not give satisfaction. But his opera "Didon," performed in 1783, met
with good success, and was considered as a masterpiece.
"Le Dormeur éveillé " and "Le faux Lord," given in 1783,
pleased very much as comic operas. In 1784 he was
nominated professor of singing in the royal school, when
his good fortune forsook him. Jealousy and envy stared
him continually in the face, several of his operas were unsuccessful, others were not performed, and, to crown the
whole, he lost nearly all the little property he had been
able to lay aside. He then decided to return to Naples.
He was somewhat consoled by the reception given him at
Lyons, and the kindness with which the court and people
of Naples [3] received him. But a sort of fatality seemed
to hover over him. Toward the end of the year 1792, he
was suspected of being a republican, because he had married one of his daughters to a young Frenchman established
in Naples.[4] This accusation, spread by two of his former

[1] The director of the opera not only over-persuaded Piccini, but promised him
that his Iphigénie en Tauride should be performed first; for Piccini well knew that the
work of Gluck would cast his own in the shade.

[2] To add to the artist's trials, the actress whom he had carefully taught to sing the
part of Iphigenia came upon the stage so drunk that she could scarcely stand : nevertheless she went through the part without making a single mistake.

[3] The king gave him a most flattering reception, granted him a pension, and
ordered several works to be written immediately.

[4] Queen Caroline of Naples, who was very homely, imagined that she resembled

pupils, excited the populace against him, and caused the failure of his opera "Hercules." However, during a sojourn of nine months in Venice, he was successful with his operas "Greselda" and "Il servo Padrone." On his return to Naples, the minister Acton[1] put him and his family in a sort of imprisonment, where he remained nearly four years. Forlorn and destitute, he employed his time in writing psalms for convents, which he was too poor to have copied. With the conclusion of the treaty of peace with the French republic, ended his captivity; and he could communicate with his friends in Paris, through whom he learned that the papers and articles of value which he had left in that city were lost. The tenor David, deeply affected by the situation of Piccini, obtained a new engagement for him with a Venetian manager; but his friends at Rome, where he remained a short time, dissuaded him from going to Venice, and he continued his journey to Paris.

The Parisians made an ovation to him at the opera; and the manager accorded him a pension of twenty-four hundred francs, besides five thousand francs for his immediate necessities. His pension as a composer was restored to him, and the consulate created a sixth place of inspector at the conservatory. The benefit of this nomination was only for the shadow of the composer, so to say. He had been suffering for a long time from bilious affection, and, moreover, he was seventy years old. He died on the 7th of May, 1800, at Passy, whither his family had taken him. He was a good husband, a tender father, and an excellent friend.

her sister Antoinette. One day when Piccini was speaking with her, she asked him if he did not think she looked like Antoinette. At first he did not answer, but on her repeating the question he said, "Majesty, there may be a family likeness, but no resemblance;" at which she was much piqued, and used her influence against him.

[1] Acton treated the gentle Piccini in the most ungracious manner.

Piccini's facility for composition was extraordinary: it is said that he wrote not less than one hundred and thirty-three operas, besides church-music, songs, and romances. Purity of style, and sweetness of melody, are the distinctive characteristics of his works.

HAYDN.

1732–1809.

FRANCIS JOSEPH HAYDN was born March 31, 1732, at Rohrau, a village about fifteen miles from Vienna, on the boundary of Austria and Hungary. His father was a wheelwright, and sexton of his parish. He had a fine tenor voice, and learned to play the harp in one of the journeys which German workmen often make. His mother[1] had been a cook in the kitchen of Count Harrach, lord of the village of Rohrau. She, too, sang well; so, on Sundays and festal days, the couple added to their earnings and amused themselves by their music. Francis Joseph wished to take part in the concert when he was five years old; and he did it in an original manner, using a piece of wood for a violin, and a stick for a bow. The accuracy with which the young Joseph marked the time attracted the attention of a relative named Franck, then on a visit to the family. He was a schoolmaster at Haimburg, and a good musician. He offered to educate the boy, and his parents gladly accepted the proposal. He took his little cousin home to Haimburg with him, taught him to read and write, to sing, play on the violin and other instruments, and Latin enough to understand the sacred text. It is easy to perceive that Haydn under-stood Latin in the accentuation of his masses, and the just

---

[1] The mother of Joseph had two other sons, both artists.

8*

expression given to his sacred compositions. The same *is* observable in the church-music of Mozart ; indeed, we can recognize it among almost all the masters of the eighteenth century.

Haydn was a diligent pupil, and made rapid progress. He found a tympanon, a sort of tambour, in Franck's house, and succeeded in performing an air on this rude instrument. It must be acknowledged that Franck was indefatigable in cultivating the musical talent of his cousin ; but, unfortunately, his was the zeal of a rough teacher, more prodigal in blows than in good music, as Haydn used to say after he left his school. But, if the master at Haimburg did not spare the blows, his severity tended, at least, to quicken the energies of his pupil.

Haydn had studied three years with his relative, when the royal chapel-master, Von Reuter, who was director of the music at the cathedral of St. Etienne in Vienna, called at Franck's house ; and, hearing him speak of the great precocity of the young Haydn, he desired to hear his music. The eight-year-old boy astonished the director, who remarked, "Only you cannot trill." — "And how can you expect me to know what my cousin does not know himself ? " said the boy. "Come here : I will teach you," said Von Reuter. No sooner had the child heard it than he began to trill as if he had never done any thing else. The imperial director was so much pleased with the boy, who gave promise of being an ornament to his church, that he took him with him to Vienna, and placed him in the boys' choir of St. Stephen's Church.

Haydn, anxious to learn, seized every opportunity of hearing music. At the age of eleven he tried to compose ; at thirteen he undertook to write a mass, of which the director made fun. Haydn felt the justice of his master's derision ; but what could he do to merit his praise ? His poverty prevented him from taking lessons ; so he resolved to study and read theoretical works instead.

He asked his father for money to replenish his scanty wardrobe ; but spent the six florins which were sent for that purpose in books.

He lost his voice, and his place at St. Etienne, when he was sixteen years old. One day, having taken it into his head to cut off the tail of the wig of one of his comrades for fun, he was dismissed for the offence. This boyish trick merited only a reprimand ; but happening just at the time his voice was changing, and he could no longer sing soprano, Reuter made it an excuse for sending him away. Biographers, however, think that the director felt jealous of a youth whose success threatened soon to eclipse his own.

Thus our young musician was suddenly thrown into the streets of Vienna without money, and with clothes so much worn that he was ashamed to be seen. However, he managed to procure the necessaries of life by playing in the orchestra, giving a few lessons, and composing. In the mean while he studied the six sonatas of C. Ph. E. Bach with the greatest assiduity and care. It is a happy circumstance, that the popular classes in Austria recognize the pursuits and feelings of dilettantism.

A poor wig-maker, who had been a great admirer of Haydn's fine voice in the religious services of the cathedral, tendered him the hospitality of his house ; and the future symphonist, somewhat freed from the material cares which preyed upon his mind, could now take more time for his studies. In the garret which he occupied, were an old worm-eaten harpsichord, and his own musical works, together with Bach's sonatas, which he performed daily.

Thus wrapped in his studies, this garret became a palace
to him. It was not long, however, before he found sufficient employment to enable him to pay rent.[1] Besides
the few lessons he gave, he played the violin in a church,
and the organ on Sundays and holidays in the chapel of
Count Haugwitz.

Metastasio hired an apartment, suitable to his rank as
a poet of the court of Vienna, in the same house where
the poor Haydn lived under the roof. Notwithstanding
the difference of their fortunes and situations, an acquaintance was soon formed between the illustrious poet
and the obscure artist. Metastasio, charmed with Haydn's
intelligence, soon made friends with him, taught him the
elements of the Italian language, and recommended him
as a teacher to Mlle. Martinez, the daughter of his host.
The poet took pains to introduce the young artist to the
beautiful Wilhelmina, who was passionately fond of music.
Haydn had no difficulty in winning the favor of the
ambassador of Venice, friend of Wilhelmina ; but that
which he had most at heart was to gain the friendship of
the old composer Porpora,[2] who lodged in Wilhelmina's
hotel. To obtain his end he served Porpora in every
possible manner, even brushing his coat and shoes daily,
and showing him such attentions as could not fail to tame
the old master, whose surly humor at length yielded to
his kindness. Porpora instructed Haydn, who in return
played his accompaniments while he was giving his singing-lessons. The Venetian ambassador gave him a pension of sixty francs monthly. About this time he wrote
some sonatas for his pupils, which attracted the attention

---

[1] Haydn left Keller the barber, and took a small attic in a large house.
In after-life he told his friend Carpani that he was never happier than in that
attic with his instrument and his books.

[2] Porpora was a famous Italian music-teacher in Vienna.

of the Countess of Thun, who, desiring to see him, was surprised by the shabbiness of his appearance. The young artist frankly told his situation; and she not only encouraged him in the most flattering manner, but presented him with twenty-five ducats.

Haydn was eighteen years old when he composed his first quartet,[1] which was received with great favor, though theorists found in it much to blame. The Baron of Fürnberg received the young artist with noble hospitality; and soon he obtained the situation of organist in a church on Leopold Street. At the request of the actor Kurtz, he composed "Der Kummer Teufel,"[2] an opera which, on account of its satirical tendency, was forbidden after its first representation.

In 1758 Haydn was appointed master of the chapel of Count de Mortzin, and in 1759 his first symphony was performed. Prince Esterhazy, who was at the concert, immediately thought of taking the composer under his special protection, and gave him the position of musical director in his chapel. It was for this chapel that Haydn

[1] "Haydn's quartets have never been surpassed; often tender, playful, and pathetic, sometimes even sublime."

[2] At night the young minstrel, accompanied by two friends, used to wander about the streets of Vienna by moonlight, and serenade his friends and patrons with trios of his own composition.

One night he happened to stop under the window of Bernardone Kurtz, the director of the theatre. Down rushed the director in a state of great excitement.

"Who are you?" he shrieked.

"Joseph Haydn."

"Whose music is it?"

"Mine."

"The deuce it is! at your age too."

"Why, I must begin with something."

"Come along up stairs."

And the enthusiastic director collared his prize, and was soon deep in explaining his mysteries of a libretto entitled The Devil on Two Sticks. The music was composed to the entire satisfaction of the director, who paid a good price for it.

composed his wonderful symphonies; here also he wrote a great part of his masterly quartets, and many instrumental pieces. Haydn wrote the symphony known as "Haydn's Farewell," for the prince when he talked of dismissing his chapel-musicians.

We must not omit to mention the first interview of Prince Esterhazy with the composer. His first words on seeing him were, "What! the music is from this Moor," alluding to the complexion of the artist. "Well, well, little Moor, from this moment I take you into my service. What is your name?" — "Joseph Haydn," was the reply "Oh! now I remember your name: you already belong to my house. Why have I not met you before? Go, dress yourself as a chapel-master. I do not. wish to see you again in this plight: you are too small. Get a new dress, a curled wig, red band, and high heels, that your stature may better correspond with your merit."[1]

Some time after, a canon from Cadiz brought Haydn a difficult problem to solve; viz., "*The seven words of the Redeemer on the cross*,"[2] which he originally wrote for instruments, and afterwards arranged for singing also.

Haydn faithfully kept the promise made in the days of his adversity, by marrying a daughter of his old host, the kind wig-maker. Want of congeniality rendered this marriage a very unhappy one. It is said that the wife was not only a bigoted religionist, but a bickering, quarrel-

[1] "Haydn now went to live at Eisenstadt, in the Esterhazy household, and received a salary of four hundred florins. The old prince died a year after; and Haydn continued in the service of his successor, Nicolas Esterhazy, at an increased salary of seven hundred and after a time one thousand florins per annum. Haydn continued the friend and companion of Prince Nicolas for thirty years, during which time he lived contented, laborious, and perfectly unambitious."

[2] "The music was composed for the solemn celebration of the Passion at Cadiz. The ceremony consisted in the bishop's enunciation of the words of the divine agony after each of which. one of these deeply pathetic pieces was performed."

some woman. Although Haydn himself was very pious, his piety was no shackle to the natural gayety of his disposition. They soon separated, but he was careful to allow her a handsome maintenance; for he was too good-hearted not to care for her who had taken his name.

Haydn, devoted to his studies, and aiming at perfection in his work, knew little of the great reputation he was gaining throughout Europe. His works were published in France, to the discomfiture of Boccherini, whose composition had previously gained public favor; but he was obliged to yield the palm to Haydn, whose music has since formed the substantial and indispensable part of all musical catalogues.[1]

Haydn frequently received letters from directors of the different European theatres, requesting him to write for them. However, they only lost their time in addressing a man who had little ambition and no thought of money-making, and felt happy living with well-beloved hosts. At length, however, he listened to the propositions of the violinist Salomon, who had made an engagement for concerts in London. Twenty concerts were to be given in one year; and Haydn was to receive fifty pounds sterling for each, and retain the proprietorship of his own works. Haydn accepted this offer, and went to London in 1791.

The English gave the illustrious artist a brilliant reception; and two years afterwards, on his return to London with more of his grand symphonies, the University of Oxford sent him the diploma of Doctor of Music, a distinction which even Händel had failed to obtain.[2]

---

[1] Haydn wrote with the greatest care. A symphony cost him a month's time, and a mass more than double that time. He rose early, and wrote all the forenoon of every day.

[2] It seems that Händel refused the title; for, "when urged to accept the degree of Doctor of Music, for which he would, of course, have to pay a small fee," his reply was, " Vat te tevil I trow my money away for dat vich de blockhead vish? I no want."

His fame abroad strengthened the esteem and admira
tion in which he was held by his own countrymen. At the
age of sixty-two he was permitted to retire to a small
house in Vienna, where he remained until his death.
Prince Esterhazy at the same time granted him a suitable
pension. Happy in the enjoyment of his little house and
garden, Haydn continued to compose ; and here he wrote
"The Creation" and "The Seasons." The latter, his
last work, was written in eleven months.

The admiration of the public drew him from his retreat
to witness the performance of "The Creation" at the
palace of Prince Lobzowitz. The assembly of the *élite*
of Vienna, consisting of one hundred and sixty chosen
musicians and fifteen hundred persons from among the
notabilities in politics, arts, and beauty, exhibited much
emotion when the old symphonist was brought into their
midst in an armchair (he was just recovering from a fit of
sickness). Immediately there was a flourish of trumpets.
Salieri, the director of the orchestra, came forward, and
shook hands tenderly and respectfully with the great master. The audience rendered their homage to the composer
by the silence and profound attention with which they listened to his *chef-d'œuvre*. We must not fail to mention a
touching feature of this memorable solemnity. Dr. Cap-
pelini, a distinguished physician, who was seated at
Haydn's side, perceiving that his legs were not sufficiently
covered, asked for wrappers : immediately ladies tendered
splendid cashmere shawls, which were wrapped about the
legs and feet of the old man. Could any action more
clearly display their attachment and veneration for the
artist ? This was the crowning day of his life's labors.

The author of "The Creation" was too feeble to resist
so many emotions. He felt that his strength was failing.

They lifted the armchair, and bore him towards the door, then stopped a moment to allow him to address a salutation of thanks to the public, after which he turned to the orchestra, raised his hands, and, with eyes filled with tears, seemed to call the blessing of heaven upon the faithful interpreters of his beloved work.[1]

The war of 1809 saddened his last days. On the renewal of hostilities between France and Austria, he was continually asking, " What news ? " Every little while he went to the piano, and sang in a feeble voice the national hymn of Austria, " God save the Emperor Francis."

On the 10th of May, the enemy arrived within half a league of Haydn's dwelling. Whilst the shells were falling around, he re-assured his domestics, saying calmly, " Why are you so afraid ? Do you not know that no harm can come to the house in which Haydn lives ? " But the strength and vigor of his mind far exceeded the strength of his body, which daily became weaker. On the 26th of May, he sang, " God save the Emperor Francis," for the last time. He died May 31, 1809, at the age of seventy-seven years and two months. He was buried in the cemetery of Gumperdorff. Mozart's requiem was executed in his honor.

Cherubini caused a funeral song on the death of Haydn to be sung in the Conservatory of Paris. The artist left no direct inheritor. His little fortune, except a legacy, passed over to one of his relations, a farrier. He bequeathed twelve thousand florins to two domestics, who had faithfully served him for many years. Prince Esterhazy purchased his manuscripts ; and Prince Lichtenstein paid fourteen hundred florins for an old parrot, which was

---

[1] Haydn considered his art a religious one, and "wrote at the beginning of his works, ' In nomine Domini,' or ' Soli Deo gloria ; ' and, at the end, ' Laus Deo.' "

said to have learned music and languages in its forty years' intimate connection with the illustrious composer, Haydn owned a watch which had been presented him by Nelson; but no one knew what became of it.

The number of his works is very large, although he did not write quickly, and always with the greatest care. He composed a hundred and eighteen symphonies, eighty-three quartets, twenty-four trios, nineteen operas, five oratorios, a hundred and sixty-three pieces for baritone,[1] twenty-four concertos for different instruments, fifteen masses, ten smaller church pieces, forty-four piano sonatas with and without accompaniment, twelve German and Italian songs, thirty-nine canons, thirteen songs for three and four voices, the harmony and accompaniments to three hundred and sixty-five old Scotch songs, besides a number of fantasias and pieces for four instruments. Haydn is a model for instrumental music; and with him begins a new epoch.

There have been many brilliant musicians; but who can compare with Haydn?

Before sitting down to compose, Haydn used to dress himself as if for a walk, and put on his finger the jewelled ring which Frederick, King of Prussia, had presented him. If he chanced to forget this ring, he could not write with ease.

Speaking with Carpani about "The Creation" and "The Four Seasons," Haydn said, "Of course 'The Creation' is superior; for the personages in it are angels, whereas in 'The Seasons,' they are only country people."

An English lord who knew the theory of music, wishing to take lessons of Haydn, commenced by saying, "We will examine this quartet, and you shall give me the reason for its modulations, which are not strictly according

[1] A kind of violoncello, entirely out of use at the present day.

to rule." Haydn, surprised, answered that he was ready to justify his work; whereupon "milord" began to criticise almost every note. Haydn soon lost his patience, and exclaimed, "I thought I was to teach you; but it seems you wish to teach me. Excuse me: my circumstances will not permit me to pay a guinea a lesson."

The celebrated Reynolds painted Mrs. Billington, the famous singer, as St. Cecilia, with her eyes turned upward, and listening to a choir of angels in the act of singing. Mrs. Billington asked her friend Haydn what he thought of the picture. "I think the painter has made a mistake," he answered. "He has painted you listening to the angels, when he should have painted the angels listening to you."

Gluck liked to write out of doors in a bright sunshine.

Sarti wished to be in a large empty room, and to write by candle-light.

Salieri collected his musical ideas while running through the most frequented streets, and eating sugarplums.

Cimarosa wished to have his friends about him, and hear a noise, when he composed.

Sacchini needed a female friend and playful kittens to inspire him.

Paisiello composed while lying in bed.

Haydn, seated at his little table alone, with his ring upon his finger, listened to the voices of angels, who inspired him with their divine harmony.

SACCHINI.

1734–1786.

A FORTUITOUS circumstance, similar to that which made a painter of Giotto, made a musician of Sacchini.

He would in all probability have been a poor fisherman if Durante, who was visiting in his neighborhood, had not heard him sing. Struck by the singular quality of his fine voice, the correctness of his intonation, and his intelligence, he felt persuaded that the boy was destined to an artistic vocation, and took him to Naples, where he placed him in a conservatory. "You have a rival difficult to conquer," said the professor to Piccini and Guglielmi, pointing to Sacchini, who was younger than either of them. "If you do not exert yourselves to equal him at least, he will stand alone, and be the musician of the century." After completing the usual course of studies, Sacchini began to teach, and compose little operas for different theatres. His productions were favorably received, and in course of time he was chosen director of a conservatory in Venice. At the age of thirty-six he had written forty serious and ten comic operas. In 1744 he brought out some of his works in Munich and Stuttgard, then went to London. Notwithstanding his good success and continued gains, he was never free from debt, owing to his inordinate extravagance. Threatened with imprisonment by his creditors, he was forced to quit England. Thinking to better his fortune in France, where his friend Framery had sounded his trumpet of fame, he went thither. This was in 1782, the time of the quarrel between the Piccinists and the Gluckists. Lucky for Sacchini, Joseph II., who was passionately fond of Italian music, and well disposed to our musician, recommended him to Marie Antoinette, who lent her influence in his favor.

The best of Sacchini's works was "Œdipe," a tragic opera in three acts, performed at the Royal Academy of Music, Feb. 1, 1789, after the composer had passed from the scene of action.

The Queen Marie Antoinette promised Sacchini that this opera should be the first performed at the Court Theatre in Fontainebleau. Placing implicit confidence in the promise of his protectress, and happy in anticipation, Sacchini contrived to see the queen every Sunday as she came from mass. She often invited him to her music-saloon, where she listened with evident pleasure to fragments of the opera on which his hopes were built. But it was not long before Sacchini noticed a change in the manners of the queen ; and at length she said to him with emotion, " M. Sacchini, they complain that I grant too many favors to foreigners. They insisted on my permitting the ' Phèdre ' of M. Lemoine to take the place of your ' Œdipe ;' and how could I refuse ? You understand my position. Pardon me."

The disappointment was more than Sacchini could bear. It made him sick, and in less than three months he died. Even his strongest opponents expressed their regret at the loss of one of the most illustrious representatives of musical art.

Funereal honors were rendered to his memory in Paris and in Italy. His bust, sculptured by Caradori, was placed in the Chapel of the Pantheon at Rome.

Sacchini wrote with great purity and elegance. He composed sixteen pieces of sacred music, besides six oratorios. Of his operas, only about forty are known ; besides these, there are a considerable number of pieces for violin, clavichord, &c.

ALBRECHTSBERGER.

1736–1809.

JOHN GEORGE ALBRECHTSBERGER, one of the most scholarly counterpointists of modern times, was born at

Klosterneuburg, — near Vienna, — Feb. 3, 1736. He was taught accompaniment and composition by the court organist Mann. After being organist in Road and Maria-Taferl, Albrechtsberger became director of the choir of the Carmelites in Vienna, and in 1772 court organist, and member of the Musical Academy; in 1792, chapel-master in St. Stephen's Church. He died in Vienna, March 7, 1809. Beethoven and Seyfried were his pupils in counterpoint. His numerous works, of which only twenty-seven were published, as well as his " Gründliche Anweisung zur Composition " (Profound Method for Composition), are of sterling value. His theoretical writings on bass, harmony, &c., were published by Seyfried of Vienna in 1826.

PAISIELLO.

1741–1816.

GIOVANNI PAISIELLO was born at Tarento, the 9th of May, 1741. His father, a skilful veterinary surgeon, placed his son at the Jesuits' College when he was only five years old, intending to make a lawyer of him. But the precocious disposition of the child for music, the delicacy of his ear, and the fineness of his voice, soon brought him into the notice of Carducci, a nobleman who had distinguished himself by his fine compositions. The child was placed under the care of a priest named Carlo Resta, from whom he received his first music-lessons. Then his father, though grieved to be separated from the beloved child, sent him to the conservatory of San Onofrio in Naples, of which Durante was, at the time, director. This celebrated teacher brought the young Paisiello forward so rapidly that at the age of eighteen he was advanced to the position of first private tutor among the pupils.

He conformed to the rules of this establishment by devoting his leisure to the composition of religious music. In 1763 he wrote an interlude bouffé, filled with grace and melody, for the theatre of the conservatory. This work crowned the hopes which had been conceived of his ability. The city of Bologna invited him to come and work for their theatre. Two operas which he wrote in that city were received with unbounded applause : so were many other pieces which were brought out at Modena and Venice. Soon after, he made a masterly stroke with a charming composition called the " Il Marchese di Tulipano," which carried his name far beyond the Alps.

The old saying, " Fortune favors the bold," was true in the case of Paisiello ; for favors really rained upon the Italian stages, so that he had nothing more to ask. In 1772 he married Cecile Pallini, a very worthy woman, who rendered his life happy. About the same time he composed his famous mass of " Requiem " with chorus and orchestra. He wrote also for concerts as well as theatres.

After a short stay in Rome, Paisiello determined to visit foreign countries. He had received invitations to go to London, St. Petersburg, and Vienna. He accepted an engagement in London, which he soon broke, and went to Russia, where the empress offered him a superb position. Whilst he was in St. Petersburg he composed, among other things, the famous " Il Barbiere di Seviglia," and two volumes of sonatas.

In 1784 Paisiello left Russia, and went to Warsaw, where he composed the music for Metastasio's oratorio of the " Passion." Thence he went to Vienna, where he composed twelve symphonies, and his famous opera bouffé " King Theodore," for Joseph II.

The Queen of France was so passionately fond of this

opera that she caused it to be performed three months at her theatre in Versailles.

Paisiello next located himself in Naples, and was made chapel-master by Ferdinand IV. He now turned a deaf ear to the enticing offers of the King of Prussia, who wished to have him settle in Berlin, and heeded not the earnest solicitations of the Russian empress.

Subsequent events wrought great changes for our composer, who had hitherto led a uniformly happy life. He was destined to experience alternations of prosperity and forgetfulness, as well as of fidelity and inconstancy; yet we do not know if we ought more to pity than to blame him. Be it as it may, his art had nothing to lose.

At the time of the French invasion in 1797, Bonaparte offered a prize for the best funeral symphony to be performed at the funeral of Hoche. Paisiello and Cherubini were the competitors, and the former won. At the breaking out of the revolution in Naples, 1799, the court returned to Sicily, and Paisiello was called to direct the national music ; but King Ferdinand, re-entering Naples the same year, withdrew his favor from our composer. After two years the king took Paisiello into favor again, but for a short time only. The first consul, who appreciated our author's talent very highly, and who had conceived an unreasonable aversion to Cherubini, sent a formal demand for him to the King of Naples ; and the artist, obliged to yield obedience to his sovereign, had to submit, notwithstanding no offers or conditions had been made with him. He arrived in Paris 1802, was handsomely received, found a furnished apartment ready for him, a carriage for his private use, and two good appointments.

Such favors shown to a foreigner did not fail to wound the feelings and excite the jealousy of the French composers, who did their best to disparage Italian music. However Paisiello behaved in the most gentlemanly manner towards them, to try to atone, as it were, for his good fortune. One day, when the consul was complaining of the chapel artists, Paisiello courageously answered, "It is impossible for me to command people who reasonably complain that they are not justly paid." His words were heeded, and there was no more complaint. Paisiello thought, and perhaps justly, that French poems were not in his line; and he did not try again. Afterwards he wrote nothing but sacred music, except an interlude performed in 1804; but several of his operas were performed in Italy. Paisiello had been in Paris more than two years when he gave "Proserpine," the failure of which grieved him so much, that he resolved to leave France forever. Ill health, which made it necessary to live in a warmer climate, was his excuse for wishing to leave. He obtained Napoleon's permission to retire, after having designated him whom he considered the right person to fill his place. Every year, however, he sent a composition to celebrate Napoleon's anniversary.

The King of Naples received his old chapel-master with much favor. In a short time, however, he fled with his court; and Joseph Bonaparte ascended the throne of Naples in 1806. From this new sovereign, Paisiello received eighteen hundred ducats salary, as composer and director of the king's music.

If the compositions of the artist became less numerous, it was not so with the distinctions he received; for he was laden with them. Among the last, he had the honor to be named Foreign Associate of the Institute of France, which caused him much joy. Academies of Italy and foreign academies manifested their appreciation of his genius, by

reckoning him among their number. The old master re·
tained his position under Murat, who succeeded Joseph,
and Napoleon continued his favors : he sent him four
thousand francs for a sacred composition written for his
marriage celebration.

The era of revolutions had not finished : Ferdinand returned to his throne, and Murat left. With this change,
Paisiello's good fortune entirely forsook him, — Ferdinand's
ʿavor, Napoleon's pensions, that of the Russian empress ;
and nothing now remained for his support but a small
income from the chapel.

He died at Naples, June 5, 1816, aged seventy-five. A
requiem for four voices and an orchestra, found among
his papers, was performed at his funeral.

Few Italian masters have written so charmingly for the
human voice as Paisiello wrote ; and he knew how to
join sweet melodies, full of grace and naturalness, to the
pure harmony of the accompaniment.

GRÉTRY.

1741–1813.

ANDRE ERNEST GRÉTRY was born at Liége the 11th of
February, 1741. When he was six years old his father,
who was first violinist at the college of St. Denis, placed
him in the choir. This was the beginning of tribulations
for the poor child, the bitter remembrance of which he has
given us in his " Essais sur la Musique." " The hour for
the lesson," he said, " afforded the teacher an opportunity
to exercise his cruelties. He made us sing, each in turn,
and woe to him who made the least mistake : he was beaten
unmercifully, the youngest as well as the oldest. He
seemed to take pleasure in inventing tortures. At times

he would place us upon a short, round stick, from which we fell head over heels if we made the least movement. But that which made us tremble with fear was to see him knock down a pupil, and beat him; for then we were sure that he would serve others in the same manner, one victim being insufficient to satisfy his ferocity. To maltreat his pupils was a sort of mania with him; and he seemed to feel that his duty was performed in proportion to the cries and sobs which he brought forth."

This picture seems to be strongly painted: yet the bad treatment then common in schools was not calculated to develop the talents of any child, much less those of a timid and sickly one. Owing to his delicate health, the young Grétry required the most careful attention; and such a method of discipline as that to which he was subjected tended rather to brutalize than make a musician of him; but happily his father took him away from this school, to place him under the instruction of a professor named Leclerc, a man as mild as his predecessor was violent.

Grétry also took his son to the representations given at Liége by an Italian troupe which performed the operas of Pergolese. Thanks to the instructions of Leclerc, and the examples of the Italian singers, the child made up for lost time, so that, when he soon after re-appeared in the choir of St. Denis, the canons highly complimented his singing, and his old master expressed surprise at the wonderful progress he had made in so short a time.

Our young artist nearly lost his life by an accident which occurred to him on the day of his first communion. It is believed in Liége that the prayers offered on this day by the communicant himself will certainly be answered. Grétry on that day prayed that he might die if he was not destined to be an honest man, and distinguished in his profession ; after which he went to play with the children of his own age, when by some mischance a beam fell upon him. He fainted, was taken up for dead, and carried in to his weeping parents. After a time he gained consciousness, and soon recovered. Grétry recollected this circumstance in his old age, and recognized that as an honest man, in the midst of a corrupt society, his prayers had been answered ; added to this, he had become very distinguished in his profession.

A mass which he composed entitled him to a fellowship in the Liége College at Rome. Travelling in those days was very difficult, particularly for a young student who had not the wherewithal to pay for riding by post. However, Grétry found compensation in the adventures of which he gives us sprightly details. His journey was undertaken in company with a young abbé, a medical student of joyful character, and an old smuggler who served them as guide : of course they all went on foot. They had gone but twenty-five leagues, when fatigue, or the extravagant gayety of his travelling-companions, obliged the abbé to turn back ; the rest of the party continued their march, enlivened by the drollery of the son of Esculapius. After having gone a very roundabout way, on account of the constant alarms of the smuggler, the travellers finally reached their journey's end.

It was 1757 when Grétry came to Rome. Here he studied counterpoint four or five years, after which he was received as a member of the Philharmonic Society at Bologna. Some of the works that he published were well received by the Roman public. Meanwhile he felt that he was unable to create a name in Italian opera, and left Italy in 1767 for Paris. Pressed by pecuniary necessities, he stopped at Geneva, where a friend procured some pupils for him. Teaching singing was very wearing to him : yet he resigned himself to it, in the hope of earning sufficient to meet the expenses he should incur in Paris until he could get to work.

That which greatly encouraged the composer was the flattering and cordial reception he received from Voltaire at Ferney, after the performance of one of his works in Geneva. " You are a musician, and you have genius : it is a very rare thing, sir, and I take great interest in you," said the celebrated author. Notwithstanding this profession of interest, Grétry could not get from him the text for a comic opera. Voltaire remembered too well the trouble he had had with Rameau about a text which he was to furnish : so he excused himself to Grétry, saying that he was too old, and too ignorant of the taste then ruling. Grétry had spent nearly a year in the obscure and ungrateful occupation of singing-master. He was twenty-eight years old, and had accomplished little or nothing ; because his renown had not extended beyond the narrow limits of the republic of Geneva. It was time to make a commencement : he hesitated no longer, but went to Paris. All his endeavors to procure a poem were useless, and the friends who were interested in him succeeded no better. No literary person of renown cared to work with a stranger. " Make yourself known," was the reply to his demand, whilst they withheld the means. All those who go to Paris in search of artistic or literary renown are obliged to pass through a similar ordeal.

After two years of expectation, a young poet gave him a text-book, but the artists cast it aside. However, Grétry was not to be discouraged. Some time after, he brought out the " Huron," which was favorably received ; this was followed by many others equally successful. The only check to which the composer had to submit was in the representation of "Amitié à l'Épreuve," which was performed only about a dozen times. Just then tableaux of country life were all the fashion. The frivolous public of Paris thought it was good taste to be passionate for rustic and *naïve* manners. It was the period in which the idyls of Gessner and the pastorals of Florian were eagerly read. Noblemen and gentlefolks took the costumes of shepherds and shepherdesses. Marie Antoinette followed the tastes of the day by making a little farm of her châlet at Trianon. It was the effort of a cloyed society, seeking for change. Grétry paid his compliment to the general lead by composing a pastoral comedy which was represented in 1774.

One evening Rousseau attended the performance of "Fausse Magie," and was so much pleased with it, that he desired to become acquainted with the composer. When Grétry heard that he wished to see him, he flew to the box of the citizen of Geneva, who received him most cordially, and begged permission to cultivate his friendship. The two went out together at the end of the performance, the artist congratulating himself upon having made the conquest of a writer whose talents he so highly appreciated, when an incident occurred which entirely frustrated his hopes. They had to go through a street blocked up by pavements; Grétry, not understanding the character of his new friend, who was very sensitive in his notions of independence, offered his arm to Rousseau to help him over the pavements. Rousseau sharply repelled the proffered help. " Let me make use of my own powers," he said. Grétry never again saw the misanthrope whom he had mortally offended without knowing it

Grétry had been much tried by the unskilfulness of his co-laborers until he met with the English humorist Hales. This man, who had passed his youth in the English marine service, eventually died of a pulmonary disease brought on by strong drink. He had managed his fortune no better than his health, and his poverty obliged him to work for the theatre. But, if he did not know how to manage himself, he knew very well how to conduct a dramatic intrigue. Grétry and he made the "Jugement de Midas." In the score there is a derisory imitation of the old music; it is a sort of drawling psalmody with which Marsyas flatters himself to gain the victory over Apollo. The success of this work was contested: the public were in favor of, and the court opposed to it.

The year 1785 marks the culminating point in the dramatic career of our artist. In this year "Richard Cœur de Lion" was performed. To say that this was a musical event, is not too much, when applied to a work which attracted all Paris, and which, after more than eighty years, is still heard with pleasure. It was the crowning work of his life: those which followed this masterpiece are all inferior. When Cherubini and Mehul introduced a more learned harmony and stronger instrumentation into their compositions, Grétry tried to alter his manner; but he did not succeed. The same desire of following the fashion of the day led Grétry to enrich the Revolutionary catalogue, although he had every reason to be well satisfied with the court of France, and had received a pension of a thousand crowns from Louis XVI. Ingratitude was of no service to him; none of the works which he composed for the Revolution succeeded.

As far as sprightliness and freshness go, Grétry was excellent, whilst for all that requires deep thought and grandeur his genius was not suited : therefore comic operas were best for the display of his talents.   Among the many works of this musician which have never been made pub-lic, were several books, the most important of which is entitled " Essais sur la Musique," written in three vol-umes.   The *naïve* self-sufficiency of Grétry goes through the entire work.

The fascination of Grétry's music was considerably lost by the changes which were made in the opera a few years before the Revolution.   He was no longer the composer in vogue, when the events of 1789, which ruined him, led to the suppression of his pension.   However, this misfortune was of short duration, as many of his works needed only a good interpretation to bring money.   Grétry, aided by the talent of a celebrated singer, again captivated the ear of the public.   Bonaparte granted him a pension.   To honor him the city of Paris named a street " Grétry."   His bust was placed in the Opera-House during his lifetime.   He was made a member of the French Academy of Arts, and inspector of the conservatory ; which office, however, he retained but a short time.

He bought the hermitage in Montmorency, where Rous-seau formerly lived, to finish his days in that quiet retreat ; but changed his mind, fearing to meet the fate of a neighbor who was assassinated there in 1811.   He went to Paris again, where he remained until he became ill, when, finding his strength fail, he requested to be taken to the hermitage, and died there Sept. 24, 1813.   Notwith-standing his vanity, Grétry possessed those qualities of the heart which endeared him to friends and acquaintance, and increased the regret of the public at the loss of one so much beloved.   Deputations from the conservatory and from the principal theatres, accompanied his last remains to the cemetery, where Méhul, the chief speaker, pronounced an able eulogy. In 1828 a nephew of Grétry caused the heart of him, who was one of the most glorious sons of Liége, to be restored to its mother city.

Grétry's daughter Lucille wrote two operas, which had good success. She died at the age of twenty-two.

Grétry, as a child of four years, had been badly scalded by the overturning of a boiling pot into which he was peeping with the childish curiosity of seeing the bubbling water. It was a long time before he recovered from the effects of the burn; indeed, his eyes were ever weak in consequence of it. Two years after his health was tolerably re-established, his father, who had been occupied with the formation of his voice, which he found to be very beautiful and of great compass, decided to have him instructed in music, and procured a place for him as choir-boy in the College of St. Denis. These choir-boys, as we have already said, were very cruelly treated by their teacher. In order to be present at the church offices, little Grétry was obliged to go the distance of a league, some two or three times a day; and the constant fear of ill-treatment rendered the poor child's life almost insupportable. In order not to be too late, he started in winter at three o'clock in the morning, sat down with his lantern at the church door, that he might be awakened by the opening of the door, should he chance to fall asleep. So it went on during five years; and, although the boy did his best to gain the love of his master, yet his faithful study and good behavior had no effect in producing a milder treatment : the only distinction that the tyrannical music-teacher made was to allow Grétry to buy his snuff, and to bestow a friendly look upon him if he found an extra quantity of snuff; for the child sometimes filled the box from his own pocket-money. The boy was told to sing a solo in public; but he failed for want of courage, and his father was requested to take him away from the choir : he did so, and gave him to another teacher, who was very kind to him. When his father saw the progress the child had made, he sought to induce him to sing publicly in the churches, although his teacher did not quite approve of such a step. The father, however, having full confidence in his son, assured the teacher that the boy would sing better than any other, and do him credit. The father encouraged his son, and promised him a present if he did well. The boy trembled as he entered the church, the musicians grumbled, the choristers whispered to each other, and cast derisive looks at Grétry. But his fond father must not be disappointed; and, besides, the honor of the family was in jeopardy. Grétry mustered all his courage, and sang an Italian air translated into Latin. After the first measure, the orchestra accompanied him carefully, the choir kept a respectful distance, the sisters listened with astonishment, his father gave him an encouraging smile. Scarcely had he finished, when the people flocked around to congratulate the father of such a talented child. As to his mother, she wept for joy. The musicians wondered where the child had learned to sing so well. In fine, he was ordered to sing another solo the following Sunday, and had a numerous auditory, among whom were the Italian singers of the opera-troupe, who were highly gratified with his singing, and prophesied that he would at some future day be a famous music an.

SALIERI.

1750–1825.

ANTONIO SALIERI was born the 19th of August, 1750, at Legnano, in Venice. His father, a well-to-do tradesman, sent him to the public school to learn Latin. His brother Francis and the church organist instructed him in music. Francis, a skilful violinist, was often invited to play at church festivals in the neighborhood; and Antonio, who even as a child manifested great talent for music, was allowed to go with his brother whenever there was room for him in the carriage. Once he followed the carriage without permission of his father, who, not being able to account for his absence, was worried about him. On his return at night, his father threatened to shut him in his room for a week, and feed him on bread and water, if he ever went again without leave. Antonio, who was ten years old, consoled himself by the following reflections: "The punishment is not so very terrible, after all, when one hears such good music to pay for it. I never take wine: I don't like it unless it is very sweet; and, as to bread, I like that as well as any thing else, if I can have sugar with it. At any rate, I will provide myself with sugar in case of need."

He had already laid aside a considerable quantity of sugar, when his brother set off again for a festival without taking him. To use Salieri's own words, "This time, I think I must have appeared very indifferent about Francis's going and leaving me. However, about half an hour after he left, I said to the servant-maid that I would go to mass. It was very early: the family were still in bed. I set off walking mechanically to a distant church near the gate through which my brother had passed. Suddenly it came

into my head, that the festival was but a short distance
from the city; that, if I went, it was only to hear good
church-music, and that was no sin. The more I thought
of it, the more anxious I was to enjoy this innocent recrea-
tion; and finally I started to go, but was stopped by a person whom my father had engaged to watch my movements,
and take me home. My father exclaimed in an angry
tone, 'So this is the way you obey my orders! You forgot what I told you, did you? Away to your bedroom!
there you may expect a good dinner.' I slunk away to
my chamber, and my father locked me in. As I conceived
that I had done no great wrong, I was not much troubled;
and, satisfied with the good breakfast I had taken with my
brother, I felt no anxiety about my dinner, especially as I
had a good stock of sugar on hand. So I amused myself
with my books and my music. As dinner hour drew near,
I was curious to see if my father really meant what he
said, though I felt that he would be likely to carry his
threats into execution. By and by the maid came with a
large piece of bread, a bottle of water, and a tumbler, which
she put before me without speaking, then fastened the
door behind her. I went to the closet to get some sugar.
There was not a particle: some one had taken it. I had
told my secret to my sister, she repeated it to mother, and
mother to father, who had taken it from me. With the
loss of my treasure, I felt the full weight of my punishment,
and cried aloud from vexation and disappointment. Soon
my father appeared saying, 'So, my fine gentleman, you
are playing a great part: you not only disobey me, but you
help yourself to sugar. What will be the end of such conduct?' I begged forgiveness, which was granted on condition, that, when it was not convenient for my brother to
take me with him, I should remain shut up in my chamber
for the day."

The following anecdote will show Antonio's ability to judge of, and his veneration for music, while yet a child. Walking one day with his father, they met a monk, whom the boy saluted very coldly. His father asked what he meant by such rudeness, to which Antonio replied, "I would salute him as a monk, but I hate his carelessness in playing the organ." — "What do you, a mere beginner, know about playing the organ?" asked his father. "It is true that I am only a beginner," answered Antonio; "but, if I were in his place, I would at least mind what I was about, when I attempted to play an organ."

Unfortunate speculations ruined Salieri, who died when Antonio was but fifteen years of age, leaving him to provide for himself with his fine voice and musical ability. Thrown upon his own resources, the boy went to Venice, where it was his good fortune to meet with an old friend of his father, a member of the family, Mocenigo, who offered him protection, and provided him with the means for continuing his musical studies. He took lessons in harmony of John Pescetti, and in singing of Ferdinand Pacini; afterward he became the pupil of Gassmann, master of the Imperial Chapel, who was interested in the young Salieri through Mocenigo's recommendation.

In 1766 he went with Gassmann to Vienna, where he studied German, French, and Latin, Italian poetry, and all that pertains to the science of composition. Although the master had desired his pupil not to occupy himself with any thing but the rules of his art, yet, as often as he was alone, he felt an unconquerable desire to compose, and even to write the text for vocal music. What he scribbled he hid away in the pillows of his bed, that he might from time to time enjoy it; but his secret was found out. Gassmann reprimanded him severely, and forbade his taking note-paper into his room without permission. Salieri carefully avoided overstepping this order, yet he soon forgot that the object was to restrict him to the theoretical study of composition : so every bit of white paper he could get was covered with notes and poetical ideas.

He was fortunate in being admitted to the chamber concerts of the Emperor Joseph II., where Gassmann was in duty bound to be present three times a week. The emperor, having heard that Gassmann had brought a boy with him from Italy, wished to see him. The master was then obliged to take his pupil to court. The monarch received him graciously, and asked several questions. Antonio, bashful and confused, hardly knew how to answer at first ; but, taking courage, he not only answered, but expressed much gratitude to his master, who was present. The emperor, greatly pleased with the boy's simplicity, asked him to sing something from memory, which he did in the most satisfactory manner.

After this, Gassmann took Antonio not only to all the concerts, but also to the theatre, that he might learn practically what he had been studying in books at home. He soon made himself useful by taking his master's place at the piano.

Whilst Gassmann lived, Salieri received no fixed salary for his services at the concerts and theatre ; but at New Year the emperor presented him with from fifty to eighty ducats.

In 1769 Salieri composed his first opera. This was the most important epoch in the life of the artist, for in this year was laid the foundation-stone of his wide renown. This opera was followed by " L'Amore innocente ;" and in 1771 he wrote " Don Chisciotto " and " D'Armida," &c.

Gassmann died in 1774, and the position of master of the Imperial Chapel was given to the pupil who did him so much honor. With this place he received a yearly salary of one hundred ducats; at the same time he was nominated leader of the orchestra of the Italian opera, with a salary of three hundred ducats.

In 1775 a great change took place in the manner of the young master. Notwithstanding the favor with which his works were received, he turned his attention to the style of Gluck, which he studied so closely, that, although an Italian by birth, his music soon became Germanized. In 1778 he brought out " L'Europa riconosciuta," a serious opera in three acts, for La Scala in Milan. The same year he wrote " La Scuola de'Gelosi;" in 1779, " Il Talismano;" and, in 1780, " La Dama Pastorella." These and several others were written in Italy; then he returned to Vienna, where a court chapel-master had no lack of work to satisfy a musical amateur like Joseph II.

The Royal Academy of Music in Paris had requested "Les Danaïdes" of Gluck, which he turned over to Salieri, his pupil and friend. The work was a complete success, and Salieri received ten thousand francs for the score from the directors of the opera, besides a rich present from the queen. He soon brought out " Semiramide " and " Il Ricco d'un Giorno," &c., in Vienna. From 1770 to 1804 the master of Legnano wrote forty-two operas, several oratorios, cantatas, duos, trios, choruses, and instrumental pieces. From 1804 he devoted himself entirely to the service of the Imperial Chapel. In 1821 he asked his dismissal, which was not given until 1824. But the musician did not live long, to enjoy the sweets of repose. He died May 12, 1825, in the seventy-fifth year of his age.

Salieri was of middle stature; his complexion was dark

eyes sparkling, hair black. He was choleric and rash, but easily appeased. He loved order and cleanliness, dressed neatly and in accordance with his age. He was indifferent to all kinds of games. He drank only water, but was very fond of sweets, such as confectionery and cakes. His amusements were reading, music, and walking. He hated ingratitude, and considered gratitude as an agreeable duty. He was generous and kind to the needy and suffering. Moderate praise he enjoyed, but flattery pained him. Sadness came over him from time to time, and he has been known to weep without having a reason for it; generally, however, he was bright and lively.

Our artist was a man of great information, and possessed the happy faculty of making himself interesting in society, where he charmed his companions by his lively conversation and his anecdotes, told in a mixture of French, German, and Italian. To his honor be it said, that even in his old age he never ceased to express his gratitude to Gassmann, the friend of his youth. He did more than talk of his gratitude: he showed it in the care he took to provide for Gassmann's two daughters.

Salieri, unbeknown to any one, had composed a requiem for himself. It was found, and performed at his funeral.

CLEMENTI.

1752–1832.

CLEMENTI was one of the greatest of piano-players, and composer for this instrument. He was born at Rome in 1752. His father, a silversmith, was so passionately fond of music, that he neglected nothing to gain a knowledge of that art. Muzio, his son, studied solfeggio before he was six years old. He was so highly gifted by nature, and

made such rapid progress, that at the age of nine years he
was able to compete with good musicians for a situation
as organist, and to gain the victory. At the age of fourteen, the precocious pianist made a voyage to England
with an English gentleman named Beckford. This gentleman resided at Dorsetshire ; and thither he took his young
protégé, affording him the means of perfecting his taste
and improving his fingering, by studying the works of
Bach, Scarlatti, and Haydn. While enjoying the hospitality of his English admirer, he wrote his second work, of
which all artists, even Bach,[1] spoke in the highest tone of
admiration. Through this work, the basis upon which all
modern sonatas for the piano are founded, he was called
to London, and engaged as pianist at the opera. Thus he
was brought into contact with the best virtuosi of Italy,
whom he heard almost daily. Under such influence the
style of his compositions and his execution naturally improved, so that, when he was eighteen years old, he surpassed his contempories in piano-playing. In 1780 he
went to Paris, where he was received with enthusiasm,
and had the honor of being complimented by the queen.
Applauses and successes awaited our young artist in Germany. In Vienna he made the acquaintance of Mozart
and other illustrious musicians who happened to be there
when he arrived : the Emperor Joseph likewise befriended
him. In 1783 Jean Baptist Cramer became his pupil.

Clementi made a second journey to France, and then
returned to London, where he remained uninterruptedly
until 1802. Although having a professorship, and the
labor of teaching in a country able and willing to pay for
foreign glory, he continued to compose, and brought out
a remarkable series of works, together with his "Introduc-

---

[1] Charles Emmanuel Bach.

tion to the Art of Piano-playing." His time was fully occupied; for everybody wanted to take lessons of him, though he had raised his price to a guinea a lesson.

However, he lost the fortune acquired by teaching, through the failure of Longman and Broderip's banking-house, which induced him to go into other business for a time, with the hope of indemnifying himself. He set up an establishment for the manufacture of pianos and the sale of music; and, as an artist, he naturally strove to have his instruments made in the best manner possible. His success was so great, that in a short time he was wholly relieved from all financial difficulties.

His love of travelling induced him to go through Europe in the autumn of 1802. He went to Paris with his celebrated pupil Field, then to Vienna, St. Petersburg, Berlin, and Dresden, through Switzerland and Italy. About this time he lost his wife and a brother, and returned to Rome, his native city, where family affairs rendered his presence necessary. During a period of eight years he composed little or nothing except one sonata. About 1810 he returned to England, where he passed the remainder of his life in the midst of artists by whom he was much esteemed, and in the bosom of a family whom fortune had given him [1] to console him for the loss he had previously sustained : [2] the remainder of his life was consecrated to the domestic joys which he had happily found in a second union. In the winter of 1822 two of his symphonies were performed in Leipzig. Clementi lived mostly at his country-seat, from whence he occasionally went to London. As an artist, he retained his power and intellectual vigor till his death, which took place March 10, 1832.

---

[1] In 1811 he married, for his second wife, Emma Gisborne, an Englishwoman.

[2] His first wife was a young and beautiful woman, whom he married in Berlin, and who died within a year after her marriage.

He left a hundred and six sonatas : of their elegance and quality of style it would be impossible to speak too highly. He is justly considered as the founder of the modern virtuoso piano-playing. Not only was his execution extremely brilliant, but he greatly advanced piano-playing by a system of fingering. He transferred his principles to a number of distinguished pupils, among whom we will mention Field, Cramer, Klengel, and Kalkbrenner. His "Introduction to the Art of Piano-playing," an excellent work, has gone through twelve editions in English, besides several in French and German. However, the symphonies, so much applauded in his time, would meet with but little favor in our day.

Moscheles says, " Clementi is one of the most vigorous old fellows of seventy that I ever saw. In the early morning we watch him from our windows, running about the garden bareheaded, reckless of the morning dew. He is too lively ever to think of rest. At table he laughs and talks incessantly."

When Moscheles went to housekeeping, Clementi made him a present of a splendid piano, on which was inscribed with his own hand, in front of the keyboard, the dedication, " Muzio Clementi e Socj all'ingegnosissimo J. Moscheles, ed alla sua amabilissima consorte."

APELL.

1754.

DAVID A. APELL, private counsellor of the prince of Hesse, member of the Royal Academy of Music in Stockholm, of the Philharmonic Academy of Bologna, &c., was born at Cassel. In his earliest childhood he studied music

alone and without a teacher, and was able to play sonatas
and concertos on the piano before he began to take lessons. At eighteen years of age he commenced a course
of study with the organist Müller. The more he advanced,
the greater was his desire to compose. About 1780 he
set himself seriously to writing, and very soon sent some
of his compositions to the Academy of Bologna. The
Academy of Stockholm gave him a diploma; and the pope,
to whom he had sent a mass, wrote him a flattering letter,
and made him Knight of the Golden Spur. He wrote
many fine pieces for the church, besides operas, sonatas,
and collections of airs in German, French, and Italian.

CIMAROSA.

1754–1801.

CIMAROSA was one of the most illustrious musicians
which Italy, classic land of melody, has produced. Domenico Cimarosa was born at Aversa, near Naples, Dec. 17,
1754. His father, a mason, fell from a scaffolding and was
killed; and his mother, a washerwoman, had not the means
to educate her seven-years-old boy. Such was the humble
origin of the future friend of Cardinal Consalvi, whose
political ability was equalled only by his virtues. Fortunately the parents of Cimarosa had settled in Naples soon
after his birth; for on that account he was permitted to
commence his studies at the Poor School in that city.

Father Policastro soon discovered that the boy was endowed with great natural abilities and a. disposition for
music. Instead of limiting his instruction to what is ordinarily taught in the free schools, he gave him lessons in
Latin and the rudiments of music. Domenico made such
rapid progress, that his protector sent him to the Conserva

tory of St. Maria di Loretto in 1761. Full of ardor for his work, remarkably intelligent, and of a charming disposition, the pupil, possessing more than an ordinary degree of such qualities as gain the affection of teachers, was soon endeared to them all. The lively and brilliant imagination which characterizes all his works displayed itself even in the essays of his early youth. He was not only a very promising composer, but an able violinist and a good singer, while at the conservatory. The expeditious methods lately invented to form artists were undiscovered at that time, when students worked in earnest, and in Italy an apprenticeship lasted many years.

Cimarosa did not leave the conservatory until 1772, after eleven years of hard study. Then he gave his first opera, " L'Extravaganza del Conte," which was soon followed by several others, both serious and comic, the rich melodies of which pleased all Italy, and were heard with delight in other countries. Time will not permit us to enter into the details of his works. Suffice it to say, that he alone furnished the music for two large theatres of Southern Italy, and his faculty in producing was equalled only by the variety and richness of his scores.

In July, 1789, Cimarosa left for the court of Catherine II. Everywhere on his route he received the greatest attentions. It was not until December that he arrived in St. Petersburg. While there, a period of about four years, he composed more than five hundred works for the court. Towards the end of 1792, the artist, feeling that he could no longer endure the rigorous climate of Russia, asked permission to leave, which was reluctantly granted.

Arrived at Vienna, the Emperor Leopold made him chapel-master, with a salary of twelve thousand florins. Whilst here, in the capital of Austria, Cimarosa wrote the work which is generally considered as his masterpiece, viz., " Il Matrimonio Segreto," or " The Secret Marriage," an opera bouffé in two acts. The orchestration of this opera is very simple : the quartet abounds in interesting details, and the wind-instruments, which are rarely used, are never noisy. The emperor was so much delighted with the first performance of this opera, that he ordered it it to be repeated the same evening.[1] This opera was received with transports of enthusiasm in Naples, whither Cimarosa went, and the next year wrote, " Astuzie Feminili " and other operas.

In 1796 we find our composer at Rome, where he brought out " I Nemici Generosi." He went to Venice in 1801, with the intention of bringing out " Artemisia ; " but death did not allow him the time. Cimarosa, whose health had been failing for some years, fell asleep on the 11th of January, 1801, aged only forty-seven.

The direct cause of the death of this great artist has never been known. He had warmly embraced the revolutionary party in Naples ; and some people suppose he was poisoned. And some even went so far as to accuse Queen Caroline of the infamous deed ; the character of the princess, unfortunately, giving some probability for suspicions which always exist in the minds of credulous people. His physician, however, thought that the artist died of cancerous tumor.

The friend and protector of Cimarosa, Cardinal Consalvi, caused funereal honors to be paid to him in Rome. He ordered Canova to execute a marble bust of the great musician, which was placed in the gallery of the Capitol

[1] The emperor gave the actors and musicians of the orchestra a good supper after the first performance, then sent them to the stage again for a second, which he enjoyed as much as the first.

All the world, at least the musical world, participated in the regrets of the cardinal. The author whose goodness of heart was equalled by his genius was so much beloved that his death was a cause of public grief.

Cimarosa was very large; but his face was handsome, and his presence pleasing. He was witty, and wrote good poetry. His eighty-two works written in twenty-eight years bear witness to his industry.

MOZART.

1756–1792.

Jean Chrysostome Wolfgang Theophile Mozart was born at Salzburg, Jan. 27, 1756. His father, Leopold Mozart, was chapel-master at the court of the Prince Archbishop of that city. There never was a child who displayed greater love for music. He was scarcely three years old when his attention was drawn to the pianoforte by the lessons given to his sister Mary Ann. At four years of age he was not only a little virtuoso full of taste, but he could compose minuets, some of which have been carefully preserved by his biographer Mr. Nissin. With Mozart, education succeeded in finishing that which nature had so happily commenced. Leopold Mozart, a distinguished musician, who deeply felt his responsibility as father of such a child, deemed it his duty to relinquish the situation at court, which offered him but a limited means of support, and devote himself exclusively to the education of his children.

The young Mozart gave himself up to study with the eagerness with which children of his age give themselves up to their daily sports; in fact, study was play for him. No sooner had he learned the elements of mathematics, of which he was extravagantly fond, than he covered chairs, tables, walls, and even the floor of his chamber, with figures. A passion for mathematics is by no means uncommon with great musicians. But Mozart's fondness for figures did not turn him from the object of his predilection; and, as to difficulties, they did not exist for him. One day his father, in looking over a concerto which the child was writing for the piano, was surprised to find the composition conformable to rules, although it was impossible to play it.[1]

The flattering attentions paid to young prodigies too frequently stimulate their pride and self-love, to the exclusion of their natural good qualities. Such, however, was not the case with Mozart: he was a *naïve* and simple child, with a most affectionate heart. When very young, he frequently said, " Do you love me ? " in a most endearing

---

[1] Mozart, not five years old, was bending over a sheet of music-paper covered with ink, when his father with a friend entered the room.

"What are you doing, my son ? " said the father.

"Writing a concerto for the piano," was the prompt reply. "The first part is nearly done."

" Let us see it."

" It is not finished."

The father took it from him. The paper was almost black with ink, as the child had here and there rubbed off a blot with his open hand or his coat-sleeve, and written the notes over the ink-spot. Tears of astonishment and joy streamed from the eyes of the father, as he observed the correctness of the writing.

" It is good, but too difficult for general use," observed his friend.

" Oh ! " said Wolfgang, " it must be practised until it is learned. This is the way it goes ; " and, seating himself at his instrument, he played it to their entire satisfaction.

One day several musicians were playing, and Wolfgang asked permission to play the second violin. His father refused, saying, " How can you ? You don't know how to play the violin."

"One needs not to study for that," said the boy, weeping with disappointment. At the request of Mr. Schachtner, he was allowed to join them, and played the second violin with perfect ease.

The sound of a trumpet had a peculiar effect on Wolfgang: he shuddered, turned pale, and nearly fainted, every time he heard it apart from other instruments. This continued until his tenth year.

manner. The private virtues which mark the honest man were as prominent in the child as the genius which rendered him a great artist.

In 1762 Leopold Mozart took his children to Munich and Vienna, that others might participate in the enthusiasm with which his son inspired him. The grace and gentleness of the six-year-old virtuoso won all hearts, whilst his wonderful musical talents excited their admiration. The Emperor Francis I., astonished by his brilliant touch, asked him, jokingly, to play with one finger, which he did with perfect ease. Maria Theresa and her children were delighted with the little Mozart. Two of the archduchesses were walking about the palace, through the galleries, the floors of which were waxed and smooth as glass. Mozart slipped and fell. One of the archduchesses, the future Queen of France, helped him up caressingly, whilst the other stood and looked on. "You are good: I would like to marry you," said the young artist. This was told the empress, who asked the child how such an idea came into his head; to which he innocently replied, "Through gratitude: she was good to me, whilst her sister was quite unconcerned at my fall."

On their return home, Mozart studied the violin and organ as well as singing, all of which he learned readily. Again, in 1763, the father took the children on an artistic tour through the principal cities of Southern Germany, to Paris. The seven-years' war was at an end; and the German population, free from warlike preparations, gladly indulged themselves in their national taste for music. Many cities fêted their guests, and presents were not wanting. The father wrote home, under date of Oct. 17, "We have swords, laces, mantillas, snuff-boxes, gold cases, and such like, sufficient to furnish a store; but, as for money, it is a very scarce article, and I am positively poor."

In Paris [1] they were very kindly received, also in London, whither they went. This journey offered the young student many opportunities for improvement, which with the tender attentions of the watchful father brought the talent of the boy to wonderful maturity. During their sojourn in England, Mozart's third work was published. His piano sonatas which he executed, and his improvisations and compositions for orchestra and song, called forth the greatest admiration.

Soon after their return to Austria, Mozart had the small-pox; and the Dean of the Cathedral of Olmütz took the child into his own house, where he could have the attention of a good physician. Thanks to this charitable intervention, Wolfgang recovered from the dreadful disease which threatened to carry off this charming bud of promise. His father took him again to Vienna in 1767, where he was presented to the Emperor Joseph, not only as a superior virtuoso, but also as a finished composer. Here he succeeded in procuring an order for a comic opera, "La Finta Semplice." He also composed an operette for a private theatre; and, at the dedication of the new Waisenhaus Church, a mass and the other pieces which were performed were all his compositions.

Mozart passed the year 1769 in Salzburg in the study of the Italian language; and the next year he made a journey through Italy, accompanied by his father. This journey, which led through the chief cities as far as Naples,[2]

[1] Whilst in Paris, the Marquise de Pompadour turned her head when Wolfgang wished to kiss her, at which he exclaimed, "Who is she, that she will not kiss me? Have I not been kissed by the queen?"

[2] The Neapolitans ascribed Mozart's rapid playing to the ring which he wore on his left hand, and were thunderstruck when they found that he could play without this charm.

was an uninterrupted chain of triumphs for the youthful virtuoso, on the piano, organ, violin, and in singing. The pecuniary gain, however, did not amount to any thing, as the concerts were given to private parties and companies. In composition he was always ready for the most varied problems. He was made honorary member of the academies of Bologna and Verona;[1] but more important to him was the order to write the opera " Mithridates," which was performed with good success in Milan, 1770. The festival play " Ascansio in Alba " followed, then the Serenade, " Il Sogno di Scipione," and many others.

Mozart met with so many contrarieties in different parts of Germany, that he decided to expatriate himself, and this time he went to Paris with his mother.

As we advance in the biography of the greatest musicians of the eighteenth century, we are surprised and afflicted by the obstacles which constantly impede their progress, the difficulties they labor under to obtain popularity, and the fruitless efforts which wear upon them.

Mozart and his mother arrived in Paris, March 23, 1778, just when the disputes between the Gluckists and Piccinists were causing a remarkable crisis in dramatic music. Except the arrangement of a " Miserere," which had poor success, Mozart found nothing to do, and was obliged to give a few lessons to pay his expenses.[2] He was living in

---

[1] He was decorated with the grand order of the Golden Spur.

[2] A letter of Mozart to his father, dated Paris, May 1, 1778: —

"The little violoncellist Zygmatofsky, and his unprincipled father, are here. Perhaps I may have already written you this; I only mention it cursorily because I just remember that I met him at a house which I must now tell you about, — I mean that of the Duchess de Chabot. M. Grimm gave me a letter to her; so I drove there. . . . I waited half an hour in a large room without any fire, and as cold as ice. At last the duchess came in, and was very polite, begging me to make allowances for her piano, as none of her instruments were in good order, but I might at least try it. I said I would most gladly play something, but at this moment it would be impossible,

sadness and disappointment, when his mother died.   This was a most terrible blow for the tender and affectionate Wolfgang.   Remaining in Paris was no longer to be thought of ; and he returned to his father in Salzburg.   He reluctantly accepted the new call as concert-master at court, though the conditions were much more favorable than at first.   Soon after he wrote his chorus and " King Thamos."   In November, 1780, he was invited by the prince electoral of Bavaria to compose the opera of "Idomeneo ;" and, thanks to his great activity, this bril liant composition was represented Jan. 29, 1781.

The Archbishop of Salzburg, a weak-minded and vain man, was not sorry to have it known that the composer so much spoken of and admired was in his service.   He

as my fingers were quite benumbed with cold ; so I asked her at all events to take me to a room where there was fire. 'Oh, oui! Monsieur, vous avez raison,' was her answer. She then seated herself for a whole hour in company with several gentle-men, all sitting in a circle round a large table ; and during this time I had the honor to wait. . The windows and doors were all open, so that not only my hands, but my body and my feet, were cold, and my head began to ache. Moreover there was perfect silence, and I did not know what to do with myself. I again and again thought that if it were not on M. Grimm's account I would leave the house at once. At last, to cut matters short, I played on the wretched, miserable piano. What, however, vexed me most of all was, that the duchess and all the gentlemen did not cease drawing for a single moment, but coolly continued their occupation, so I was left to play to the chairs, the tables, and the walls. My patience gave way under such unpropitious circumstances. . . . Give me the best piano in Europe, and listeners who understand nothing, or don't wish to understand, and who do not sympathize with me in what I am playing, — I no longer feel any pleasure.

"You write to me that I ought to pay a good many visits, in order to make new acquaintances and to renew former ones. This is, however, impossible from the dis-tances being so great ; and it is too muddy to go on foot, for really the mud in Paris is beyond all description. To go in a carriage entails spending four or five livres a day, and all for nothing. It is true the people say all kinds of civil things ; but there it ends, as they appoint me to come on such and such a day, — when I play, and hear them exclaim, 'Oh! c'est un prodige, c'est inconcevable, c'est étonnant!' and then, *adieu!* At first I spent money enough in driving about, and to no purpose, from not finding the people at home. Unless you lived here, you could not believe what an annoyance this is. Besides, Paris is much changed : the French are far from being as polite as they were fifteen years ago."

sent for Mozart to come to him at Vienna, where he was on a visit. He lodged the composer at his hotel, treating him as a valet, and obliging him to take his meals with the domestics. In this situation Mozart's pecuniary interests suffered as much as his pride; for his master would not allow him to play in concerts which would have yielded him some profit. In a letter to his father, written at this time, Mozart says, "His grace does not wish that his people should make any profits." Mozart submitted to the indignities of the prelate, in consideration of his father's situation. One day, however, driven to extremities, he ventured to complain, when he received only these impertinent words, "Get you gone, if you can't serve better." He took the archbishop at his word, and asked his dismissal.

But he must live, and teaching was insufficient:[1] therefore he turned his attention to writing for the theatre. Whilst at Mannheim he had been introduced to a beautiful young singer, named Aloysia Weber, who made so deep an impression on him, that, encouraged by the reception he met with from her family, he went to Munich, where she was, with the intention of offering her his hand. The result, however, was very different from what he had anticipated. It would have been very difficult to recognize the artist of genius in the thin young man, with a long nose, great eyes, and small head. Aloysia eyed her suitor from head to foot in such a manner as to deprive him of all hope. However, he soon transferred his affection to Aloysia's sister Constance, whom he married Aug. 4, 1782. The marriage took place in the house of the Baroness Waldstetten, a protrectress of the musician.

---

[1] He writes, "I have only one small room. It is quite crammed with a piano, a table, a bed, and a chest of drawers."

This was not a money match ; and our young house-keepers were often inconvenienced for the means of living. Meanwhile the King of Prussia offered Mozart an appointment as chapel-master with a salary of three thousand crowns ; but he refused, preferring to remain with his prince, although this prince did not appreciate his music, and left him to vegetate in a situation bordering on misery, for he was obliged to give lessons, and write contra-dances and waltzes for balls. To be named Mozart, and thus waste the time which should have been devoted to masterpieces !

Leopold Mozart, being in Vienna in 1785, begged Haydn to tell him sincerely and frankly what he thought of his son. "I tell you, upon the word of an honest man," replied the author of "The Creation," "that I consider your son as the greatest composer whom I have ever heard. He writes with taste, and possesses a thorough knowledge of composition."

We see Mozart at the culminating point of his artistic development in the year 1786. With the "Marriage of Figaro," he commenced the series of his immortal works, alas ! too soon interrupted. The emperor, notwithstanding his predilection for Italian music, justly upheld and supported Mozart against enemies, who, from motives of interest, continually attacked him. The "Marriage of Figaro," performed at Vienna for the first time in 1786, was more highly appreciated in Prague ; and it was there that he offered his most popular work, "Don Giovanni." The inhabitants of Prague, who seemed to understand Mozart better than those of Vienna, were wild with enthusiasm when it was performed. At a meeting of musical critics, Haydn, called upon to express his opinion, replied, "All that I have to say is, that Mozart is the greatest composer of our epoch."

About this time Mozart began to feel the first symptoms of a pulmonary affection, which filled him with melancholy. Then vanished the flattering prism of youth and coming glory, which had hitherto filled his soul with joy. Like many other artists, he was no financier; and, though temperate in living, he was often so pressed for money, as to be obliged to borrow. Unfortunately for him, the frequent sicknesses of his wife, and the maintenance of a large family, caused expenses disproportionate to his means, so that he was in a continual state of anxiety. Musicians at that time derived little profit from their works, and the last three grand symphonies composed in 1788 brought him much more glory than money.

Mozart's reputation in Vienna was chiefly based on his mastery of the piano; and he was everywhere recognized as the first virtuoso and composer for this instrument. He laid the foundation for the development of modern pianoforte-playing in his seventeen concertos for piano and orchestra, as well as in a large number of compositions with and without accompaniments.

In 1790 he wrote "Così fan tutte;" and in 1791 the festive opera "La Clemenza de Tito," for the coronation of Emperor Leopold. The same year he wrote the score of the "Enchanted Flute"[1] at the request of a manager, who had prepared the text from a fairy tale, the fantastic fundamental elements of which were not only interwoven with traits of popular humor, but had also a Masonic tendency. Mozart, who was a zealous Mason, took hold of this work with much earnestness, and made it the first great German opera which expressed the essentially intellectual elements and kindly feelings of German popular life.

[1] Zauberflöte.

For this splendid work, Mozart made no charge : he only reserved to himself the right of selling his score to other theatres. But the manager, despite his agreement, gave away copies : all the theatres thus had an opportunity to bring out the work. When Mozart learned that he had been the victim of his disinterestedness, he merely exclaimed "The scoundrel ! " It seemed to be the destiny of Mozart, to be continually cheated in business affairs.

About this time a mysterious circumstance contributed to strengthen the feelings of melancholy which were wearing upon him. A stranger, singularly dressed in gray, came to him desiring that he would compose a requiem in consideration of one hundred ducats paid in advance ; the work to be completed in a month, without fail. He departed without telling who he was, who had sent him, or for whom the requiem was to be written.

One day, as Mozart was stepping into a carriage, the unknown person again presented himself, and asked if the requiem was finished.

It has since been discovered that the person who thus disguised himself was no other than Count Walseck. This gentleman had lost his wife, and wished to have the honor of composing the work that he had engaged the author of " Don Giovanni " to write for the funeral obsequies of the countess. Mozart, thinking of his own end, easily persuaded himself that the gray man was no other than a messenger of fate, and that the requiem he was composing must be for himself. This foolish infatuation can only be accounted for by the reigning superstition of the times. Many people believed in the intervention of spirits. Exhausted by labor and sickness, the great musician saw a revelation in a simple event.

Shortly after, his health appeared to be improving ; and

he took advantage of a respite from pain, to write a cantata for the Masonic lôdge of which he was a member.
Feeling better, he set about writing the requiem, but soon
grew worse, and was confined to the bed from which he
was to rise no more. He died on the 15th of December,
1792, in the arms of his wife, and surrounded by children
and loving friends. He was in his thirty-seventh year.
Lussmayer, one of his pupils, finished the requiem. He
was buried in the common burial-ground of the poor,
without even a stone to mark the spot.

Of Mozart's six children, only two survived him. His
widow married M. de Nissen for her second husband.
This gentleman, it will be remembered, published the
"Biography of Mozart."

"If Mozart by his manifold gifts, the fertility of his
invention, the beauty of form, and the exactness of method,
can stand a comparison with the highest masters in his art,
he stands alone in that perfected harmony where his genial
nature and artistic taste seem to be clasped together in
insoluble union."

In a letter from Mozart's father, dated Vienna, 1768, he
details the manifold difficulties which prevent the "Buona
Figliuola" from being brought before the public, and de-
clares that the enemies of his dear child have taken every
possible means to keep it back. Even Afflegio, the stage-
manager, after flattering and praising the twelve-years-old
composer, and promising a certain amount for his labor,
absolutely refused to put the opera upon the stage ; and
this was in Vienna.

Mozart wrote to his sister from Naples, 1770, —

"I am still alive and well, and very fond of travelling. I am surprised that you compose so well. In a word, your song is fine. **Try
it often.** Send me the other six minuets from Haydn.

12*

"M'lle, j'ai l'honneur d'être votre très humble serviteur et frere, Chevalier de Mozart.   Addio."

To his mother from Milan in the same year he wrote, —

"I cannot write much, for my fingers ache from writing so many recitatives.   I beg you, dear mamma, to pray for me that the opera may succeed, and that we may soon be together again.   A thousand kisses."

Mozart to his sister, from Rome : —

"I am, thank God! except my miserable pen, well, and send you and mamma a thousand kisses.   I wish you were in Rome : I am sure it would please you.   Papa says that I am a little fool, but that is nothing new.   Here we have but one bed : it is easy to understand that I cannot rest comfortably with papa.   I shall be glad when we get into new quarters.   I have just finished drawing the Holy Peter with his keys, and the Holy Paul with his sword, and the Holy Luke with my sister.   I have had the honor of kissing St. Peter's foot ; and, because I am so unfortunate as to be too small to reach it, they had to lift me up.   I am the same old

WOLFGANG."

Notwithstanding the contrarieties to which Mozart was subject, he often met very kind friends where it was least to be expected.   For example : a dyer in Vienna named Rindum, who knew Mozart only through his music, which he greatly admired, procured the services of a physician, and apartments for his wife, when she had a lame foot, thus saving much expense to the *maestro*.

Mozart was very anxious when any thing ailed his wife. Once he was sitting by her bedside composing : she lay in a profound sleep, when a rough servant suddenly entered. Mozart, fearing that the sleeper would be too suddenly awakened, beckoned him to withdraw.   In doing so, the pen that he held in his hand fell, and struck deep into his leg ; but he uttered not a sound, only went very quietly out of the room.

Mozart's father wrote to his daughter in April, 1786, —

" ' Le Nozze di Figaro ' will be brought out on the 28th. I shall be surprised if it succeeds, there are so many working against it. Salieri with all his crew will set heaven and earth in motion to put it down. I am told that your brother has so many enemies on account of the great reputation he has gained."

Mozart tenderly loved his sister Nannerl. Some of his letters written to her, in the playfulness of his boyhood, are a mixture of German, French, and Italian, interspersed with Swabian dialect.

When fifteen years old he wrote the following : —

"Dearest Sister, — I have not written to you for so long a time, because I have been so busy with the opera. Now that I have more time, I shall be more punctual in writing. The opera, thank God, was well received. People say that no opera before has drawn such full houses. Papa and I are well, thank God, and I hope by Easter to see you, and tell you all. *A propos*, yesterday the copyist was here, and said that he was to copy my opera for Lisbon Court. Keep well, my darling mademoiselle sister. I have the honor to be, and to remain from now to eternity, your loving brother."

In a letter from the Hon. Daines Barrington, F. R. S., written Nov. 28, 1769, he says, —

" I was witness of the most extraordinary abilities of the young Mozart as a musician, both at some public concerts and likewise at his father's house.

" I carried to him a manuscript duet, which was composed by an English gentleman to some favorite words in the opera of 'Demofoonte.' The whole score was in five parts ; viz., accompaniments for first and second violin, the two vocal parts, and a bass. The score was no sooner put upon his desk, than he began to play the symphony in a most masterly manner, as well as in the time and style which correspond with the intention of the composer.

" I mention this because the greatest masters often fail in these particulars on the first trial.

" The symphony ended, he took the upper part, leaving the under one to his father.

"His voice was thin and infantine ; but nothing could exceed the masterly manner in which he sung. His father made some mistakes, which our artist immediately pointed out.

"When he had finished the duet, he expressed himself as well pleased, and asked if I had brought any more such music."

"Every thing went swiftly with him. He thought swiftly ; his feelings were swiftly aroused, to thrill and quiver long afterwards ; the blood sped swiftly along his veins, so that, at the smallest excitement, his heart knocked loudly on his breast ; even in eating, drinking, smoking, talking, every motion was quick and sudden. He could scarcely stand still long enough to wash his hands, but would seize the towel, and wander up down the room, knocking one heel against the other, and composing in his head. Hands and feet were continually in motion. He must be playing on something, — on his hat, or his watch-chain, or the chairs and tables, as if they were the piano. But it was in composing that his rapidity was the most surprising. The thoughts flew, and the pen drove on to keep pace with them, till he seemed almost working like a madman. The instant that a musical idea flashed across him, he grasped it at once in its relations to what must precede and follow, and with its full harmony.

"It was his custom to rise every morning at five o'clock, usually from the lounge where he had thrown himself down after half the night spent in writing, and take a ride on horseback. It was an expensive habit ; but he worked hard, and needed both the exercise and the refreshing breath of morning. Before he left the house, he always would slip into his wife's chamber, and leave a light kiss on her sleeping forehead ; then he would write a little note in pencil, and lay it on the stand by the bedside, that Constance might find it there when she waked. The note was generally something like this : —

Good-morning, dear little wife! I hope you have had a good sleep and pleasant dreams. I shall be back in two hours. Behave yourself like a good little girl, and don't run away from your husband.'"

Speaking of his last child when an infant, Mozart said, "The boy will be a true Mozart, for he always cries in the very key in which I happen to be playing."

One of his relatives, who was with him much of the time in the latter part of his life, says he was ever kind and in good humor, but always thoughtful, attentive to what was said to him, he answered carefully though he seemed to be thinking of something else all the while.

"Mozart's favorite composers were Porpara, Durante, Leo, and Alexander Scarlatti; but he esteemed Händel more than any of them. He knew by heart most of the works of this great master. 'Of all of us,' he would say, 'Händel understands best how to produce a grand effect: when he chooses it, he can strike like a thunderbolt.'

"It is well known that the Baron von Swieten, a great friend of Haydn's, said, 'that if Mozart had lived, he would have plucked from Haydn the sceptre of instrumental music.'"

At the rehearsal of "Idomeneus," Karl Theodore, Elector of Bavaria, cried out, "One never would think that so great a thing was hidden in so small a head."

"Mozart was a king and slave, — king in his own beautiful realm of music; slave of circumstances and the conditions of this world. Once over the boundaries of his own kingdom, and he was supreme; but the powers of the earth acknowledged not his sovereignty."

CHERUBINI.

1760–1842.

MARIA LOUIS CARLO ZENOBIO SALVADOR CHERUBINI was born Sept. 8, 1760, in musical Tuscany, where speech

is so sweet that it seems almost like song. Imbued by
nature with a love of music, and taught by his father, a
professor of that art, the child learned the first elements
before he had attained his sixth year. At nine years of
age he commenced harmony, and very soon after took up
composition. Such was his progress, that he was able to
write a solemn mass, and an interlude for a private theatrical, when he was only thirteen years old. Encouraged by
his success he began to write operas; but at seventeen,
when intoxicated, as it were, with the glory which shone
around him, he suddenly tore himself away from his public
career, and retired to Bologna that he might devote himself to study. The Grand Duke of Tuscany generously
granted him a pension, which enabled him to take lessons
of the learned Sarti. In order to overcome all the difficulties of harmony, he confined his writing for two success-
ive years to counterpoint and fugue.

Cherubini finished his studies in Milan, whither Sarti
went; and in the autumn of 1780 he commenced the
career of dramatic composer. He was not in the least
discouraged by the ill success of his first work, but continued to compose so that he brought out several works during the years 1782 and 1783.

The Venetians called him *the Cherubim;* alluding more
to his pretty face, his thick curly hair, and his name, than
to the angelic grace of his songs. The Jesuits of Florence
made parodies of his operas for their oratorios, hoping
thereby to attract the faithful into their churches.

The enthusiasm of the English for the great masters of
the Continent induced Cherubini to go to London in 1784,
where he brought out an opera bouffé in two acts, which
had great success. On the contrary, "Giulio Sabino,"
which he gave in 1786, was such a failure that the disap-

pointed composer left England, and took up his abode in Paris. However, his commencement in this city was any thing but encouraging; for, after composing a grand cantata for the concert of the Olympic Lodge, he could not get it performed. In 1787 he went again to London, and then to Turin, where his " Ifigenia in Aulide " was performed with great success. On his return to Paris, he wrote the score for "Demophoon," a lyric tragedy from the pen of Marmontel. This was his first French opera, and it was not very successful.

In 1789 Leonard, coiffeur of Marie Antoinette, obtained the privilege of establishing a theatre in Paris in which the Italian opera could be performed; and Viotti was sent to the Peninsula to engage singers of renown. Cherubini, as director of the new troupe, put the best works of the Italian masters upon the stage; but this charge did not prevent him from working upon different operas, among which was " Lodoïska," which created much enthusiasm. Under this artist a new way was opened to dramatic music; for he, by his constancy and the perfection of his works, made a principle of that which Gluck had only imagined. Thus he was enabled to found a wise, conscientious, and distinguished school, particularly favorable to the development of the musical imagination. In fact, Cherubini, by writing the operas of " Demophoon " and " Lodoïska," opened the way for Mehul and Spontini.

Cherubini composed the music for many of the songs which were sung at Revolutionary festivals. Among others let us notice a funeral hymn upon the death of Gen. Hoche, sung at the Champ de Mars. All persons of musical taste were in raptures over the beauty of this composition; but Bonaparte was annoyed at hearing the master so much praised, and did not fail to make him feel the effects of his impatience.

In 1795 Cherubini gave the important dramatic work known as " Elisa, or Mount St. Bernard ; " in 1797, " Médée," a grand composition ; in 1798, " The Portuguese Hotel ; " in 1799, " The Punishment ; " in 1800, " The Two Days ; " 1803, "Anacreon, or Fugitive Love ; " in 1804, the great ballet " Achille at Scyros."

However, Cherubini's chief dependence for the maintenance of his numerous family was upon the moderate salary appropriated to him as inspector of the Conservatory. How was it that France showed so little hospitality to the stranger who did so much to enrich her national repertory ? Unfortunately for Cherubini, he had offended Bonaparte by having the march which he had composed for the funeral of Gen. Hoche performed in his (Bonaparte's) presence, and without his order. He had even ventured to express an opinion contrary to that of the First Consul, when he was praising Paisiello and Zingarelli in the most extravagant manner. " It may do for Paisiello," said Cherubini ; " but for Zingarelli ! " Now, Bonaparte did not allow any one to oppose him in a matter of music, or any thing else ; and from that day forth there was great antipathy between the two.

When the First Consul escaped the infernal machine of *nivôse*, he was the object of general felicitations, as is usual in such cases. The conservatory sent a deputation to the Tuileries. Cherubini, who was one of them, not caring to have an interview with the man who did not like him, kept himself in the background. " I do not see Mr. Cherubini," said Bonaparte, affecting a French pronunciation of his name. The composer was obliged to show himself, but he did not speak. Some time after, he was invited to dine at the Tuileries. The repast finished, Bonaparte began talking about music as he marched about with rapid strides ; and, quoting the famous air " Ambre Adorée" of Zingarelli, he complained of Cherubini's accompaniments being too loud. Then he expressed his preference for Paisiello's music, which he said was very soothing to him. " I understand," replied Cherubini, with more spirit than a courtier is wont to manifest, " I understand that you like such music as will not prevent your thinking of state affairs." How could Bonaparte forgive any one who dared to use such language ?

It now became difficult for Cherubini to live in Paris, where the dislike of Bonaparte left him almost without the means of gaining a livelihood. Receiving an order to fulfil an engagement in Vienna, he accepted, and removed thither with his family. The first opera which he put upon the stage in that city was " Lodoïska." The events of war led the French to the gates of Vienna before he had finished his " Finiska." After the battle of Austerlitz and the peace of Presburg, Napoleon, who wished some relaxation from the fatigues of the campaign, requested Cherubini to arrange some musical *soirées*. The master complied with this request, which, in reality, was no other than a command ; but he obtained only a slight pecuniary indemnity for services rendered to the emperor, who could not forget the grudge of the First Consul.

Both Haydn and Beethoven expressed their admiration of the opera " Finiska," represented in Vienna in 1806. But, unfortunately for the artist, this splendid opera was put upon the stage at a time when both court and people were plunged in despondency by the disasters of the late war. Under the circumstances his engagement was broken; and he felt obliged to return to Paris, to resume the employment which scarcely sufficed for the support of his family. The most distinguished musicians of the conservatory received him with spontaneous affection, whilst Napoleon remained cold and inflexible in his resentment.

In 1809 he wrote the charming opera of " Pygmalion " for the theatre of the Tuileries ; but Napoleon could not or would not appreciate it.   At length Cherubini became tired of his continued injustice, and gave up writing altogether.   He then turned his attention to the study of botany, and from time to time amused himself by tracing faces and scenery upon playing-cards ; and this continued until an unforeseen circumstance roused him again to action.   Whilst at the country-house of the Prince of Chimay, the Harmonic Society of that place begged him to write a mass for the festival of St. Cecilia ; but he said " No " in such a decided manner as to deprive them of all hope.   However, after a few days, he appeared very thoughtful, was observed to walk about the grounds unoccupied, and to be moody.   The result of his reveries was the " Kyrie " and the " Gloria " of the grand mass in *fa*, executed at the festival of St. Cecilia.

On his return to Paris, 1809, Cherubini composed the rest of the mass.   This new production of the master was listened to with indescribable pleasure.   The pure style and exact harmony in which he wrote being better adapted to sacred than dramatic music, he happened to light upon that which was best suited to his musical temperament and his genius.   The kind of persecution by which he was oppressed ceased with the empire ; and, in his new position as superintendent of the king's music, he wrote many masses, and hymns for the royal chapel, thus exercising the special talent which had lain almost dormant until his visit to Chimay.

From this time the composer confined himself to sacred music, only now and then writing an opera to order

Cherubini, admired and favored by the Bourbons, was made director of the royal school ; but the service of the chapel had been his chief occupation, until suppressed by the government of July, 1830, which interrupted his habitual labors.   In 1833, when he was seventy-three years old, Scribe gave him the text of " Ali Baba," upon which he wrote a charming score.   This opera was brought out July 22, 1833, and obtained the highest applause from artists, who were astonished at the vigor of this aged composer.

In the exercise of his duties as professor,[1] and director of the conservatory, Cherubini was reputed as severe and blunt.   However, all agree in acknowledging that, thanks to his passion for exactness, and his requirements of the professors, the level of study was considerably raised.

His pupils could not help feeling that he was devoted to his duties, that he did not disdain to compose simple and progressive lessons in solfeggio and harmony for their benefit, and that his respectable and laborious life was a fit model for their emulation.

" Ali Baba " was his last great dramatic work.   After that he gave himself up to repose, only writing occasionally, for the pleasure of friends, as his Muse inspired.   He resigned his duties at the conservatory in 1841, and died March 15, 1842, at the ripe age of eighty-two years.

He was a knight, then commander, of the Legion of Honor ; a member of the Institute of France, also of Holland ; and of the Academy of Music in Stockholm.   It is to be regretted that he occupied himself so little with pure instrumenta music, since the overtures he did write are of the highest order.

[1] Among his pupils were Auber and Halévy

DUSSEK.

1761–1812.

LADISLAS DUSSEK was born at Czaslau in Bohemia, Feb. 9, 1761. His father was a talented artist, and he soon manifested the quality of his inheritance. At five years of age he played the piano ; and, five years after, he was able to accompany upon the organ. He was sent to the Convent of Iglau as a choir-boy. At this convent he studied the classic languages under the Jesuits, while continuing his musical education. Afterward he was called to Kuttenberg to take charge of an organ, and remained there two years and a half. He then pursued a course of philosophy at the University of Prague with great assiduity, passed a successful examination, and obtained a degree.

Dussek's society was always courted on account of his varied and solid learning, as well as his very amiable character. His entertaining and instructive conversation retained those near him who had been attracted by his reputation.

A captain of the Imperial Artillery, whose *protégé* the young musician was, took Dussek along with him, and procured for him the situation of organist in the Church of St. Rombant de Malines. Dussek retained this situation for a considerable time, then went to Amsterdam, where he gave so great satisfaction by his performance, that he was invited to La Haye to give lessons on the piano to the children of the stadtholder. Whilst in Holland he wrote his first three works, the best which he has composed.

Despite the favor which he enjoyed from the public,

and which was sufficient to encourage any young man of twenty-two years of age, his artistic future was uncertain. Doubtful as to the best course to pursue, he decided to go and consult Chs. Emanuel Bach. This master gave him serious and friendly advice, and then he went to Berlin. The harmonica with a key-board had just been invented by Hessel ; and our young artist showed no less skill upon this new instrument than upon the piano. He met with equal applause at St. Petersburg, whither he went intend- ing to make a long sojourn there ; but Prince Charles de Radziwill made him such advantageous offers, that he went to Lithuania to reside in the château of the noble Pole.

In 1786 he made his first visit to France, and played to Marie Antoinette with his usual success. She tried to hold him at court with golden chains ; but, having been already reproached for using his talents among foreigners, he resumed his wandering life, and went to Italy. His concerts in Milan created a perfect furore, which was so much the more astonishing, as the Italians at that time, not being very good judges of instrumental music, were hardly capable of appreciating its charms.

It would have been an unpropitious time for the artist to return to France, for just then appeared the first symp- toms of the Revolution ; so Dussek went to London, where he married in 1792. He tried to establish himself as a music-dealer ; but he was too fond of pleasure, and, being a careless person withal, was not in the least calculated for a business of this kind. His affairs were embarrassed : he soon got into debt, and was forced to take refuge on the Continent to escape from his creditors. Then he entered the service of Prince Louis of Prussia, who was killed in the battle of Saalfeld in 1806, after which Dussek engaged himself to the Prince d'Ysenbourg. In 1808 this nomadic existence gave way to a more tranquil life. Prince Talleyrand, by naming Dussek master of concerts, put an end to the agitated career of our artist.

In this same year the virtuoso obtained a most brilliant triumph at a concert given at the Odeon, where he played his sixth concerto in *fa*. In the rondo, one of the most brilliant imaginable, every repetition of the delightful air perfectly carried away the audience; but their enthusiasm knew no bounds, when Dussek improvised an entire fantasia, in which he reproduced all the ideas with wonderful harmony and skill. The next morning an editor of music gave him one hundred louis for this fantasia, which was engraved in a new edition of the concerto.

In his last years Dussek grew very obese, and, as is generally the case, he became inert. Wishing to rouse himself from the sort of apathy into which he had fallen, he had recourse to wine and other stimulants, a dangerous régime which proved very injurious to his health; for the artificial means which he used soon carried him to his grave. He died at Paris, in the hotel of Prince Talleyrand, the 20th of March, 1812.

Dussek was very fond of Grétry's music, and chose several airs from his operas as subjects for pianoforte variations. But he, too, knew how to find original themes, and work them out delightfully. All pianists are familiar with the melancholy rondo called "Canzonetta," the charming andante "L'Adieu," the first sonata in B-flat, the "Consolation," and the sonata in G-major, all of which are written with exquisite taste.

MÉHUL.

1763–1817.

HENRY ÉTIENNE MÉHUL, a celebrated French composer, was born June 24, 1763, at Givet, in the Department
of the Ardennes. His father was a cook in the regimental
barracks. The child manifested so much taste for music
that the blind organist of Givet took him under his instruction, and procured for him the situation of organist in
the Franciscan Church in Givet, when he was only eleven
years old. The young organist soon became a subject of
conversation; and the good fathers rejoiced to think that
they had encouraged him. People came from all quarters
to hear him, and were astonished at his skilful performance.

Soon Méhul became anxious to take lessons of the celebrated German organist Wilhelm Hanser, who was then at
La Val Dieu, near Givet. But it was too far for him to go
every day; and, even if he could, his father was too poor
to be at the least expense for him. The Abbé Lissoir
showed the greatest kindness to the young artist: he generously invited him to the monastery, thus sheltering him
from pecuniary difficulties. Méhul in a delightful situation among the mountains, surrounded by comrades of his
own age, had nothing to hinder him from studying composition with Hanser.

It was not long before the pupil became almost a master;
and, from his earnings as associate organist, he had the
satisfaction of being able to pay for the kind hospitality he
had received.

All this time his parents were looking forward to his
becoming a monk; but in 1778 an officer in the garrison

of Charlemont was so charmed with Méhul's improvisation upon the organ, that he proposed taking him to Paris.[1] He found no difficulty in persuading the sixteen-years-old artist to go. Having studied literature at the Abbey of Val Dieu, he gave lessons in Paris whilst he studied with an able pianist.

In 1781 he published his first and second works, which were of no great value: then he turned his attention to dramatic music, which was his real vocation. Gluck, who was in great repute at that time, was particularly kind to the promising youth. The contest going on between Gluck and Piccini[2] served to strengthen Méhul's passion for art.

The Sacred Ode of Jean Baptiste Rousseau had been written without regard to music, and was therefore a difficult subject for him; yet when it was executed, in 1782, it was highly praised by the journals of the day. At twenty years of age, Méhul offered his opera "Cora et Alonzo," which was accepted, but not then performed. The difficulties and length of time required to have it produced caused him to turn his attention to comic opera. His "Euphrosine et Conradin," put upon the stage in 1790, had brilliant success. A number of operas, received with more or less favor, followed during seven years, when he gave the opera of "Le Jeune Henri." Meanwhile Méhul had turned his art to politics, and became composer for the Revolution.

[1] Méhul went to Paris when he was sixteen years old. Anxious to hear the music of the celebrated Gluck, then in vogue in that city, and not having means to buy a ticket, he slid into the theatre during rehearsal, and was nicely ensconced in the corner of a box when an officer discovered and drove him out. Fortunately Gluck perceived what was going on, and heard from the lips of the weeping boy, how anxious he was to know something of the music of such a composer. Gluck not only gave him free admission to all his rehearsals and performances, but invited him to his house. The joy of the young artist at being able to make such an acquaintance can easily be conceived.

[2] The detractors of Gluck gave his address as "Street of the Great Howler," and those of Piccini gave his as "Street of Little Songs."

He wrote the powerful melodies of the " Chant du Départ," " Chant de Victorie," " Chant de Rétour," and many other pieces for republican festivities.

At the first representation of the " Young Henry," the royalists were ready to applaud, and the republicans to hiss. As to the enthusiasm which the overture excited, it is indescribable : it was scarcely ended when the public demanded it again, and the orchestra bravely recommenced. But, the moment the curtain rose, they began to hiss, and cry out, " Down with the tyrant ! " for it was a sort of episode of the youth of Henry IV. It was impossible to continue the piece, and the curtain fell ; but the audience insisted upon the third performance of the overture, which was certainly one of the greatest triumphs a composer ever had. One may well say that this magnificent overture is perfect in its kind. As inspector of the conservatory, and also as professor, Méhul had little time to work for the theatre. However, he brought out the opera of " Adrian," which was received by the Academy of Music, but stopped many times just as it was about to be performed. " Adrian" was a spectacular piece. The Roman emperor was receiving the honors of a triumph in Antioch. The people, always on the alert, thought they recognized some of the horses as those which had belonged to Queen Marie Antoinette, and hooted at the poor animals. Even David, the artist, declared that he would set the opera on fire, rather than see the triumph of a king. Naturally the opera, though containing many beauties, had to be sacrificed when such feelings were manifested. During the two years which Méhul mostly devoted to the conservatory, the uprightness of his character and the kindness of his feelings enabled him to exert a very useful influence in this establishment.

In writing the opera " Joseph," which is his masterpiece, and certainly one of the best that ever has appeared upon the stage, Méhul entered fully into that species of composition more fitting to his grand and severe style. More than seventy years have passed since " Joseph" was put upon the stage: yet it is always fresh and new, because the author, having only the unchangeable principles of beauty in view, paid no regard to the fashion of the day. The French amateurs of Méhul's time were not capable of appreciating the beauties of this opera, though it made a triumphant tour throughout Germany.

Méhul, who had been suffering many years from a pulmonary disease, grew melancholy, and inclined to solitude. He owned a small estate near Paris, where his favorite amusement was to cultivate the flowers of his garden. Becoming seriously ill, he was advised to seek a more genial climate in the island of Hyères. He met with a warm reception from the *dilettanti* in all the cities through which he passed. At Hyères he regretted having left Paris, his pupils and colleagues of the institute. In writing to one of his friends at the end of a month, he said, " I have broken up all my habits; I am deprived of all my old friends; I am alone, at the end of the world, surrounded by people whose language I can scarcely understand : and all this sacrifice to obtain a little more sun. The air which best agrees with me is that which I breathe among you." He could not remain without his friends ; who, though glad to see him, were sorry that he had not remained long enough to improve his health. Once more he was present at the academy, but only once. He breathed his last Oct. 18, 1817, aged only fifty-four years.

In mourning for Méhul, the people mourned for the good, the honest, disinterested, benevolent man, who was bound up in his art. Méhul abhorred intrigue, and ever tried to serve·a rival. It is well known that he lost the situation of chapel-master because Napoleon hated Cherubini, whom Méhul desired to have for a partner. A funeral chant was performed in his honor at the Royal Academy of Munich. The newspapers of Germany vied with each other in sounding his praise. Writers and artists belonging to the comic opera felt it a duty to be present at the crowning of his statue, which was brought upon the stage at the performance of his opera "Valentine de Milan," 1822. No composer from the time of Rameau merited the glory of being considered one of the chief founders of the French school of music as much as Méhul. Notwithstanding the difficulties he encountered in early life, and his premature end, he wrote forty-two operas. He honored art by his industry as by his genius.

KREUTZER.

1766–1831.

ALTHOUGH we occasionally meet with a rapid writer who is a genius, yet all rapid writers are by no means geniuses. For example, Rodolphe Kreutzer, who wrote no less than thirty-five operas and ballets, held but a second rank among the lyric masters of his day. His talent for the violin was the admiration of all his contemporaries : the works he wrote for that instrument are classic. As a virtuoso he had no equal. He was born at Versailles, where his father, who was first violinist at the royal chapel, began to teach him the rudiments of music. The signs of what he would be at some future day showed themselves in the five-year-old boy, who was put under the instruction of Aubon Stamitz, a German violinist in good repute.   Kreutzer improved rapidly under this master. His natural talents were such that he wrote good concertos without a knowledge of the principles of harmony.

At Trianon the young musician delighted Marie Antoinette by the purity of his singing, and his skill upon the violin.   It was fortunate for him that he had gained the favor of the royal family; for his parents both died before he was sixteen years of age, and he, being the eldest of five children, was obliged to earn the living of the whole family.   In this extremity he was assisted by the queen, who made him first violinist to the King's Chapel.   This appointment not only freed him from want, but enabled him to continue his studies.   Thanks to the frequent opportunities he had of hearing Viotti, he could also perfect himself in execution.   While thus striving to improve, he composed a great deal of instrumental music.   Meanwhile he became ambitious to write for the stage; but found no suitable text, until the poet Desforges gave him the historic drama of "Joan of Arc."   It is pretended by some biographers, that Kreutzer wrote the music for it in a few days; which would be almost impossible, since it would require weeks, instead of days, even to copy it.

The rich music and pleasant airs of "Paul and Virginia," which Kreutzer put upon the stage in 1791, gained him great applause; but the writer of the text, in his endeavor to give pleasure to the audience, spoiled the beautiful romance of St. Pierre, by substituting a happy close for the final catastrophe.   This opera is said to be the best which Kreutzer ever wrote.

"Lodoïska," a comic opera in three acts, and "Werther," which soon followed, were favorably received.

In composing, Kreutzer allowed himself to be guided by his inspiration, walking rapidly, and accompanying his melodies either by the violin or singing. Notwithstanding that he had been violinist to the Royal Chapel, he assisted other musicians in the Revolutionary work called " Congrès de Rois."

Soon after the treaty of Campo Formio was signed, Kreutzer set out for Italy, passing through Germany and Holland, where he received much applause. On his return to his native country, he was named violin-soloist at the opera, and in 1816 leader of the orchestra of that theatre.

At the commencement of his career, Kreutzer made up for what he lacked in harmony and composition by his natural talent. But, when he became a professor in the conservatory, he felt that he must be a learned musician : from that time forth, he sacrificed that naturalness and freshness which rendered his music so delightful ; and his compositions, in consequence, became stiff and formal.

His " Francis I.," performed in 1807, did not meet the approbation of the public. In 1824 Kreutzer received the cross of the Legion of Honor. Some time after, the director of the opera refused to put " Mathilde " upon the stage.[1] This was an affront which Kreutzer felt very sensibly ; for by his labors he had contributed largely to the success of that theatre. A prey to chagrin, his health was impaired. He gradually declined, and died at Geneva, where he had been carried for the benefit of the climate of Switzerland, and the treatment of a celebrated physician. As an instrumentalist he owed more to his own feelings than to any school ; but, although he was in a measure a self-made musician, he ranks very high as a virtuoso.

---

[1] The retired composer desired to take leave of the public with " Mathilde."

ATTWOOD.

1767–1838.

THOMAS ATTWOOD, an English composer, the son of a coal-merchant, was born in 1767. At the age of nine years he entered the Royal Chapel as choir-boy, and studied under Drs. Nares and Ayrton. After he had been in this school five years, he chanced to sing before the Prince of Wales, who took him under his protection, and sent him to study composition and singing in Naples. From Naples he went to Vienna, where he took lessons of Mozart till 1786. On his return to England, he was employed as music-teacher of the royal family, and organist of St. Paul's Church. 1796 he succeeded M. Dupuis as composer of the Royal Chapel; and in 1821 he was made member of the King's Chapel at Brighton. Among the many operas which he wrote we will mention "Poor Sailor," "Smugglers," "Castle of Sorrento," "Old Clothes Man," "True Friends," &c. Besides these works Mr. Attwood composed sonatas for the piano, and church music. His music which was performed by the choir and orchestra at the coronation of King George IV. is exceedingly fine. His style is tasteful and pure, and the music is very effective. It seems a pity that so good a composer should have been forced to teach, instead of pursuing the career of glory for which Nature seemed to have intended him.

MÜLLER.

1767–1835.

WENZEL MÜLLER, composer of popular comic operas, was born at Türnau 1767. He studied music under Dittersdorf, after which he went to the Brunner Theatre as violinist. In 1786 he was leader of the orchestra at the

Theatre Marinelli, in Leopoldstadt, at Vienna. Besides cantatas, symphonies, &c., he left two hundred and twenty-seven works for the stage, the first of which, "Das Ver-fehlte Rendezvous," he composed at the age of sixteen. His "Sonntagskinde," "Feste der Braminen," "Die Schwestern von Prag," "Die Teufelsmuhle," "Der Alpen König und der Menschenfeind," &c., are so jovial and natural, that they have gained him a high reputation throughout Germany and elsewhere.

BEETHOVEN.

1770–1827.

LUDWIG VON BEETHOVEN was born Dec. 17, 1770, at Bonn, where his grandfather Ludwig was chapel-master, and his father Johann was tenorist in the chapel of the Elector of Cologne. At a very early age the child showed a remarkable talent for music, which even under unfavorable circumstances developed itself in a most extraordinary manner. His father was addicted to drink,[1] his excellent mother was sickly ; and, after the death of his grandfather in 1773, the means of the family were very limited. Such sad circumstances tended to make the boy gloomy and reserved. Naturally obstinate and headstrong, his faults were aggravated by the corrections he received from his brutal father, who, aided by Pfeiffer, leader of the orchestra, was his first teacher. Through his talent the boy became acquainted with the noble family Von Breuning,[2] who sympathized with and assisted him in the culture of his

[1] Often in the night, when Pfeiffer came with Beethoven from the drinking-saloon, they would wake the little Louis to make him take a lesson, and keep him at the piano for hours.

[2] It was Beethoven's good fortune to have such a friend as Mme. Breuning, who understood his character, and appreciated his work.

mind and manners. In the boy's character was a singular mixture of roughness and gentleness, of brooding reserve and harmless gayety, of silent distrust and devoted friendship, which rendered it difficult for even his friends to understand him.

An organist of the court, who offered gratuitous lessons to the young Beethoven, succeeded remarkably well with the boy, who was any thing but amiable. He it was who made the child feel that music was his vocation. The ice was now broken, and Beethoven became a zealous and devoted student. Neefe, instead of making him go through a series of elementary exercises, initiated him into the masterpieces of Bach and Händel. Neefe had well judged, and the result was most satisfactory. At the age of thirteen the boy composed several quartets which were afterwards published by Artaria.

Beethoven greatly admired Mozart, who was then reigning over the musical world ; but little did he foresee that he should at some future day become his peer. Anxious to make the acquaintance of the author of so many masterpieces, he made a journey to Vienna in the spring of 1787. Furnished with a letter of introduction, he was at once admitted into the presence of the great composer. Mozart, curious to know if the youth really was such a prodigy as they boasted of, gave him a very difficult piece to perform. Beethoven seated himself at the piano, and played with a power and originality which quite astonished Mozart, who, turning to a friend standing near, said, " Mark that boy : some day you will hear of him."

In 1792 the Elector Maximilian Francis, brother of the Emperor Joseph, sent Beethoven to Vienna to study composition. Baron Swieten, friend of Mozart and Haydn, immediately took the boy under his protection ; and by him Beethoven was introduced into some of the best families in Vienna. Prince Lichnowski gave an annual sum of six hundred florins towards his support. Unfortunately Beethoven disregarded such marks of sympathy. The patience of his kind friends was sadly tried by his bad humor, his despite of the customs of society, his extravagant self-conceit. He was the pupil of Haydn from 1792 to 1794; but he gave no heed to the advice of the old master, and was anxious to be free from him. Afterwards he became acquainted with Schenck, of whom he took lessons in counterpoint. It is said that Haydn once desired Beethoven to write " Pupil of Haydn " on a piece he was about to publish; but the young man refused, saying, " I have learned nothing from you." His nature was so independent that gratitude seemed an insupportable burden to him.

Beethoven received instruction from seven professors, so that he was really favored in a special manner. But it was not their instruction which made him what he was: it was his own free movement in the great world of art.

Prince Lichnowski and Count Rafuwowski gave alternate musical entertainments for him in their palaces. This unrestrained social intercourse gave free play to the moods, yes, even incivilities, of the young artist, who felt himself so much at home in Vienna, that he only left the city occasionally for a journey. However, it was his regular custom to pass the summers in the country, sometimes with friends in some of the pleasant towns in the neighborhood of the city.

The happiest period in Beethoven's life was from 1793 to 1800. He competed with the pianist Woelfl in improvisation, and bore off the prize in the eyes of those who preferred his strange and powerful genius to Woelfl's

natural and gentle talent. Then he had a sympathetic
audience, capable of understanding his works; and he
enjoyed the benevolence of his admirers with more care
less ease and frankness than he afterwards displayed, when
his character, naturally sombre and defiant, was soured by
suffering. And, again, at that time he had no pecuniary
embarrassments, his pension sufficing for his modest
wants.

Beethoven was imbittered to the last of his days by the
griefs and chagrins which came to him with the beginning
of the nineteenth century. The conquest of Rhenish
Germany by the armies of the French Republic, and the
fall and death of the archduke, blasted the hope he had
cherished of establishing himself at Cologne. Worse still,
he had an attack of deafness which soon assumed an
alarming character. To think of an artist who seemed
born expressly to make his music heard by enthusiastic
multitudes, losing the sense of hearing! The wonderful
enchanter of the most polite society of Europe to become
deaf! How crushing to a man like Beethoven, who had
such a multitude of ideas to express, so many conceptions
to be brought forth, that were working in his brain like an
harmonious sea! Need we seek any other explanation of
his character, and the life he led?

In 1801 he wrote "Die Geschöpfe des Prométheus;"
1802, "A Funeral March;" 1803, the cantata "Christus
am Œlburg," besides songs and small pieces; 1804, the
symphony of "Eroica;" 1805, the opera "Fidelio," which
in an abridged form, as given in 1806, had but little suc
cess, but, when partly rewritten in 1814, was received with
general acclamations, and performed in all German thea
tres. It was the first since Mozart's "Zauberflöte" which
prognosticated the further development of the German
opera. Alas! Beethoven never wrote another opera.

In 1806 he wrote three Russian quartets, and the symphonies in B-major and C-minor; in 1807, the "Pastoral;" 1810, the music to Goethe's "Egmont;" 1812, the symphonies in A-major and F-major, — all of which fully designate with distinctive marks the great master's course, and show his individuality completely separated from the influence of his great teachers.

The history of the circumstances which led to the composition of the symphony "Eroica" deserves our notice. Although Beethoven was a good German, and living on intimate terms with the heads of the aristocracy of Vienna, he was a republican at heart, and strongly sympathized with the Revolutionary party in France. He looked upon Bonaparte as the victorious arm of the French Republic; and, in his admiration of the First Consul, he was pleased with the proposition of Bernadotte to write a symphony in glorification of this hero. He was about to put a part of the score of "Eroica," with the dedication to the First Consul, consisting of two words, "Napoleon Bonaparte," into the hands of the general, to be sent to Paris, when the news of Bonaparte's causing himself to be proclaimed Emperor of the French reached Vienna. Prince Lichnowski and Ferdinand Ries informed Beethoven, who immediately seized his score, angrily tore off the title, and threw it upon the floor, uttering imprecations against the new tyrant, as he called the Emperor Napoleon. Afterwards he gave the symphony this title: "Per festeggiare il Sovenire d'un Gran Uomo."

The epoch in which Beethoven brought out his magnificent symphonies marks the culminating point of the progress of music in Germany. All honor to Germany and to Italy, which have given the world so many musicians of genius! Even while the rich and fruitful genius of

Beethoven was shining with its greatest brilliancy, he was tormented with a thousand cares about his livelihood, which he believed to be precarious and insecure. However, very few composers, even among the greatest, have been favored as Beethoven, who while living enjoyed great renown, who was constantly surrounded by devoted and enthusiastic friends, and whose quartets hardly finished were executed by princes, and at the houses of princes, even before the ink with which they were written was dry. Meanwhile he considered himself very unhappy, which was enough to render him so; and therefore we sympathize with him.

The concerts in which his music was performed naturally involved expenses. Like many illustrious artists, he was entirely wanting in business tact; and although he covered the walls of his lodging with arithmetical calculations, to the great annoyance of his hostess, this man of genius became an easy prey to the avidity of editors, who profited by the sale of his works.[1] While under the influence of these pecuniary annoyances, he came near falling out with Prince Lichnowski, by asking him for the capital of the six hundred florins which this generous amateur allowed him yearly. In this extremity Beethoven suddenly determined to seek his fortune in Italy; but Jerome Bonaparte, King of Westphalia, offering him the situation of chapel-master in Cassel, he did not go. The aristocracy of Vienna, fearing to lose a musician of whom they were very proud, took his case into consideration; and the Arch-

[1] "Beethoven was always poor; but in his poverty he never forgot to be generous. At a concert given in aid of wounded soldiers, he supplied music, and conducted. When some offer of payment was made, he wrote, ' Say, *Beethoven never accepts any thing where humanity is concerned.*'

"His charity was not merely for show. His friends never applied in vain for money as long as he had any to give; and his purse-strings were often loosed for those who had injured him deeply."

duke Rudolph and two other princes agreed to secure an
annual pension of four thousand florins to the author of
"Fidelio." These generous stipulations were a proof of
their intelligent patriotism. To free the mind of the great
master from pecuniary cares, was to give him up to art.
Pleasantly situated in the pretty village of Baden, a few
leagues from Vienna, it seemed that his only care hence-
forth would be to note down, in his immortal scores, the
harmonious songs which were resounding in his soul.

But such was not his fate. After 1810, the year in
which Beethoven had written so many *chefs-d'œuvre*, his
pecuniary position underwent a change in consequence
of that of the Austrian finances, and his pension was reduced from four thousand florins to eight hundred. Notwithstanding this reverse of fortune, he wrote the music
to three of Goethe's songs in 1811 ; and in 1812 he composed the overtures of "König Stephan" and "Ruinen
von Athen" for the opening of the theatres in Pesth.
But grander still was "The Battle of Victory,"[1] a military
symphony for two orchestras, performed December, 1813.
This may well be said to be the decisive hour of Beethoven's career. His friends triumphed: his enemies, reduced
to silence, hung their heads. "The Musical Gazette" of
Leipzig is only the echo of universal opinion when it says,
"As regards 'The Battle of Victory,' nothing can be better
fitted to express the changes of combat by sound, than the
means employed by the author in this composition. He
who is able to conceive the idea of the writer is astonished
and delighted at the same time, by seeing the elements of
art applied with so much genius and effect. It may be
safely affirmed, that in the whole domain of imitative music
there is no composition to equal it."

[1] George IV., then Prince Regent, never acknowledged the dedication of the battle
symphony, or took the slightest notice of its composer.

In the spring of 1821 Beethoven was nominated honorary member of the Royal Academy of Arts and Sciences in Sweden. At that time a person could not accept such a mark of distinction without first obtaining permission of the Austrian Government. After many hinderances it was granted ; and Beethoven sent two letters to his friend Schindler, that he might announce the fact in the journals of the day, which proves that he valued the title. Meanwhile the poet Bernard, who had been commissioned by the composer to publish certain musical notices in the journals, thought it right to add the honorary titles to the name " Beethoven," which drew upon him a severe reprimand. " Such follies make me appear ridiculous," wrote Beethoven: "you will please leave out the titles in future."

Our great composer was not only troubled by sickness and suffering aggravated by hypochondria ; but the difficulty in his hearing, which commenced when he was about thirty years of age, increased to a degree of deafness which drove the artist almost to despair. Finding no relief, he became gloomy, distrustful, and solitary. With a warm heart, and a longing for that domestic happiness of which he was deprived, and being totally unfit to regulate the affairs of daily life, he was continually annoyed, and his temper soured. The death of his brother Charles in November, 1815, weighed heavily upon him. This brother, a cashier of a banking-house, left his only son to the guardianship of Beethoven. Another source of perplexity and trouble was the long and serious difficulty with his brother's widow, who, despite the father's will, during five years contested his right to the guardianship of her child. During this expensive lawsuit, full of quibblings as usual, they disputed the right of the artist to use the aristo-

cratic *Von* before his name. " My nobility is here," said
Beethoven, pointing to his heart and his head alternately.

The pretensions of the widow were set aside by the
judges; and the young Charles Beethoven, in virtue of the
judicial decision, was placed with his uncle, who adopted
him, and from that time forth spared no expense for his
education. We can form some idea of the kindness and
affectionate tenderness concealed under the rough exterior
of the great composer, by the manner in which he understood and fulfilled his duties towards the child of his
adoption. Alas! that such a prodigality of tenderness
should have been wasted upon an ungrateful child! Whilst
Beethoven became avaricious in his desire to make the
boy rich, whilst he wearied himself with mercantile and
arithmetical calculations for that purpose, whilst he refused
brilliant offers from London, that he might be near and
superintend the instruction of Charles, what was he, the
unworthy object of such devotion, doing? He studied
philology in Vienna; but dissipation and the love of
pleasure prevented him from passing his examinations.
Then he turned his attention to commerce, but was too
idle for business. Finally he enlisted in the army.

The excitement and anxiety caused by his nephew's
bad conduct were very unfavorable to Beethoven's artistic
labors. The interruption of his writings, with the increased demands upon his purse, rendered his position
still more uncomfortable. The good friends of former
times were either dead or estranged : the unfortunate artist
became more and more isolated, and many a one supposed
that he had lost his musical power.

In 1818 Beethoven conceived the idea of writing a
mass, to be performed at the installation of the Archduke

Rudolph as Archbishop of Olmutz, and set himself to
work with the most devoted enthusiasm. The mass which
he had composed for Prince Esterhazy, in 1808, retained
the Haydn and Mozart character; whilst this expressed, in
the artistic manner peculiar to himself, the religious feelings and conceptions of the sorely tried man. No sooner
had he completed this mass than he began with equal zeal
to carry out a long-cherished plan for a symphony,
which should conclude with Schiller's "Lied an die
Freude."

In answer to a letter from Beethoven, desiring to have
the mass and symphony above mentioned performed at a
grand concert in Berlin, Count Bruhl warranted him good
success. But when the *dilettanti* among the nobility, and
the admirers of the good artist, heard of his proposition,
they were much excited, and immediately drew up a petition in which they begged him to spare their capital from
such a disgrace. The petition was signed by more than
thirty distinguished persons, among whom were Czerny,
Kuffner, the Abbé Stadler, Kiesewetter, &c. Beethoven
was deeply affected by this manifestation. His friends
overcame such difficulties as the character of the master
was likely to raise; and the execution of the two colossal
works took place at Vienna, May 7, 1822.

Beethoven stood at the right of the leader, and gave the
movement of each piece during the performance; but he
heard little or nothing of what was passing around him.
He stood with his back to the audience, and some one was
obliged to motion to him when he ought to answer to the
applauses. On learning that the pecuniary results of this
performance were next to nothing, he was seized with an
ill turn, and carried home. He did not speak a word during the whole night. His domestics, who left him when he

fell asleep, found him next morning just as they had left him, in his concert-dress.[1]

The managers of the Imperial Opera and of the theatre of Berlin begged Beethoven to compose a German opera, and set his own price upon it. At first he accepted the proposition, which he afterwards refused, alleging the want of good German singers. In this he was right; for at that time, 1822, the best singers in Vienna were all Italian. It is said, that, when he examined Rossini's score of the "Barber of Seville," he was much pleased, and praised it highly. Praise from a man sincere as Beethoven was a great honor to Rossini.

His last works were five grand quartets, which even at the present time are subjects for study.

Beethoven's last works, with few exceptions, remained almost unnoticed by his contemporaries, who preferred lighter and easier studies : in fact, they were disinclined to make the exertion necessary to follow in the tracks of this wonderful composer. It was not until after the death of Beethoven, March 24, 1827, that they became conscious of having lost one of the greatest artists of all times. Since then lovers of music, and students, have exerted themselves in conquering the difficulties with which his works are replete. The study of Beethoven's works has tended greatly to the development of music. He had that aspiration for individual freedom which pervades our times, combined with musical energy, truth of feeling, and charm of expression, which one cannot help feeling while listening to his artistic productions.

Beethoven died at the age of fifty-seven, of a pulmonary

1 "His dress on such occasions usually was a sea-green frock-coat, green breeches with buckles, white silk stockings, shoes with black ribbon bows, embroidered white vest trimmed with gold cord, white cravat, hair curled with cue, black hat under the left arm dagger with a silver hilt worn on the left side."

affection, although he had previously been treated for dropsy. On his death-bed he manifested great interest in religion, partook of the sacrament, and was reconciled to his rival Hummel.

In his private life Beethoven was full of odd humors, which made him very unsociable. We need hardly speak of his defiant and irascible spirit: it is too well known. He would sometimes allow himself to fly into a rage, and be very rude to those performers who were so unfortunate as to make a mistake in the concerts which he was directing. At times he was angry with and suspicious of his best friends. Of course his manners checked the sympathy that would otherwise have been accorded to him as a genius.

It seems almost impossible to believe some of the caprices [1] which are related of him, such as not attending to his pupils, or composing while he should have been teaching, or taking pay in advance for music that he promised, but never wrote. Odd as he may have been, we believe him too high-toned for such unjust conduct.

It was difficult for a stranger to get access to the great musician, who did not in the least resemble those illustrious persons who have a friendly word especially for young talent in search of protection. However we must acknowledge that the false kindness of many masters, jealous of their own popularity, has made more victims than the rough humor of the misanthrope. That Beethoven did not go into ecstasies over the talent of the precocious young

[1] " When we hear it recorded of Beethoven, that he was a morose, churlish, ill-tempered man, full of caprice, and devoid of all complaisance, let us rather remember one who in the midst of sufferings which we cannot estimate, and trials which we have not known, never lost his reverence for God, his deep and tender devotion to all that was highest in man, his patient forbearance with the weak and selfish, and a certain indomitable courage, wideness of vision, and power of will, which has raised him, the lonely worker, to one of the most solitary pinnacles of fame."

Liszt, is not surprising ; but it is much to be regretted that he twice refused to see Rossini, notwithstanding he was much pleased with his " Barber of Seville," as has already been mentioned. But one must understand the suscep-tibilities of such a man as Beethoven, before he can judge correctly of such peculiarities. Perhaps there never was an artist so conscious of his superior talents, and of his future renown, as Beethoven. He repeatedly read Plu-tarch's Lives, and wished to have some one write the history of his own life and works. During his last sick-ness of four months, he was asked whom he would like to have for a biographer ; to which he answered without hesi-tation, " Rochlitz, if he outlives me." But Rochlitz gave up the project of writing the life of Beethoven, on ac-count of ill health. The task then devolved upon Schindler, whose sincere attachment to his teacher had never changed.

Boileau tells us that he found the word he had lost, at the end of the wood : like him, Beethoven sought inspira-tion in walking either in the country, or in the streets of Vienna. Whatever the weather might be, he walked and walked, always glad to be in the open air. As soon as he entered his house, he began to write and cipher on the walls, the blinds, tables, every thing, with his habitual carelessness.

He was subject to fits of distraction and forgetfulness. At one time he had forgotten the date of his birth. At another time he went into a restaurant in Vienna, and called for the bill of fare ; but, instead of asking for what he had chosen, he turned the paper, and began to note down some musical ideas which had come into his head. There he sat thinking, writing, totally unconscious of the place in which he was, or what had brought him there. Then after having written a while, he rose, looked about him, and asked how much he owed. "You owe nothing, sir," said the boy in attendance: "you have not yet dined." — "What! do you think that I have not dined?" — "Most assuredly." — "Very well, then, give me something." — "What will you have?" — "Any thing."

If we mention these things, it is with no idea of belittling a person who will always remain one of the highest in the sphere of art. How much justice in these words of Goethe! — "It is all the same whether one is great or small: he has to pay the reckoning of humanity."

CRAMER.

1771–1858.

PERHAPS no man of our time has rendered greater service as a teacher of the piano than Cramer. He was a superior teacher and fine composer for this instrument.

Johann Baptist Cramer was born at Mannheim, Feb. 24, 1771. His father, William Cramer, a skilful violinist, removed to London when our artist was but a year old. A few years sufficed to discover the musical taste of the boy,[1] who was put to the study of the violin. However, he displayed so great an aptitude for the piano, that his father judiciously allowed him to follow the bent of his inclination, and confided him to the care of Benser, of whom he took lessons for three years. In 1782 he studied with Schroeter, and the following year with Clementi. On the departure of this last pianist in 1784, which deprived Cramer of the rare advantages of his instruction, he set himself to the study of Händel and Sebastian Bach. His

---

[1] "While still a mere boy, he attracted the notice and regard of Haydn, during one of his visits to England."

talent for execution was manifested in several public concerts, when in 1785 he initiated himself into the theory of
his art, under the direction of Fred. Charles Abel. His
musical education completed, Johann Baptist Cramer was
soon known as a virtuoso of the first class, and acquired
a legitimate reputation by performing in different cities.
He also labored to establish his name as a composer by
publishing many sonatas. In 1791 he returned to England, the country which had been the cradle of his infancy:
here he married, and began to teach. He made London
his home, but travelled upon the Continent, and lived in
Vienna and Paris at different times. He died at Kensing-
ton, April 16, 1858, at the age of eighty-seven.

Cramer wrote forty-three works containing one hundred
and fifty sonatas, also a great variety of duets, concertos,
&c.; but his last two books of studies, and his sonatas, are
considered as his best productions. The style of Cramer
was perfection with all its qualities, — correctness, harmony, delicacy of shade, and good taste. He had great
skill in the art of modifying sound so as to detail all the
inflections of song; and his execution was brilliant.[1] He
played the "Das wohltemperirte Klavier" (Well-tempered
Clavichord) of Sebastian Bach, and the fugues of Händel,
with wonderful clearness and skill.

The long life of this excellent professor offers but few
incidents. May we not say of artists what Fénelon said of
people, "Happy are those whose history is not interesting"? If the recital is short, it is easy to make the praises
long: we should only have to notice separately the rare
qualities displayed in the course of sixty years' teaching, as
well as the particular merit of each composition, from the

---

[1] Moscheles says, "His Mozart-like compositions are like breathings from the
sweet south."

piece entitled "The Little Nothing" to his most learned studies.

In the case of Cramer, it might come into the head of some one to say, "What's a sonata?" To which the sonata might reply, "A friend who wishes to make your house more pleasant; who wishes to go into competition with your clubs and other outside attractions, by showing you the talent and taste of your wife, and the grace and intelligence of your daughters; who wishes to find a place in your heart, which cannot help being moved at finding how much sonata is valued by those so dear to you; a friend whose wish it is to contribute to your well-being by making a useful diversion of your serious thoughts. Humble sonata that I am, I wish to banish scandal from your parlor, and cause politeness, kindly and harmonious feelings, combined with refined pleasure, to reign there."

SPONTINI.

1774–1851.

LUIGI GASPARDO PACIFICO SPONTINI was born Nov. 14, 1774, at Miolati, near Ancona. His parents, common farmers, anxious that he should enter into holy orders, confided him, when eight years old, to the care of his Uncle Joseph, curate of Jesi, who undertook to teach him Latin.[1] But one of those incidents, insignificant to all appearance

[1] To teach the boy Spontini Latin was no easy task; for that was not what Nature intended him to learn. The only thing that interested him in the Church of Santa Maria was the ringing of the bells. In many churches, and particularly in Italy, the bells are toned so as to sound harmoniously together: the bells of Santa Maria were noted for their harmonious tones. As soon as they sounded, Gaspardo disappeared; and when they sought for him they were sure to find him stretched out in the belfry, listening with delight to the harmonic chime. One day he nearly paid with his life for his favorite pleasure. The bells were rung during a severe thunderstorm; the boy lay, as usual, in the belfry, enjoying his roaring orchestra of metal. In his delight he somewhat resembled Quasimodo, the celebrated bell-ringer of Notre Dame, only that

which often puts the child of genius in the way of his real
vocation, prevented the young Gaspardo from following the
career marked out by his family. It so happened that an
organ-builder named Crudeli was employed to put up an
organ in the church where Gaspardo's uncle officiated.
The young Gaspardo was charmed with the sounds
Crudeli brought out of his instrument,[1] and tried to
imitate them. This showed his musical taste, and proved
to Crudeli that the boy possessed the germ of real talent.
The artist informed the curate, who, far from displaying a
willingness to foster the talent of his nephew, determined
to use every exertion to turn his mind from music. Spontini tried to reason with his uncle ; but, not succeeding, he
ran away.[2] A brother of his mother kindly received him,
and allowed him to commence his musical studies with the
chapel-master of the place. At the end of a year, Uncle
Joseph had changed his mind, and desired the return of his
nephew, whose talent he was forced to acknowledge. He
no longer hesitated to give him the masters best qualified
to guide him in the attainment of the art to which he
devoted himself. Gaspardo studied for a while at his
uncle's, then entered the Conservatory of Naples : this
was in 1791. His progress was such that he was soon
made tutor.

the boy was neither one-eyed, hunchbacked, nor bandy-legged. On this day, however,
he had the advantage of Quasimodo, in that he distinctly heard the uninterrupted
rolling thunder, as an accompanying bass to the harmonic chime ; and nothing seemed
wanting to fill the measure of his happiness, when suddenly a stroke of lightning
entered the belfry, and precipitated the young *dilettant* from the upper story to the
next below. It was lucky for him that the opening of each story was in a different
place, or he would have fallen to the ground-floor, and been killed : as it was, he
received but a slight injury.

[1] Crudeli had a spinet on which he allowed Gaspardo to play, and even gave him
some instruction.

[2] It was in the winter season, and the boy's clothes were thin : yet he ran as fast as
he could, and scarcely stopped until he reached Monte Sante Vito, where his uncle
lived.

In 1796 he wrote his first opera, "I Puntigli delle Donne," which was brought out at Rome with good success, so that he was encouraged to continue writing. Meanwhile the French army invaded the territory of Naples, which obliged the court to take refuge in Palermo. As Cimarosa was sick at the time, Spontini was chosen to charm the sad leisure of exiled royalty; but, his health failing, he left Sicily, and went first to Rome, then to Venice. Several of his works performed in those two cities were well received, though in after-life he judged harshly of these, his youthful productions.

Spontini left Italy in 1803, and went to Paris. The reputation of a great number of Italian composers well known in Paris had preceded them, so that, as a general thing, they met with little difficulty in making themselves known. With Spontini, however, the case was very different: his works were not known beyond the Alps; and, when he first went to Paris, he was obliged to give lessons in singing, to earn his living. In February, 1804, he put one of his works, "La Finta Filosofia," upon the stage, and had the satisfaction of having it well received. In the course of the year, he brought out a French operetta, "Julie ; ou, le Pot des Fleurs." This was unsuccessful ; and the operetta "La Petite Maison," attempted to be performed in July, 1804, was not even played through. The opera of "Milton," in one act, performed at the end of 1804, met with more success : in this opera he first stepped out of his Italian mannerism, and began that transformation of his talents that afterwards shone forth so brilliantly in the opera "La Vestale." Spontini's want of success at the beginning was partly owing to the French musicians, and chiefly those of the conservatory, who, seeing the national stage invaded by Italian artists, formed a league destined to drive away, as intruders, all those musicians whose name ended with an *i* or an *o*. This coalition had commenced its operations when Spontini arrived. It is doubtful whether he could have overcome the difficulties thrown in his way when he was ready to bring out the opera " La Vestale," if he had not applied to the Empress Josephine.[1] A cantata, that he performed in honor of the conqueror of Austerlitz, served him admirably ; and the artists of the Academy of Music who had refused to perform " La Vestale," declaring it could not be sung, were obliged to yield when Napoleon ordered.

It was put upon the stage Dec. 15, 1807, after nearly a year's study. A few months previous, Napoleon requested the author to perform some parts of it at the Tuileries. At the conclusion he said, " M. Spontini, your opera abounds in fine airs and effective duets. The march to the place of execution is admirable. You will certainly have the great success which you so well deserve." More than a hundred consecutive representations confirmed the justice of this prediction.

At the rehearsals the first singer, who took the part of the grand pontiff, acquitted himself so badly, displayed so much ill-humor, and was so impertinent withal, that Spontini in his impatience snatched the pamphlet from his hand, and threw it into the fire. Dérivis, who chanced to be present, rushed to the fireplace, put his hand into the flame, and drew out the part. " I have saved it, I will keep it !" he cried. The composer gladly consented, and had no cause to be sorry for it.

His next opera, much admired, was " Ferdinand Cortes," in three acts, performed in 1809 with great success.

---

[1] Josephine loved music, and was not insensible to the merits of the elegant young artist who claimed her protection.

The scene of the revolt is one of the most beautiful passages in music which has ever been written.

About this time Spontini married the niece of D'Erard, the celebrated pianoforte-maker, and soon after was called to the directorship of the Italian opera. Many things combined to render his new situation disagreeable, so that at the expiration of two years he gave it up in disgust. In 1814 he wrote the opera " Pelage ; or, The King and Peace." In 1816 he assisted Perseus, Berton, and Kreutzer in writing the ballet opera " Les Dieux rivaux." Neither of these last two operas, however, was much noticed. On the other hand, he was very successful in 1817 with the numbers which he added to Salieri's great opera " Danaïdes : " one, that of the Bacchanal, is particularly worthy of notice. Afterwards he introduced it into his opera of " Nurmahal." At the same time Spontini was very busy composing the opera " Olympia," which was performed in December, 1819. This excellent work, on the same plan with " La Vestale " and " Cortes," was not well received, owing partly to the changes which had taken place in Paris, and partly to the libretto.

Not meeting with the success he expected, he decided to listen to the propositions which were made by Frederick William, King of Prussia. In 1820 the author of " La Vestale " went to Berlin with the title of " Director of Music." He filled this post satisfactorily from 1820 to 1840.[1] Among the works which he brought out were the opera " Nurmahal," partly taken from " Lalla Rookh," a poem by Thomas Moore ; in 1825, "Alcidor ;" and in 1829, " Agnes von Hohenstaufen," and various other works

[1] " Spontini has been represented as stiff, proud, and arrogant. He loved to be called the ' Napoleon of music.' By his adroitness and iron will, he not only maintained his position as director, but he held the sole sceptre of musical supremacy in Berlin."

written for different occasions. As a director of music, Spontini had great influence upon the lyric theatres of Berlin. He had the glory of forming singers among the Prussians, who until his time had taken more pains to play their parts well than to vocalize correctly.

However, Spontini's residence in Berlin was imbittered by the enmity which he had brought upon himself in a great measure by his pride and arrogance. The native musicians were indignant at being ruled by a foreigner. A league headed by Count Brühl, superintendent of the Royal Theatre, was formed against him.

The artist redoubled the hatred of his enemies by paying them back in their own coin. Adding the intolerance of genius to his ill-feelings at their bickerings, he doubtless went too far. Finally, on the death of Frederick William III., he determined to leave the country forever. The new king, finding it impossible to conquer his resolution, generously granted him a pension of sixteen thousand francs, and allowed him to depart.

Spontini had been named member of the Academy of Fine Arts in Paris, on condition that he would return to that city at the expiration of his engagement with the King of Prussia. He kept his promise ; but, when he tried to make an arrangement with the manager of the opera, for the representation of his old works, the manager would not listen to his proposals. Spontini seemed to have lost his friends : only the Society of the Conservatory Concerts remained faithful to the old musician, who more than once had the satisfaction of hearing his works applauded in the very hall in which the councils of his enemies were held thirty years before. Laden with honors, decorated with all the orders of Europe, Spontini had guarded in his heart a real love for the country of his birth. When his memory began to fail, and deafness warned him that he was on his way to a far-off journey, he felt that he could not go without seeing his native place once more. He left Paris in 1850, passed some time at Jesi, and then went to Maiolati. This cradle of his infancy was destined to be his tomb.

After having founded several benevolent institutions (for he had amassed considerable wealth), he led a happy and quiet life with the amiable and affectionate partner of his joys and his sorrows, until he took a violent cold, his last illness. Not willing to change his habit of going to church, he exposed himself one severely cold day, and went home with a fever which carried him off Jan. 24, 1851.

BOIELDIEU.

1775–1834.

The latter part of the eighteenth century furnished a great number of celebrated men, among whom is the immortal Boieldieu, justly considered the prince of light music in France.

François Adrien Boieldieu, the favorite of all the French composers of opera, was born at Rouen, Dec. 15, 1775. His father was secretary in the archbishop's office ; and the young François received his first notions of the art of music at the Metropolitan Church, where he sang as choir-boy. The head master was a severe, — yes, a violent man. It is said that the little Boieldieu, having soiled one of his master's books, ran away, to obviate the punishment which awaited him. He was caught on his way to Paris, and brought back.

At the age of sixteen he played well upon the piano, and attempted composition. He was so fond of the dra·

matic art, that he spent all that he could save for the theatres at Rouen, where he heard the operas then in vogue. More than once, when his money failed, he had recourse to stratagem ; as, for instance, getting into the hall by stealth, and concealing himself under a bench, that he might hear the rehearsals. Hearing the works of others incited him to renewed efforts in composition ; and it was not long before he wrote a comic opera, which was performed at Rouen.

The Revolution had made such sad havoc with the churches, and the property of the clergy, that Boieldieu's family were ruined. But our young artist of nineteen, rich in hope and courage, saw the future under the colors which concealed the present. He had thirty francs in his pocket, and a score under his arm, when he set out for the capital, with his head full of charming and brilliant air-castles which were soon to be blown away. The companies of the comic opera refused the work of an unknown artist ; and poor Boieldieu soon learned from experience that it was no easy matter for a young man from the provinces to bring himself before the public. While waiting for something to turn up, he set himself to tuning pianos, and in this way came to the house of Erard, where the *élite* of artists were in the habit of meeting. Boieldieu soon felt his need of more knowledge, and made good use of such opportunities as presented themselves for his improvement ; and he found sympathizers, and received good advice. The celebrated Garat sang several of his romances, at first in Erard's saloons, and then elsewhere, thus gradually leading the way to the stage. The poet Fiévée furnished the young artist with a libretto for an opera in one act, "La Dot de Suzette," which he composed in 1795. Its success encouraged the youthful aspirant to continue ; and

in 1796 he wrote "La Famille Suisse;" 1797, "Mon-
breuille et Merville," and "L'Heureuse Nouvelle;" in
1879, "Zoraïme et Zulnare," "Les Méprises espagnoles;"
in 1800, "Baniowski."[1]

"The Caliph of Bagdad," which he brought out in
1801, was far more successful than all the other operas
which he had previously written. It had more than seven
hundred representations in Paris alone, and spread the
name of the composer far and wide. In 1802 he wrote
the lovely score of "Ma Tante Aurora." But the amiable
artist of distinguished manners and fine person, possessing all the qualities which render a man agreeable in
society, admired and applauded in public for his musical
gifts, was very much to be pitied in his private life. His
wife, the opera-dancer Mafleuroy, whom he married in
1802, rendered him so unhappy that he found it impossible to live with her. A separation took place, and Boieldieu decided to leave Paris. He set out for Russia in company with his friends Rode and Lamarre. Immediately
upon his arrival, the Czar Alexander made him master of
the Imperial Chapel, which brought him honor but no
profit. However, the emperor engaged him to write three
operas a year, on such subjects as he himself might
choose. But dramatic literature had made very little progress in Russia ; and the composer was limited to setting
to music some pieces which had been performed in Paris.

During the seven years the artist remained in St. Petersburg, the only works he wrote worth mentioning are, "Ab-
derkan," "Calypso," "Les Voitures Versées," "Aline,"
and "Rien de Trop." Although laden with favors by the
Emperor Alexander, and dear to the *élite* of Russian
society, Boieldieu was nevertheless entirely out of his

---

[1] About this time he obtained a professorship at the Conservatory.

natural element. And, if his talents were highly recognized by the court and nobility, he was not free from the surveillance of the police, always suspicious of foreigners, and more particularly of the French during the war of Napoleon against the Czar. The artist was neither a politician, nor a meddler in politics ; yet he unwittingly drew suspicion upon himself by preparing a package of manuscripts to be sent to a friend in Paris. An employee opened the package, according to custom, and to his astonishment read the words "si, mi, sol," upon the first paper. This was evidence sufficient for the detective, who clearly understood the words "si, mi, sol," to mean "*six mille soldats*" (six thousand soldiers). Boieldieu was a spy, and he had caught him. It is but just to say that the mistake was easily explained, and the serious affair terminated in bursts of laughter.

Early in 1811 Boieldieu returned to Paris,[1] where he composed the opera, "Jean de Paris," which he put upon the stage in 1812. It was and is very much admired for its charming fresh music. This opera was soon followed by "Le Nouveau Seigneur de Village," also a delightful composition. Then he took part with others in writing occasional operas ; and in 1816 he wrote "La Fête du Village Voisin."

The death of Méhul in 1817 left a vacant place in the section of fine arts at the Institute. Boieldieu was called to fill the chair of him whom he had for a long time considered as one of his masters, and whose rival he had become. In 1818 his opera "Le Chaperon Rouge" had brilliant success. After this he retired for a few years to his country residence, Jarcy, on account of his health,

---

[1] On his ret :rn to Paris, a class in composition was formed for him at the Conservatory.

doing very little with music except looking over the compositions brought to him from the Conservatory ; but in 1825 he came out from his resting-place, bringing with him "La Dame Blanche," [1] a masterpiece which crowned his reputation.   Such is the charm of this work, that for forty years it has held its place in the first rank of French comic operas.   In 1829 he brought out his last opera, "Les Deux Nuits."

The health of Boieldieu was failing.   He had the habit of singing while composing, which tired him very much ; then, the duties incumbent on a teacher, the interminable conversations at the theatre, the rehearsals, — all these combined had injured his organs of respiration. He needed rest, but was not wise enough to take it in season.

Finally he was obliged to relinquish his duties as professor at the Conservatory.   He obtained the usual pension, though he had not served the time required by the regulations.   Charles X. made a liberal addition from his private purse ; and Boieldieu had no real financial difficulties until the Revolution of 1830, when he lost the pension of the Conservatory, as well as that of his royal benefactor. At the same time there was a change in the government of the comic opera ; and he was deprived of the income which had been allowed him [2] in gratitude for the master-pieces with which he had enriched its repertoire.   The anxieties caused by such reverses of fortune preyed upon his already feeble health.   He went to Pisa, but received no benefit from the journey.   On his return to Paris, the minister of the interior granted him a pension of three thousand francs.   Then he thought he would go to the

[1] Boieldieu chose the air of Robin Adair on which to found this charming opera.
[2] Twelve hundred francs.

watering-places of the Pyrenees, but was unable to get farther than Bordeaux. Feeling that his end was approaching, he begged to be carried to his country-house in Jarcy, near Gros-bois, in the Department of Seine et Oise. He died Oct. 8, 1834. His obsequies were celebrated in the Church of the Invalides. Cherubini's Requiem had been prepared for the occasion; but the ecclesiastical authorities opposed its execution, because it required female voices.

After the death of his first wife, in 1826, Boieldieu married again, and enjoyed much domestic happiness in his second union. His son Adrien, by his first wife, born in Paris, Nov. 3, 1816, was a talented musician. He wrote romances and operas, the most successful of which was " La Bouquet de l'Infante," brought out in 1847.

The loss of the composer was great to the musical world especially, for he was one whom all esteemed and admired. No one knew better than he how to discover obscure talent, and to aid in bringing it to light. Hérold never forgot his kindness in time of need; and Catel was indebted to his exertions for the Cross of Honor bestowed upon him. Boieldieu was free from jealousy. In a letter that he wrote to the author of "Zampa," he displayed his love of justice, and hatred to any thing which savored of detraction. A disposition like his could never harbor any thing like envy With his brother composers he was always on the most friendly terms.

HUMMEL.

1778-1837.

THE greatest eulogium that can be made of Hummel is to say that he was Mozart's first pupil, and for several years the rival of Beethoven. If he was wanting in the sublime accents of the great master, his thoughts were grand and very rich, his harmonies full, and always agreeable to the ear. He was second, only because the comparison was established between his talent and the extraordinary genius of Beethoven. Had he been born at another period, with the rich musical qualities he possessed, he would have been distinguished in the rank of talented musicians.

Johann Nepomuk Hummel was born Nov. 14, 1778, at Presburg, where his father was a professor of military music. He began to learn the violin at the age of four, and piano and singing when he was but five years of age. The rapid progress he soon made revealed his musical ability. Meanwhile his father lost his situation ; and, having no other resource, he went with his son to Vienna, where he became leader of the orchestra in a theatre. The child, then scarcely seven years old, was so skilful a virtuoso upon the piano, that he attracted the attention of the best musicians, even Mozart himself. It is well known that Mozart had a great aversion to 'teaching ; but the pleasure of cultivating the taste of an exceptionally gifted pupil overcame his repugnance ; and he offered to teach the young Hummel, on a condition that was very advantageous to the pupil, viz., that he should reside in his (Mozart's) family, so that he should not lose sight of him during his studies.

Such a proposition was eagerly accepted by the grateful father of the precocious child. Under the direction of Mozart, the boy acquired prodigious ability in two years, so that at nine years of age he was the good pianist, who excited the admiration of all who listened to him ; and his public career may be said to have commenced at that time. Mozart gave a concert at Dresden in 1787, in which the talent of his young pupil displayed itself to good advantage. The success he obtained inaugurated a series of triumphs in Germany, England, and Holland. Whilst in Scotland, he published his first work, "Variations for the Piano."

Hummel was fifteen years old when he returned to Vienna. It seemed that there was nothing more for him to learn in regard to execution ; but his father, who was excessively severe, insisted that he should apply himself assiduously to study. Then he turned his attention to composition, studying under distinguished masters. In 1803 Prince Nicholas Esterhazy wished to obtain the services of the young artist. Hummel gladly accepted a situation which permitted him to satisfy his taste for church music. His first mass gained the approbation of Haydn. This work was succeeded by other sacred compositions, as well as operas and ballets, all of which were well received by the public. His reputation as a composer soon passed beyond the Rhine. Cherubini introduced his music into France in 1806, by causing some of his compositions to be performed at the Conservatory. It is useless to say that they were highly appreciated by those capable of understanding their elevated character.

In 1811 Hummel went to Vienna, where he gave lessons in composition and on the piano till 1816, in which year he accepted the call of chapel-master to the King of Würtemburg. He now gave concerts, and astonished his hearers by his masterly performances on the piano, and his wonderful improvisations. In 1820 he went as chapel-master to the court of the Grand Duke of Saxe-Weimar ; and in 1822 he obtained leave of absence for a visit to Russia, where he was received in the most cordial manner.

For a long time there had been enmity between Hummel

and Beethoven which the bitter humor of the great syin-phonist made irreconcilable. But, when Hummel heard that the author of "Fidelio" was at the point of death, he hastened to his bedside to seek a reconciliation. Tears flowed from his eyes at the sight of his former friend, his expiring rival. Beethoven extended his hand, and they tenderly embraced each other. It was a touching scene, and caused profound emotion in those who witnessed it.

Hummel went again to Paris in 1829, but was not successful as on his first visit. Afterwards he went to Poland; then returned to Weimar, where he died Oct. 17, 1837, aged fifty-nine years.

Although Hummel was in some respects inferior to such succeeding artists as Listz and Thalberg, he has never been surpassed in correctness, elegance, and proficiency in harmony. His improvisations, owing to their clearness and order, resembled meditated studies more than pieces com-posed and executed *extempore*.

His dramatic works are not his best; but his sacred and instrumental pieces have classed him among the most dis-tinguished masters of this century. The grand septet in *ré*-minor is his masterpiece, and has for a long time served as a type for analogous compositions. His concertos are well known to all good pianists. His trios for violin, violoncello, and piano are still in vogue.

Hummel loved the quietude and calmness of the coun-try; never, like the Titan Beethoven, seeking savage wilds and abrupt precipices. If the inflexible will of his father had not made a virtuoso of Hummel, no doubt he would have directed all his energy to sacred music, his taste for which led him to prefei the employment of chapel-master to the Prince Esterhazy to that of director of the music of the Imperial Theatre, offered him by Baron Braun.

Hummel is really the author of the most beautiful German sacred music ; and it is much to be regretted that so little of it is left to us. Three solemn masses and some motets are about all that we know of him. These works are characterized by grandeur and piety, as well as by their sweet and varied harmony.

Hummel's compositions, all of a high order, are divided into dramatic, sacred, and instrumental.

"Weber received Hummel at Prague in the most courteous and friendly manner, introduced him into all the aristocratic houses, and helped to arrange his concert with true artistic sympathy. He said of him, ' Hummel's best qualities consist in his wonderful neatness of execution, his brilliancy, and his great powers of endurance ; but he cannot play an adagio, though he astounds by his rapid passages.' "

AUBER.

1782–1871.

DANIEL FRANÇOIS ESPRIT AUBER, a celebrated French composer of opera, was born at Caen, Jan. 29, 1782. His father, a Parisian merchant, was an educated man and a great lover of music. He entertained artists at his house in Paris, so that his parlors resounded with continued concerts ; and a taste for music was early cultivated in the young François. Like most artists, he displayed a talent for his true vocation while yet a child ; but his father intended to make a merchant of him.

However, he allowed the boy to take music-lessons as an accomplishment, and was gratified by his progress ; for in a short time he composed several pieces which were performed for the entertainment of friends, and much admired.

François, who was in a banking-house, soon became disgusted with his employment, and set out for London, in company with a young banker, ostensibly for business purposes; but, when they arrived, Auber left his companion to frequent commercial establishments, and inform himself about business matters, whilst he accepted the flattering invitations extended to him by those lovers of art whose parlors were ever open to musical talent.

Thus pleasantly passed a year and a half, when he was obliged to return to Paris, much less qualified for the banking-house than he was before he left home.

He now composed some concertos for his friend Lamare, the violoncellist, who published them under his own name. Then he wrote a concerto for the violin, which was brought out by Mazas at the Conservatoire. Meanwhile he made his first attempt at a dramatic composition, taking the libretto of the old comic opera " Julie," and setting it to new music. It was performed at a private theatre, and well received by his friends.

Another little opera was performed at the house of the Prince of Chimay. Auber's father, perceiving Cherubini among the artists present, thought it a good opportunity to ask him what he thought of his son's works. " He has talent," replied Cherubini; " but it is easy to see that his musical studies are incomplete." — " But how? I have put him under the best masters." — "·My dear sir, don't you know that artists do not sell their secret? they give it." After further conversation it was concluded that Cherubini should direct the young man in his course. Auber subscribed to the engagement, and studied arduously under the guidance of the master, who knew so well how to unite French taste with Italian form, and who transmitted his own musical science to his pupil.

Among other pieces which he wrote at this time was a mass, a number of which (the prayer) he afterwards transferred into his "Masaniello." In 1813 he put "Le Séjour Militaire," a comic opera, upon the stage. Although he was then over thirty years old, it was his *début*. Few composers have commenced their lyric career so late in life; but none have regained lost time so effectually.

The cold reception given to this work, the death of his father, and material cares, prevented our artist from coming before the public for several years : it was not until a change of fortune made it necessary for him to try to earn something by that which he had previously looked upon more as a pastime than a means of gaining his livelihood, that he set himself seriously to work.

In 1819 he produced the comic opera in one act, "Le Testament et les Billets-Doux." This second work succeeded no better than the first ; but he did not allow himself to be discouraged : on the contrary, he seemed to write with more vigor, and in 1820 brought out "La Bergère Châtelaine" with good success. This was followed in 1821 by the opera, "Emma ; ou, la Promesse Imprudente," which was equally successful. In 1822 he united himself with Scribe, who furnished the greatest number of librettos for his compositions ; and from this time forward he gained continually in public favor. The first work after his union with Scribe was the opera "Leicester," written in 1822 ; then followed thirty others, "Le Maçon" (1825), "La Muette di Portici" (1828), "Fra Diavolo" (1830), "Gustave" (1833), "Le Lac des Feés" (1839), "Le Part du Diable," &c. "La Muette di Portici" ("Masaniello"), an opera in five acts, represented the 29th of February, 1828, was his crowning glory.

This opera is considered as his masterpiece. The

libretto, written in part by Scribe, has for its subject, as is generally known, the rise and fall of Masaniello. The introduction of a mute girl upon the stage and in an opera was an inspiration as happy as it was bold. The score of this opera is extremely rich. Airs, duets, prayers, cavatinas, barcarolles, choruses, dances, orchestration — all are characteristic ; and the whole is wonderfully effective. One of the singular merits of this opera is the musical language which so admirably expresses the sentiments that the poor Fenella can only render by gesticulation. The overture is original and brilliant: in fact, it is a perfect feast for the ear. In 1830 the king sent for Auber to come to the palace. "Ah, M. Auber," he said, taking him aside, "you have no idea of the good your opera has done." — "How, sire ? " — "All revolutions resemble each other : to sing one is to provoke another. What can I do to please you ? " — "Ah, sire, I am not ambitious." — "I am disposed to name you director of the court-concerts. Be sure that I shall remember you. But," added he, taking the arm of the artist very cordially, and leading him into the centre of the room, "from this day forth, you understand me well, M. Auber, I expect you to bring out the 'Muette' but *very seldom.*"

It was fortunate for our composer, that he had united with Scribe, who, like himself, was endowed with a flexible, varied, and popular talent : the two assisted and supported each other. What admirable works they have given us !

The compositions of our artist from 1830 to 1840 are distinguished by variety of effects, combinations in rhythm, delicacy of detail, and brilliant, rich, and clear instrumentation. "Fra Diavolo" was written in 1830, "Gustave" in 1833, and "Le Lac des Fées" in 1839. Among these, "Fra Diavolo," a comic opera in three acts, performed Jan. 8, 1830, stands out in bold relief, so to say. The libretto is one of the most amusing which Scribe has written, and the score, one of Auber's best. Time has not changed its sparkling melodies : what surer sign of origin- ality ? And who has not listened with pleasure to the overture ? The overture of "Le Dieu et la Bayadère," an opera-ballet in three acts, performed in the same year, is one of the most charming that this composer has written. Many other operas equally successful followed. "Le Domino Noir," in 1837, and "Les Diamants de la Cou- ronne," in 1841, place Auber in the foremost rank of the masters of piquant and graceful music.

The necessity of making a choice among so many *chefs- d'œuvre* obliges us to pass over a great number of his productions. But we will give an anecdote to show the facility with which Auber composed. At the last rehearsal of the "Sirène," after listening to the overture, he struck his forehead, exclaiming, "That is hateful : I will never keep such music. It must be changed." — "But this is quite impossible, sir," said the manager. "There is no time to make a change : the bills announce the opera for to-morrow." — "Bah ! inform the leader of the orchestra." The clock struck nine. Auber sat down in the theatre, composed another overture, directed the copyists, and at midnight had completed a new and magnificent overture, which was rehearsed the next morning.

The rejuvenated talent of Auber, the head of the French school, reached its height in 1847, with the comic opera "Haydée." Scribe had arranged some affecting situations upon a new and original subject ; and of course the musi- cian must write one of his richest scores to correspond. The general effect of it is dramatic, and perfectly appro- priate to the nature of the subject. The instrumentation

is highly colored, always elegant ; and the harmony is not
wanting either in novelty or effect.   There is a charming
hautbois solo in the overture.   Louis Philippe was so much
pleased with this opera that he sent the cross of the
Legion of Honor to the *maestro*.   Let us add that Frederick William of Prussia sent Auber a magnificent ring,
when he heard the opera "Le Lac des Fées," in 1839.   The
same prince sent him a snuff-box covered with precious
stones, when " La Muette " came out.

The composer was less felicitous with " L'Enfant Pro-
digue."   But his works produced some time after met with
public approbation, particularly "Le premier Jour de Bon-
heur," which he composed at the advanced age of eighty-
seven, and which was hailed as almost a miracle.   There
were many crowns woven for the white head of the musical
Anacreon, many happy similitudes used to celebrate this
eternal spring, and these primroses of genius that bloomed
out from under the snows of old age.

The indifference of Auber for musical renown is worthy
of remark.   Auber never was present at the performance
of his own pieces.   He did not care for the pleasure of
being applauded.

This famous artist obtained the highest and most valued
distinctions.   He was a member of the Institute, commander of the "Légion d'Honneur," successor to Cherubini
as director of the Conservatory.   He had enjoyed perfect
health to the day of his death, May 12, 1871.   He presided assiduously at all the general exercises and meetings
of his pupils.   He made it a duty to be present at all the
official ceremonies to which he was invited ; and, notwithstanding his numerous occupations, he knew how to arrange
his time so as to save several hours a day for composition,
having for a faithful companion one of Sebastian Erard's
good little pianos of four octaves and a half.

Auber was delicate in appearance, of distinguished manners, and very witty. It would be easy to fill a book with his *bon-mots*. He even joked about his own age. He was directing a musical *soirée*, when, on a gentleman's taking a white hair from his shoulder, he smilingly said, "That hair must belong to some old man who passed near me." He was then over eighty years of age.

Many musicians who in their time made much noise in the world, have long been forgotten, whilst melodies like those of Auber are floating in the air, fresh, lively, and sparkling as when they were first written. Whilst we have parlors and pianos, Auber lives.

FIELD.

1782–1837.

JOHN FIELD, the celebrated pianoforte-player, was born in Dublin. He received his first musical instruction, when very young, from his grandfather; but his artistic culture he had from Clementi in London. Clementi was proud of such a talented pupil, and brought him before the public in 1798. In 1802 Field accompanied his master to Paris, where he delighted all who heard him.[1] Clementi then took him to Petersburg, where he left him for a while. When the master returned to Petersburg the next year, he found his pupil enjoying the highest reputation: his concerts were well attended, and he was in great demand as a teacher. In 1833 he revisited London and Paris, and made the tour of France and Italy with great applause. He was detained in Italy by sickness until 1835, when he returned to Russia. He died Jan. 11, 1837.

Field has published many concertos of considerable

[1] He played the great fugues of Sebastian Bach with precision and wonderful taste.

merit, and much other music for the pianoforte ; **also** several nocturnes, considered his best works.

PAGANINI.

1784–1840.

NICHOLAS PAGANINI was born at Genoa, Feb. 18, 1784. His father, who kept a small haberdasher's shop, had, like many Italians of his class, a decided taste for music, and played the mandolin acceptably. Perceiving that his child had likewise a taste for music, the father at once resolved to cultivate it ; but he was so brutal in his teaching that any other than the little Paganini would have been disheartened by the bad treatment he received, and perfectly disgusted with an art which was to be acquired only through suffering.

After his first lessons with his father, he studied with Giovanni Servetto, and then Giacomo Costa, under whom he made wonderful progress. The child seemed born to be a musician.[1] At six years of age he played the violin, and at eight he could write a sonata for his instrument. At nine he executed variations of his own composition upon the air of " Carmagnole," in a concert given at Genoa. Soon after, his father took him to Parma, where he studied with excellent masters. Ghiretti taught him counterpoint ; however, he was not very docile. The precocious boy, already in search of new effects, was not willing to accept those traditional uses which form the basis of teaching.

When he returned to Genoa, he composed several pieces so filled with difficulties, that it cost him much labor to

---

[1] " His mother, Teresa Bocciardo, dreamed that an angel came to her, and told her that her son would be a wonderful performer."

learn to execute them. He sometimes worked ten or twelve hours upon a single passage, before he could play it satisfactorily to himself; and it was by this heroic application that he laid the foundation of a talent which defied all comparison.

He commenced his artistic circuit in 1797, by travelling through the principal cities of Italy, in company with his father. Wherever he went, he gained admirers by his astonishing skill; but, at his lodging, he received more ill-treatment from his father than marks of affection. By dint of entreaty, Paganini after a while obtained his father's permission to go to Lucca, to attend the musical festival of St. Martin.[1] Emancipated from the paternal yoke, the young artist marched with giant strides in the path of celebrity and of glory; but the maturity of his reason was far less precocious than that of his genius. Though but a child of fifteen in years, he was more than a man in art, when he was left to direct his own course.

The greatest fault of Paganini was his passion for gambling, and his choice of associates, who more than once stole from him in one evening the product of several concerts. Setting aside the injury of such habits to his reputation, the young musician got into financial difficulties that obliged him, from time to time, to sell his violin.

On one such occasion, having engaged to give a concert at Leghorn, he begged a Frenchman, who was much devoted to music, to lend him his violin, a splendid Guarnerius. After the concert, the Frenchman refused to take back the violin, saying, " I will not profane the chords

---

[1] "The youth gained large sums of money, and proposed to give his father a part; but the selfish man threatened to kill him if he did not give up all he earned. Then the son proposed to allow his father an income, which was finally agreed to. After the father's death, Paganini took care of his mother, which, to use his own words, he considered 'a sweet duty.'"

which your fingers have touched. The violin was mine : now it is yours." Paganini determined never to give up the violin so handsomely offered him, and to make use of it in all his concerts. At Parma, Pasini, a painter, and amateur of music, defied Paganini to play a very difficult concerto manuscript, promising to give him a very fine Stradivarius violin if he succeeded. "If that is the case," said Paganini, "you may as well take leave of your violin." And he played the concerto at sight, in such a skilful manner, that Pasini could not hesitate to give him the valuable instrument.

The youth of Paganini may be summed up in two words, — disorder and genius. If he loved his art extremely, he loved pleasure as well. As a remedy sometimes springs from an excess of evil, so his unbridled passion for gambling cured itself. We give our readers his own account of the manner in which he was cured : —

"I shall never forget," said he, "that one day I placed myself in a situation which was to decide my future career. Prince X. had for a long time wished to become possessor of my excellent violin, the only one that I then had, and which I still have. One day he begged me to set a price upon it ; but, not wishing to part with my instrument, I declared that I would not give it up for less than two hundred and fifty gold Napoleons. A short time after, the prince said he had no doubt that I was in jest when I set so high a price upon my violin, but added that he was willing to give me two thousand francs for it. It happened that that very day I was in great need of money, in consequence of a heavy loss I had met with at play, so that I was sorely tempted to accept the offer of the prince. Just then a friend came to invite me for the evening. My capital consisted of only thirty francs : I had lost my jewels, watches, rings, — every thing of value but my violin. Immediately I resolved to try my luck with my thirty francs, and, if fortune was contrary to me, to accept the count's offer, and leave for St. Petersburg, without instrument and without means, with the view of re-establishing my affairs in that city. Already my thirty francs were reduced to three, and I imagined that I was *en route* for the great city, when, in the twinkling of an eye, my fortune changed. With my three francs I gained a hundred. This favorable moment saved my violin, and set me on my feet again. From that day forth I have withdrawn from gambling, to which I had sacrificed so much of my youth. I was convinced that a gambler is everywhere despised, and so renounced that fatal passion."

If Paganini ceased to be a gambler, he was still a fantastic and odd being. Strange to say, he suddenly gave up his violin-playing, and took to his guitar, at the same time studying agriculture in the castle of one of his protectors. Four years passed in this manner, when the violinist, suddenly coming to the consciousness of his own ability, resumed his violin and the course of his travels. In 1805 he went to Lucca, where he remained three years. One of his feats at this time is the " Scène Amoureuse," written for two strings of the violin, the treble and the fourth. Afterwards he succeeded in executing pieces wholly on the fourth chord. Lombardy had been the only theatre of our illustrious virtuoso until 1808, when he left Lucca, and roved about the peninsula during nineteen years. He was like a meteor which suddenly shone brilliantly in one place, then was lost from sight until it re-appeared elsewhere with renewed brightness. All was mysterious in his existence, alternating with brilliant apparitions and profound eclipses. The frequent indispositions of the artist would have sufficed to explain why he at times remained so long secluded from public view ; but popular credulity and the love of the romantic would not permit the public to be satisfied with simple reasoning. They preferred the foolish calumnies propagated by the hatred and jealousy of his rivals.[1] There were those who pretended that the musician had killed some one in a fit of vindictive humor. Others represented Paganini as a murderer who had perfected himself in his art in the forced leisure of a prison.

These detractors declared that he had acquired his marvellous skill on the fourth chord while in prison. The life of the artist was for some time tormented by the lying rumors, of which the newspapers of France and Germany were but the too complacent echoes. Finally M. Fetis published an article in the "Revue Musicale," which put an end to the scandal.

But, if no one could deny his genius, there was enough about him to furnish a pretext for those who were inclined to denigrate his character, — for example, his haughtiness, and the disdain with which he treated his rivals, his despite of the conventionalities of society, forgetfulness of services rendered, and a certain charlatanism in getting up a dramatic scene. The inhabitants of Leghorn, who had been the first to encourage him with their bravos, did

[1] In a letter published in Paris, justifying himself against the aspersions of malign and ill-disposed persons, Paganini says, "After I had played the variations called ' Le Streghe ' (The Sorcerors), at a concert in Vienna, a gentleman said that he could find nothing that would astonish him in my playing ; for he himself had distinctly seen the Devil near me, guiding my arm, and conducting my bow while I played. His striking resemblance to my features was sufficient proof of my origin. He was clothed in red, had horns on his head, and a tail between his legs. Of course, after so minute a description, there can be no doubt of the correctness of the gentleman's statement ; and many people are persuaded that they have found out the secret of what they call my *tours de force.*"

not give him a very friendly reception on his return to
them. Speaking of a concert that he gave at Leghorn,
he said, "As I was about going upon the stage, a nail
stuck into my heel, which made me limp : the public
began to laugh. Just as I was beginning my concerto,
the candles on my music-stand fell down : another burst
of laughter from the audience. After I had played the
first measure through, the treble string of my violin broke,
which still further excited their gayety ; but I played
through the piece on three strings, and brought down the
house." It is only a pity that this accident of the broken
treble-string has had so many editions. There are people
who report it as a trick played to display the artist's
great skill more effectually.

The artistic tour through Italy[1] being finished, Paganini
was ready to gratify the desire he had long had of visiting
Austria. The ovations he had received in his own country could not be compared to those of which he was the
object when he arrived at Vienna, March 16, 1828. Some
people felt a sort of superstitious terror at seeing this
Mephistopheles-looking man playing the famous variations
of the " Sorcière " with a power possessed by him alone.
At this time, when photography was unknown, the portrait of celebrated men had its place marked upon snuff-
boxes and cigar-cases. Paganini not only had this honor,
but also that of giving his name to the new-fashioned
hats, dresses, gloves, &c. From Vienna he went to
Prague, where he was not so warmly received ; but the
indifference of the Bohemians was more than overbal-
anced by the flattering receptions he met with in all other
cities of Germany.

In March, 1831, Paganini gave his first concert at the

[1] Pope Leo XII. decorated our artist with the grand order of the Golden Spur.

opera-house in Paris, and immediately became the idol of the French *dilettanti*. During the year, he travelled in England, where he levied a tax upon British curiosity; which the journals of that country had the bad taste to find too heavy, and therefore accused the great artist of cupidity. His performances in Belgium and Holland created unbounded enthusiasm. Laden with riches, Paganini returned to Italy in 1834. He bought the Villa Gajona, in the neighborhood of Parma, to which he retired, only going occasionally to Milan and Genoa.

In 1836 he went again to Paris, to attend a lawsuit which had been instituted against him by the proprietors of a casino, who had engaged his services. It was in vain that he pleaded ill-health as the cause of his breaking his engagement: the tribunal condemned him to pay the sum of fifty thousand francs, under pain of imprisonment. Paganini was then suffering from phthisis, which finally carried him off. One of the last acts of his life grandly refuted the reproach of avarice, that had so often been cast upon him.

In 1838 he sent Berlioz twenty thousand francs, as a token of his appreciation of his two symphonies, to which he had listened with pleasure at the Conservatory. Could the career of the violinist be crowned more honorably? Growing feebler, he went farther south; but neither the climate of Marseilles, nor that of Nice, afforded him any relief. He died at Nice, May 27, 1840, at the age of fifty-six years.

As if every thing that regarded Paganini was to be singular, the clergy refused him the honors of Christian burial, either because he would not receive the sacraments, or for some other reason. The difficulties arising from their refusal lasted several months. Finally, after a long parley between the episcopacy of Nice and that of Parma, and the friends of the defunct, permission was given to bury the body near the church in the village of Gajona.

Paganini left his fortune, estimated at two millions, to his only son Achilles, with the reservation of a few legacies ; but he left no inheritor of his genius, and the secret to which he attributed his wonderful ability was buried with him. However, we have only to ask ourselves if this secret was any thing more than a very remarkable organi zation favored by indefatigable perseverance.

" As a composer, Paganini stands very high. His works are rich in invention ; " and he everywhere displays a scientific knowledge of his art.

While under the instruction of Giacomo Costa, director of the orchestra, and first violinist of the principal churches of Geneva, Paganini made rapid progress. At eight years of age he wrote his first violin sonata, which, with some other of his youthful compositions, was unfortunately lost. During the six months he was with Costa, he was obliged to play a new concerto every Sunday. At twelve years of age he played for the first time in a concert at the Grand Theatre at Geneva, where he executed variations of his own composition, upon the air of " La Carmagnole," with great success. Paganini published the anecdote of his first interview with Rolla, about that time. His father had taken him to Parma, that he might study composition with Rolla. " When we came to Rolla's house," he says, " we found that he was sick in bed. His wife invited us into a room adjoining his chamber, that she might speak with him, as he appeared disinclined to see us. While waiting, I took up a violin that lay upon the table, and played the music I found with it, viz., a concerto of

Rolla's, the last he had written. The composer, astonished
at what he heard, sent to know the name of the virtuoso
who had performed his music   When told that the virtuoso was the boy who had come to him for instruction, he
was much astonished, and said that he could teach me
nothing."

SPOHR.

1784–1859.

LOUIS SPOHR was born at Brunswick, April 5, 1784.
He was the son of a physician who established himself in
Seesen, 1786 ; and in this small town our composer passed
his early years. The love of music was born with the child ;
for his father, who was passionately fond of it, excelled in
flute-playing, whilst his mother had much talent for the
piano. The social concerts held in the paternal house
were of great assistance to the young Spohr in awaking
his growing faculties.   Unlike those artists whose aspirations were opposed by ambitious or interested parents,
Louis met only continual kindness and encouragement.
His parents sent him to Brunswick to study under the
direction of Maucourt, violinist of the Prince's Chapel.
He performed at a court concert when he was but twelve
years of age. Like Kreutzer, his instrument was the violin,
the composition his own. After the boy had been with
Maucourt a year, his father, pleased with the progress he
had made, and his excellent performance on the violin,
thought him able to make his own way in the world as an
artist. He therefore gave him what little money he could
spare, much good advice, and some letters of recommendation to friends in Hamburg. The boy, then only fourteen
years old, set out with buoyant and hopeful spirits. At

Hamburg he presented himself to Prof. Büsching, who, after reading the father's recommendation, exclaimed, "Your father is, then, still the same as ever! What madness to send a boy into the world, trusting merely to good luck!" He then explained the difficulty and expense of getting up a concert, at which poor young Spohr was so cast down that he could scarcely refrain from tears. On his way back to Brunswick, the idea of applying to the duke, who was himself a violin-player, occurred to him. No sooner thought than done: he wrote, making known his situation and wants, and ending with a request for a place in the ducal orchestra. It was his good fortune to meet the duke, who, on looking over the petition, asked various questions, to which the boy answered unhesitatingly. But when the duke said, "Who wrote your petition?" the boy, piqued that his ability should be doubted, answered, "Well, who but I myself? I need no help for that." The duke smiled, and said, "Come to me to-morrow, and we will see what we can do."

After having heard Spohr play, the duke said, "There is a vacant place in the orchestra: I will give it to you. Be diligent, and behave well: I will befriend you." Three years after, the young musician studied with François Eck, reputed the best violinist in Germany at that time; afterwards, furnished with the means by his royal protector, he accompanied Eck in his journey to Russia.

In St. Petersburg, Spohr made the acquaintance of Clementi and his pupil Field, both of whom he found at the washtub; and Clementi advised him to follow their example, and wash his own clothes, not only to save expense, but also the linen, which the Russians, he said, spoiled in washing.

He also met with a Madame Meier, who played a con

certo of her own composing ; and Remi, of the imperial orchestra, with whom he frequently played duets. One evening Remi embraced Spohr, and insisted upon their exchanging violins, though his, a genuine Guarneri, was much the best. Our artist, overjoyed with the possession of such an instrument, packed it carefully among the linen in his trunk. In travelling he could not refrain from putting his head out of the window of the coach, from time to time, to see if the trunk, which was strapped on behind, was all right. What must have been his disappointment, on arriving at an inn after dark, to find that his trunk was gone ! Next morning he heard, through the police, that an empty trunk, violin-case, and some sheets of music, had been found.

He borrowed a violin, and gave a concert, the proceeds of which enabled him to procure the necessary clothing to continue his journey. He visited the chief cities of Saxony and Prussia, and was everywhere well received as a composer and a virtuoso.

In consequence of the brilliant success Spohr obtained in Gotha, 1805, they offered him the situation of concertmaster at the ducal court.[1] This he accepted, but not without having asked permission of his protector the Duke of Brunswick.

In 1806 he married Dorette Scheidler, considered the best harpist in all Germany ; and in 1807 the newly married couple made a musical tour. The artist received marks of general admiration wherever he performed. At Vienna they gave him the leadership of the orchestra of the principal theatre ; but he resigned in 1816, being disappointed because the managers of the theatre refused to

---

[1] Spohr was introduced as twenty-four years of age when he was only twenty, as it was thought his youth would be an objection to his having the position.

put his opera of " Faust " upon the stage. Then he went to Italy, where his reputation had preceded him. He was as well received in the different cities of Italy as he had been in those of his own country. On his return he was appointed director of the Frankfort Theatre, and chapel-master in the same city. The first representation of his opera of " Faust," in two acts, took place 1818. " In point of harmony, this work is one of the *chefs-d'œuvre* of the German school. It has maintained its place in the musical catalogue for more than thirty years. We still remember what success the singer Devrient[1] obtained when this opera was performed in Berlin."

Spohr went to France in 1819; but, finding that the French did not appreciate his music, he went over to England, where he excited much enthusiasm. Perhaps his great success in London re-acted upon his countrymen, disposing them to accept him as a musical oracle and prince of the artists of his time. Two of his operas, " Der Zweikampf mit der Geliebten," and " Zémire and Azor," were put upon the stage in Frankfort during the year. In 1821 he wrote his celebrated mass for ten voices. In 1822, through the influence of Carl Maria von Weber, he was appointed conductor of the orchestra of the newly built theatre of Cassel, which proved a most favorable position for his artistic labors. The first thing he did was to re-organize the chapel, and elevate its standard, thus cultivating the public taste for good music. Of the opera of " Jessonda," written in 1823, Spohr wrote to a friend, " The chorus and orchestra, scenery, dances, spectacle-combats, storm, decorations, costumes, every thing, was excellent. This work has made me very happy." (See note.) In 1825 he composed " Die letzten Dinge."

[1] " E. P. Devrient, a bass-singer born at Berlin, was noted for the beauty and freshness of his tone."

His labors were from time to time interrupted by hort journeys taken for his health. He went several times to England, where his popularity seemed ever on the increase.

His wife Dorette died in 1834 ; and the following year he married Marianna Pfeiffer, daughter of his good friend Pfeiffer of Cassel. This lady was a very fine pianist.

In 1835 he finished the oratorio of " Des Heilands letzte Stunden." [1]

Spohr at the pinnacle of fame, by the sort of tacit magistracy which his contemporaries conferred upon him, became the arbiter of his art in Germany. The power that he exercised over that musical country lasted at least thirty years without any sort of interruption. There was no artistic solemnity at which Spohr was not called upon to preside. In every place where music was needed to celebrate a great anniversary, it was Spohr who held the baton of director of the orchestra ; and this baton, in his hands, had the appearance of a sceptre. The words of his mouth were words of authority.

He made a second journey to Paris in 1843, and was well revenged for the previous indifference of an ignorant and frivolous public, by the marked attention, deference, and respect of such men as Halévy and Auber. The Conservatory complimented him by performing for him alone his own fourth symphony. France felt that she must submit to the supremacy imposed upon her by all Europe.

The dramatic works of this master have perhaps contributed less to his renown than his instrumental compositions, which were scattered in great profusion during the course of his long career. Besides, he founded a school for the violin, and laid down the principles of this instru-

---

[1] " The Lover's Duel " was composed in 1840.

ment in a classic work called "School for the Violin." The celebrated Joachim chose one of Spohr's concertos with which to appear before the public. This grand composition was as a revelation of the master's music to the thousands of delighted listeners.

Louis Spohr, the admired and esteemed, was honored with many orders, and was a member of various academies. He ended his days at Cassel, Nov. 25, 1859, at the age of seventy-five years.

Spohr and his wife played at the Court of Weimar, and won great applause. Goethe and Wieland were among the auditory. When they played in Munich, King Maximilian perceiving that there was no stool for Mrs. Spohr, brought his own gilded armchair, surmounted with the royal crown, and in his friendly manner insisted upon her seating herself in it, nor would he consent to have it removed until she explained that she could not play her harp without the free use of her arms.

Herr Winter, director of the royal orchestra, was a large and powerful man, but timid as a hare. His housekeeper, who tyrannized over him, used to drive him to the piano, and order him to practise the music he was to perform.

While in Vienna, in 1813, a gentleman introduced himself to Spohr as Herr von Tost, a proprietor of manufactories, and a lover of music, and offered a suitable consideration for all the music that he (Spohr) had composed or should compose in Vienna for the term of three years, said music to be his sole property during that time, after which it should be returned to the composer, to publish or otherwise as he should think fit. The arrangement was made; Herr von Tost paying the price stipulated by Spohr, and lending him such music as he needed from time to time.

It afterwards appeared that the gentleman wishing to be present at all concerts and *soirées* given by his favorite composer, and also to be able to boast of possessing the music, hit upon this plan.

At Vienna Spohr became acquainted with Beethoven, who frequently visited him. At one time when Spohr had not seen him as usual, he said, " You were not ill, I hope ;" to which Beethoven answered, " No ; but my boot was, and, as I possess only one pair, I was obliged to remain at home."

Speaking of Hummel, whom he heard play for the first time in Vienna, Spohr says, " I was charmed by his improvisations, in which no other pianoforte virtuoso has ever yet approached him."

Spohr was living on the banks of the Wien at the time of the fearful inundation caused by the overflowing of the Danube. After some hours of excitement, his wife, overcome by terror and fatigue, fell asleep amid the roar of the waters and the howl of the storm ; and he, in order the better to keep himself awake, went from time to time to the piano, at which his landlord, who was praying overhead, became very indignant, and exclaimed, " That Lutheran heretic will bring yet greater misfortune upon us with his unchristian singing and playing."

Spohr was in the habit of taking his daughter Theresa, a child of nine years of age, to all his rehearsals ; which she seemed to like so well, that he argued therefrom a great love for music. He was, moreover, greatly delighted when the child expressed especial pleasure in the concluding number of the oratorio, " Die letzten Dinge," a fugue on the words, " His is the kingdom, the power, and glory." His wife sympathized with him in the happy disposition of their child. But upon questioning Theresa more closely respecting her preference for the fugue, she informed them, to their great surprise and mortification, that she only liked that part better than all the rest, because she knew that the rehearsal was near at an end, and that they should soon *go home to dinner*.

The first concert which Queen Victoria attended after her coronation was that of Spohr's. When he made his appearance in the orchestra, both the queen and Prince Albert bowed, and clapped their hands warmly.

"In his seventieth year Spohr wrote one of his finest masterpieces, the septet for pianoforte, two stringed and four wind instruments. This septet is replete with the freshness of youthful thought in every part, with a *larghetto* which has scarcely its equal in bewitching harmony, and beauty of modulation."

In 1855 a deputation from the Royal Chapel at Hanover presented Spohr with a leader's baton. It consisted of a beautifully grooved ivory staff, with a golden handle richly set with costly stones, ending in a knob likewise set with stones. Soon after he received a shirt-pin, with the emblems of an oak-leaf in green gold, with an acorn of pearl set in gold. He was always gratified with such artistic testimonials of esteem and approbation.

Nov. 12, 1857, Spohr received permission to retire from his duties as chapel-master and director-general of the court music of Cassel, with a yearly pension of fifteen hundred thalers.

Some time previous to his demise, Spohr was very low-spirited, and told his wife, that, as he could no longer be doing, he was weary of life, and ardently wished for death before the infirmities of old age should prostrate him completely.

WEBER.

1786–1826.

THREE great works, " Freischütz," " Euryanthe," and " Oberon," have placed Weber in the first rank of the modern composers of Germany. The genius which inspired these works is incontestable. Though sometimes abrupt, the character of this genius is profoundly individual, and indebted to no school. Weber is more original perhaps than any other musician. Imagination plays a greater part than feeling in all his conceptions. We are surprised, astonished, even charmed, by the brilliant qualities of his orchestration, the boldness of his thoughts, the picturesque color of his music, and the graceful turn of certain airs ; but all this does not touch our heart.

Charles Marie Frederic Ernst Baron de Weber, was born at Eutin in the Duchy of Holstein, Dec. 18, 1786. His father, Franz Anton, a strolling musician and actor, was anxious to make a prodigy of his youngest son, Carl Maria, who became acquainted with orchestra and stage arrangements before he knew his primer.

That the character of the child should have escaped the bad influences attendant on the instruction he was daily receiving, must be owing chiefly to the influence of that " sweet, pure, simple-minded mother," who strove to shelter her darling from the evil effects of a life so uncongenial to her gentle nature.

The anxiety of the father to make something wonderful of the child was a constant source of worriment, both to him and his mother.

His father had at first followed the career of arms ; then he was employed in the administration of finances ; but he had such a love for music, that all business annoyed him. When he lost his position as employé in the treasury, in consequence of his negligence in fulfilling its duties, he turned his whole attention to that which was uppermost in his mind, viz., music. From the year 1768 he was, in turn, attached to the orchestra of a theatre, director of a play, master of the Bishop of Lubec's chapel, town musician, wandering player, going from one place to another, with a family of eight children, whose patrimony he had wasted by his carelessness and bad speculations.

With this simple *exposé* of his adventurous life, we are led to suppose that Major Weber was an imaginative man, and that he transmitted his disposition as well as his passion for musical art to his son Carl. We must do him the justice to say that he neglected nothing for the education of the future composer. He not only procured for him good teachers in singing and piano,[1] but also in drawing and engraving ; and the boy, fully occupied, grew up a recluse in the midst of his studies. For a time his parents led a very quiet and retired life : he had no young companions, no playmates, during those early years in which a child has so much need of childish society. For want of some one to whom to communicate his thoughts, the young Weber turned them inwardly, and peopled the world with the ideal creations of his fertile imagination.

The spirits which have met with no contrarieties at the moment of their spontaneous flight, and which have not suffered by contact with society, gain, by this education, or rather by the want of education, a prouder independence, and a more strongly marked originality.[2] But such advantages are counterbalanced by grave defects, that sometimes

---

[1] Unfortunately for the young student, he never remained long enough with one teacher to acquire any fixed method or style.

[2] Weber, naturally pensive, has been accused by some writers of morbid pride.

exercise a fatal influence upon the whole course of one's life. In 1797 Weber studied piano under Hauschkel in Hildburghausen, and laid the foundation for a thorough and ready player. Hauschkel was a young man whose superior talent had early won for him the position he then filled as conductor of the orchestra of Duke Friedrich. Though amiable, lively, and agreeable, he was strict and zealous in the exercise of his art. Much pleased with Carl Maria, he begged to be permitted to give him lessons on the piano and in thorough bass. He soon found, however, that he had imposed upon himself a somewhat difficult task, viz., that of undoing all that Franz Anton had done in the way of musical instruction. Carl, though greatly attached to the genial young teacher, was almost discouraged by the laborious plodding through thorough bass, and the drilling system of execution, so entirely different from the off-hand performances of his father.

Scarcely had the boy begun to value the advantages he was enjoying, when the restless spirit of his father deprived him of them. It was in 1798 that Franz Anton took his family to Salzburg : while there, he succeeded in placing Carl in a musical institute, directed and taught by Michel Haydn,[1] brother of the great composer Joseph Haydn.

Michel Haydn, although sixty years of age, was much attracted to the puny, limping little boy, and bestowed every care on his musical education without remuneration. In a letter written by Carl Maria to Hauschkel, to wish him a happy new year, he says, "I was in luck to get lessons from a master who no longer takes pupils because he has so much to do." Meanwhile the pecuniary troubles

---

[1] Johann Michel was brother of the celebrated composer Haydn. He had a fine voice, and received a musical education at Vienna. He was for a long time chapel-master to Count Esterhazy.

of the Weber family increased. Franz Anton was unsuccessful in his theatrical undertakings; and, as want stared him in the face, he became rough and morose to those around him. Genofeva, his wife, suffered from the severity of the climate, consumption set in, and sne felt that she was near her end: her only regret was, that she must leave her boy entirely to the reckless guidance of his father. "On the 13th March, 1798, the poor, sickly, sorrowing Carl Maria knelt by the bed-side, and held for the last time the cold hand of his deeply beloved, sweet, beautiful, young mother." At first it seemed as if the poor child's heart would break; but his aunt Adelheid, an excellent, noble-hearted woman, not only found means to soothe and comfort him, but she used her influence in educating him according to the wishes of his mother. Carl Maria composed six short fugues before he was twelve years old, which his ambitious father immediately published. Towards the end of the year the family removed to Munich. Evangelist Wallishouser, or Valesi as he called himself, the greatest singing-master of his time, was then giving lessons in Munich; and Franz Anton, whose maxim it was that "no man could write well for the voice, or compose a good opera, who could not sing well himself," directly applied to him to teach his son. Then he went to Kalcher, the organist, for lessons in composition; but, however good Carl Maria's teachers may have been, properly speaking, Nature was his only master. Thence it arises that we find many imperfections, much to criticise, in the beautiful scores we all the while admire, and which would in all probability have been fully corrected with the habit of writing, if he had lived longer.

He who wrote "Freischütz" and "Oberon" seems to have had some hesitation about entering the musical

career. We learn from a sort of biographical notice, that
he was very much interested in lithography at the time of its
discovery, and that he and his father had serious thoughts of
perfecting Sennefelder's invention. Happily these fancies
were of short duration, and the young artist soon gave himself up entirely to his true vocation. Whilst he was studying harmony and composition with Kalcher he wrote a
solemn mass, sonatas for the piano, trios for violin, and
then tried his powers in an Opera, " Die Macht der Liebe
und des Weins." [1] Afterwards, when ripened by experience,
the author made an *auto-da-fé* of these youthful compositions.

In 1800 Weber, then fourteen years old, composed the
opera "Das Waldmädchen," which was brought out in
Chemnitz, and then performed in many other places. [2]

In 1802, whilst in Salzburg, he wrote "Peter Schmoll and
seine Nachbarn," an opera in two acts, of which his teacher,
M. Haydn, spoke highly. In 1803 he accompanied his
father to Hamburg. In Leipzig he bought several works on
harmony, but could not gain from them the assistance he
needed. The Abbé Vogler, with whom he became acquainted
in Vienna, was the only one among his teachers who was
able to render him a real service by clearing up the chaos
which so many contradictory studies had made in his
head. Weber studied most assiduously with Vogler,
whose favorite pupil he was for a year, during which time
he composed only a few variations for the piano.

In 1804 Vogler procured the situation of director of
music in Breslau for the young musician. The nomination of a youth of eighteen to fill a place for which long
practice is deemed necessary seemed a great injustice, and

[1] " The power of love and wine."
[2] It is said that he wrote the whole of the second act in ten days.

could not fail to displease the elder and more experienced artists of the city. Instead of endeavoring to gain their esteem, Weber foolishly aggravated them by his disagreeable manners. His conduct, particularly in regard to Schnabel, a distinguished violinist, was, to say the least, very impolite and unkind.[1] As far as the developing of his talents was concerned, this situation was very useful in permitting him to acquire the art of guiding the orchestra and chorus.

One evening his friend Berner called at his room by appointment: he knocked at the door — no answer. There was light in the room ; he must be within. Berner knocked the second and third time ; receiving no answer, he walked in. The candle was on the table, the piano open. Stepping forward, Berner stumbled over the body of his friend, which lay as if dead. He raised the body, and called for help. The father hurried from a neighboring room, physicians were sent for, the boy was with difficulty restored : he had been poisoned. When he had sufficiently recovered, he explained, that, feeling cold, he reached out his hand for a bottle of wine, and took aquafortis, which he had been using in his engraving, instead. For weeks his life was despaired of : when he recovered he had lost the power of his voice.

In the beginning of the year 1806, Weber accepted the invitation of Prince Eugéne of Würtemberg, to settle at his little court in Silesia, where, although he remained but a short time, he composed two symphonies for the chapel, and several concert pieces. But war caused the suppression of the chapel, and prevented Weber from giving con

---

[1] The trouble was, he forgot that he was only a lad, and that he sat for the first time in a conductor's seat. Notwithstanding all this, the young director did better than could have been expected from his age and inexperience.

certs in different parts of Germany, as he had intended.
Then, being invited to Stuttgard by Prince Ludwig of
Würtemberg, he became his secretary for a while. Here
in a corrupt court,[1] as manager of the affairs of the king's
brother, the inclination inherited from his father to play
the cavalier led Carl Maria into errors the after effects of
which he never ceased to regret.

"Weber hated the king, of whose wild caprice and vices
he witnessed daily scenes, before whose palace-gates he
was obliged to slink bareheaded, and who treated him with
unmerited ignominy. Sceptre and crown had never been
imposing objects in his eyes, unless worn by a worthy
man; and consequently he was wont, in thoughtless levity
of youth, to forget the dangers he ran, and to answer the
king with a freedom of tone which the autocrat was all
unused to hear. In turn he was detested by the monarch.
As negotiator for the spendthrift Prince Ludwig, he was
already obnoxious enough; and it sometimes happened,
that by way of variety to the customary torrent of invective,
the king, after keeping the secretary for hours in his anti-
chamber, would receive him only to turn him rudely out
of the room, without hearing a word he had to say.

The royal treatment roused young Carl Maria's indigna-
tion to the utmost; and his irritation led him one day to
a mad prank, which was nigh resulting in some years' imprisonment in the fortress of Hohenasberg, or of Hohen-
haufen. Smarting under some foul indignity, he had just
left the private apartment of the king, when an old woman
met him in the passage, and asked where she could find
the room of the court washerwoman. "There!" said the
reckless youth, pointing to the door of the royal cabinet.
The old woman entered, was violently assailed by the king,

---

[1] The court was very corrupt, and the family of the prince in debt.

who had a horror of old women, and, in her terror, stammered out that a young gentleman who had just come out had informed her that there she would find the "royal washerwoman." The infuriated monarch guessed who was the culprit, and despatched an officer on the spot to arrest his brother's secretary, and throw him into prison.

To those who have any idea how foul a den was then a royal prison, it must appear almost marvellous that Carl Maria should have possessed sufficient equanimity to have occupied himself with his beloved art during his arrest. But so it was. He managed to procure a dilapidated old piano, put it in tune with consummate patience by means of a common door-key, and actually, then and there, on the 14th of October, 1808, composed his well-known beautiful song, "Ein steter Kampf ist unser Leben."

Through the influence of Prince Ludwig, the young man soon obtained his pardon and release. But the prison had not cured him of his boyish desire to play tricks upon the hated monarch. Notwithstanding the disagreeableness of his position, Carl Maria had the faculty of finding himself in his right place in every kind of society, and gathering from all around new food to add to his storehouse of instruction, talent, or humor. Franz Danzi, conductor of the royal opera, appreciated the young man's talent, and became his good genius, endeavoring to lead him on, not only to the perfection of art, but to the nobility of truth. His constant maxim was, "To be a true artist, you must be a true man."[1]

Unfortunately Carl Maria conceived an ardent affection for a celebrated singer named "Gretchen," who completely absorbed his mind. For her he neglected his

[1] At this time Weber made the acquaintance of Dannecher, the famous sculptor of the Ariadne.

jovial companions, and the family circles where he had been pleasantly received. For her he neglected his studies, and rushed into extravagances far beyond his means.

Then came his father very unexpectedly from Carlsruhe with his bass-viol, two poodle-dogs, and a load of debts. As a matter of course, he installed himself in his son's room, made his dogs comfortable, and took quiet possession. Poor Carl was nearly desperate, for the manners and behavior of the arrogant old gentleman were almost unbearable. Disease had made great ravages in his memory and judgment, without changing his proud and bombastic manner. He interfered in his son's doings so far as to send off some of his compositions without his knowledge, and to sign a letter " Baron von Weber, Chamberlain to his Imperial Majesty."

Finally the weak-minded old gentleman sent to Carlsruhe certain sums of money which Carl María, as secretary, had received from the duke for the payment of some obligations on the family estate in Silesia. Carl at once confessed the whole affair to the duke, and promised speedy reparation. Then a villain, under the guise of friendship, offered to procure a loan of money for a slight consideration. Carl accepted and paid the bribe, without stopping to ask by what means the money was obtained. However, it soon appeared that an inn-keeper had been induced to loan the money upon the promise that Weber would obtain a post at court for his son, and thus free the boy from the terrors of conscription. But when the boy was drafted into the army, January, 1810, the matter was made known to the king.

On the 9th of February, Carl Maria, while rehearsing with an orchestra, was arrested in the name of the king, and dragged off to prison, without being allowed even to speak to his friend Danzi. His father, he learned, was under arrest in his own apartment.

Bitter were his sorrows during the sixteen days of his imprisonment, when only one among his many so-called friends dared to take his part, and proclaim his innocence. This real friend was Danzi, who petitioned, entreated, and even demanded a personal interview with the king.

After an examination, in which Weber proved his innocence, the king had him transferred to the debtor's prison, from which he was soon released. Then the king gave orders that the Webers, father and son, should be banished from Würtemberg for life. All the money the exiles had at the time was forty florins ; but the police-officer who accompanied them pressed twenty-five florins more in Carl's hand by stealth, and gave him several letters of introduction for Manheim, which the good Danzi had confided to his care. Such an end to his official position was the greatest benefit which could have happened to Weber as an artist.

Weber went to Manheim and Heidelberg, and in April, 1810, to Darmstadt,[1] where he met his teacher Vogler, Gänsbacher, and the young Meyerbeer, in whose company he recommenced his studies. Vogler,[2] an able author and good composer, was just the man to govern the talented, ambitious, and forward young Weber, who, conscious of his own powers, and feeling the need of instruction, yielded to the superior judgment of his teacher. His productions

[1] In a letter from Darmstadt, Weber writes, " I only take up my dull goose-quill to tell you in the dullest words, how dull I feel, in this dull Darmstadt."

[2] Vogler possessed great musical talents, was a man of much learning and good understanding. It is said that he exclaimed, " Had I been forced to leave the world before I had found these two, Weber and Meyerbeer, I should have died a miserable man."

as an author, were, however, of little value to his art.
While in Stuttgard, in spite of his not having a musical
position, and the irregular life he was leading, he composed
several pieces.   The cantata " Der erste Ton," songs, the
first of his great piano sonatas, with other works for the
piano, overtures, symphonies, and the opera " Sylvana,"
which in its music and groundwork (life in the woods, and
knights) was a forerunner of his great works " Der Freischütz [1] " and " Euryanthe."   The first performance of the
opera " Sylvana " in Frankfort,[2] Sept. 16, 1810, was as important to the future life of the composer as the opera
itself ; for Miss Caroline Brandt, who took the chief character, afterwards became his wife.   In November, 1810,
while in Manheim, at the house of Gottfried Weber, he
wrote the operette " Abu Hassan," from a poem by his
friend Hiemer.   This poem treated of events in Stuttgard,
between pressing creditors and troubled debtors.

In 1811 he gave concerts in Munich,[3] Leipzig, Gotha,
Weimar, Berlin,[4] and other cities.   In 1813 he was called

[1] While in Manheim, Weber, with a friend, sat all one night planning the
foundation of " Der Freischütz," the story of which they had found in Apel's ghost-
stories.

[2] The balloon ascent of Mme. Blanchard, which took place on the very day
"Sylvana" was to be performed, absorbed the interest of the entire population, and
carried off the victory.   Nevertheless the opera pleased those who heard it, and the
composer was called for at the end.   Carl Maria drew back, anxious and afraid ; but
Caroline Brandt took his unwilling hand, and dragged him before the curtain.   The
profit of this opera was a hundred florins.

[3] Danzi, the well-tried friend, he " who shed one unremitting sunshine upon Carl
Maria's life in Munich," was his daily companion.

[4] While at Berlin, Carl Maria received the news of his father's death.   In his
note-book stand the words, " He fell asleep at last they say.   May heaven grant him,
in another world, the rest he knew not here !   It is an almost intolerable pain to me
to think that I have not been able to bestow on him happier days.   May God in his
mercy bless him for all the love he bore me, all the love I so little deserved, and for
the education he bestowed upon me ! "

Heinrich Lichtenstein, a great admirer of Carl Maria, writes in his memoir,
" Young artists fell on their knees before him ; others embraced him wherever they

to Prague [1] to succeed Wenzel Miller as director of the music of the German opera, and remained in this city nearly three years. Among the works which he then composed was a grand cantata upon the battle of Waterloo.

At this time, 1813, the biography of the musician becomes mixed up with general history. France had its Rouget de Lisle, Germany its Koerner and its Weber.

Weber wrote his " Freischütz " in Dresden.[2] This work performed in Berlin, June 18, 1821, suddenly raised its author to the head of all the lyric artists of his country. The subject is taken from the legend of the hunter Bartosch of the sixteenth century, who was famed throughout the countries along the Vistula for his great skill in shooting.

The following letter full of the most affectionate sentiments was addressed by Weber to the poet Kind, the author who composed the poem of the opera, on the evening of the second representation of " Freischütz."

" The free-shooter has hit the mark. The second representation succeeded as well as the first : there was the same enthusiasm. All the places in the house are taken for the third, that comes off tomorrow. It is the greatest triumph that one can have. You cannot imagine what a lively interest your text inspires from beginning to

could get at him ; all crowded around him, until his head was crowned, not with a chaplet of flowers, but with a circlet of happy faces." " The devoted circle of friends that clustered around him in Berlin," he continues, " the success of his opera, and the remuneration received from his publisher, effected a change both in his moral and material condition."

[1] As early as the seventeenth century instruction in music and singing had been made a part of popular education of the Bohemians, even in humble village schools ; so that there was not a school throughout the country, that could not afford abundant material for choristers wherever needed. "A visitor in a Bohemian family might see the man-cook appear as violinist, the jäger as horn-players, the footmen as flute-players, while the steward would take his place as chapel-master, and the master of the house would play ' second,' perhaps, to his own valet."

[2] The pianoforte arrangement of " Der Frieschütz" was sold to Schlesinger, after much haggling on the part of the publisher, for two hundred and twenty thalers.

end. How happy I should have been if you had only been present to see for yourself! Some of the scenes produced an effect which I was far from anticipating; for example, that of the young girls. If I see you again in Dresden, I will tell you all about it, for I cannot do it justice in writing. How much I am indebted to you for your magnificent poem! I embrace you with the sincerest emotion, returning to your Muse the laurels I owe her. God grant that you may be happy! Love him who loves you with infinite respect.

"Your WEBER."

This letter shows us the modesty of the composer, and is sufficient to prove that Weber's pride was not innate, but rather the result of the singular education which he had received. Soon after he gave "Preciosa," also a masterpiece.

The great success of " Freischütz " drew the attention of all managers of theatres upon Weber : all were eager to bring out his works ; but Weber, in his desire to substitute new forms of orchestration, worked slowly. It took him a year and a half to write the opera of " Euryanthe." It was not too much time for a deep thinker aspiring to renovate harmony. However, his efforts at first were scarcely appreciated, and it was not until some years after that justice was rendered to this beautiful score.

Weber wrote " Oberon " for Kemble, manager of the Covent Garden Theatre in London. The unhappy artist, overcome by constant application and excessive labor, had become very weak and melancholy, despite his glory and domestic affections. He felt his strength diminish from day to day, and knew that he was in a critical situation. What with his exertions to have his score ready at the fixed time, and the trying climate of England, it was feared that he would not live to see his " Oberon " put upon the stage.

It was in March, 1826, when he arrived in London,

George Smart took him to his own house, where he was the object of the most tender care and solicitude, as well as of the admiration and sympathy of the most distinguished person in London.

"Oberon" was performed for the first time, under the direction of George Smart, April 12, 1826. Weber thought of leaving England after he had seen the first performance, and wrote to inform his wife of his immediate return. But death intervened.[1] He expired June 5, 1826.

The celebrated composer died in the house of George Smart, surrounded by friends whose tender cares soothed and comforted him in his last moments. This Mr. Smart died in London, after a long and honorable career as an artist. He had been singing-master to Mme. Sontag and Jenny Lind.

The poem of "Oberon" is from the celebrated Wieland: its subject was borrowed from the romance of Huon of Bordeaux. The action is in Fairyland. Oberon is the king of dwarfs, and the husband of Titania. The character of Weber's music in this opera is as original and as peculiar as that of "Freischütz" and of "Preciosa," but much sweeter, and slightly stamped with melancholy. Weber is well known by his overtures for instrumental music as well as his pieces for piano. All our lady readers are acquainted with his "Invitation to the Dance," a charming piece, in which melancholy is allied to the enticing rhythm. They also are familiar with the rondo called "Perpetual Movement," the Polonaise in "mi major," &c. But the superiority of his operas has almost cast his other works into the shade. Weber excels in making all the voices of

---

[1] "God reward you for all your kindness to me," he said to Sir George Smart and Fursteneau, as they led him to his chamber. "Now let me sleep." The next morning they found him asleep in death.

nature speak and sing; and so he deserves to be called the father of the romantic and descriptive school.

Extract of a letter from Carl Maria to his friend Gottfried Weber in 1810.

"The Little Bear (Meyerbeer) writes canzonets and psalms. The old gentleman (Vogler) consumes enormous quantities of snuff. Mariane snivels, and Therese sings as out of tune as ever. The family is increased by an abominable black poodle, which Beer's servant is always thrashing, and his master always hugging. And here you have a full account of the household."

In another letter to the same, he writes, "André, my publisher, gave back my sonatas, saying, 'They are far too good, and must be made more commonplace for sale.' I declared I could not write trash, and would not; so we parted in the sulks."

In another he says, "My whole life through I have owed much to hostility: it has been my best spur to excellence."

HÉROLD.

1791–1833.

Louis Joseph Ferdinand Hérold, the celebrated French opera composer, was born at Paris, Jan. 28, 1791, of a family who had cultivated music for generations. His father, a professor, was a pupil of Charles Emanuel Bach. The child soon learned to understand the voice of song; and, guided by his instinct, he composed little pieces for the harpsichord when only six years old: at the same time he manifested great intelligence and aptitude in learning. He studied the classics at eleven years of age, and figured constantly among the first of his class, where he took fourteen prizes for different things, and all this without interfering with his musical progress. He studied piano with Louis Adam, harmony with Catel, and composition with Méhul.

After the death of his father, in 1802, Mme. Hérold, fearing the chances her son might run as an artist, was not disposed to encourage his musical taste. But, before deciding upon what course to pursue with him, she consulted Grétry upon the value of one of the boy's compositions. The musician calmed the anxieties of the widow, by declaring that he would be responsible for the good success of her son ; and it was by his advice that she sent the boy to the Conservatory.

In 1812 he received the prize for the composition of a cantata, and was sent to Rome as stipendiary of the government, afterward to Naples, where he composed an opera " La Gioventù di Enrico V," which gained him a good repute. Desirous to become acquainted with German works, he went to Germany ; but unfortunately at an unpropitious time, as the return of Napoleon from Elba had rekindled the general war, and increased habitual distrust towards foreigners. Hérold, who had been in Venice, waiting more than a fortnight for his passports, grew impatient, and resolved to go without them as far as Vienna, let what would happen. At the worst he would be taken for a spy and shot. But Hérold was just at the age when a foreseen danger is but an attraction. Besides he was not sorry to infringe upon police regulations.

At Vienna the young man encountered unexpected annoyances : for want of papers to establish his identity, he was in danger of being driven out of the city as a vagabond. In this emergency he sought the intervention of Prince de Talleyrand. No sooner had the ambassador taken the case of his countryman in hand, than all difficulties were at once removed, and our young musician could give himself up to the study of the great masters without fear of molestation.

After three years of leisurely study he returned to Paris, thinking only of obtaining a good libretto through which to appear before the public. But he had to learn that what was easy to a foreigner in Italy was difficult even to a native in France. The literati were unwilling to associate with persons of uncertain notoriety. Hérold, finding that he should be obliged to wait, and becoming tired of war, gladly accepted a situation in an Italian theatre. In the mean time he received a letter from Boieldieu, who was suffering from sciatica, and needed some one to help him on an opera which he was preparing for the marriage of the Duke of Berry. We may conceive of the joy of Hérold, so long anxious for work and finding nothing to do, now associated with a master of brilliant talents, under whose patronage he would have no difficulty in making his appearance upon the French stage. Hérold never forgot Boieldieu, who had been the first instrument of his fortune.

In 1816 he brought out "Les Rosières," a comic opera, with tolerable success; then followed "Les Clochettes" and other operas, not well received on account of the weakness of their text. Then he abandoned the dramatic career for a while, and devoted himself to writing for the piano. About this time he was requested to go into Italy, and recruit singers for the Italian theatre in Paris. He acquitted himself of this delicate mission with the intelligence of an artist, and the probity of an honest man. Soon after he accepted several texts, and set himself to work with his accustomed vigor. But the troubles he had had, owing to bad speculations, were injurious to his musical inspirations : very few of the pieces he composed at that time are still in the musical repertory.

In 1827 the managers of the Italian Theatre gave Hérold the direction of the singing. Whilst in this employment he composed six ballets, without neglecting those labors which tended to extend his reputation, such as "Le dernier Jour de Missolonghi." Two other operas that he composed soon after were not popular, despite the many beauties they contained.

We have now come to that period in the life of the master, when, about to join the celestial choir, he left as his last farewell two admirable scores, "Zampa," heard for the first time at the comic opera in 1831, and ever since a favorite. The overture of "Zampa" is a succession of brilliant descants, and the orchestration of the best kind, though taken from the voice part, after Boieldieu's method.

The first representation of the comic opera, "Pré aux Clercs," took place Dec. 15, 1832 : this opera accorded with the predominating fashion of the sixteenth century. The refinement and elegance of the Valois, united to the violent passions of the time, tended to the pleasures of theatrical emotions. Through Sainte-Beuve, the sixteenth had become a literary century. The author of the libretto worked out an exciting drama. As to the score, it is hard to say which we most admire, — the musical painting of the scenic situations, or the varied coloring of the instrumentation. All is combined to please the most fastidious ear, and satisfy the most critical taste. The success of "Pré aux Clercs" was immediate, and crowned the reputation of the artist.

Hérold was much fatigued by the rehearsals for the opera. Consumption, which he had inherited from his father, had long been wearing upon him ; and extra exertion told so seriously upon his wasting strength as to cause great alarm to his friends. He died Jan. 19, 1833, not less regretted for his private qualities, than for the talents which gave him a place in the first rank of composers.

Hérold was married in 1827. He left three children, one of whom, a son, distinguished himself at the bar.

Hérold was a pleasant companion, often inspired, always interesting and ingenuous. His instrumentation is very fine. Thoroughly conversant in all the resources of his art, he was enabled to write excellent music upon any subject proposed.[1] Short as was his life, this master had the glory of having elevated the style of comic opera.

ROSSINI.
1792–1868.

GIOACHIMO ROSSINI, said to be the most popular dramatic composer of his time, was born Feb. 29, 1792, at Pesaro, in Romagna. His father, Giuseppi Rossini, was town trumpeter and inspector of butchery. His mother, Anna Guidarini, was a handsome woman, and possessed a remarkable voice. When the French army passed through Pesaro in 1796, Giuseppi Rossini, who was hot-headed, became very enthusiastic over the new ideas imported from beyond the mountains by the troops of the Republic. The vivacity of his language, and his imprudence, soon caused a re-action, and he was thrown into prison. Madame Rossini, obliged to provide for her child during the incarceration of her husband, followed the dictates of maternal love in going to Bologna to seek an engagement as singer in the theatres. Finding she could not take

---

[1] His unfinished opera, "Ludovic," was completed by Halévy.

her son with her to the different places where she had to sing, she confided the care of his early education to friendly hands. Notwithstanding that the young Rossini was a remarkably precocious child, he was too giddy and wild to apply himself earnestly to study. All his teachers, even Prinetti his music-master, complained of his lack of application. Meanwhile his father came out of prison, and joined the orchestra of the theatre in which his wife displayed her talent. But when he found out that his inheritor could scarcely read and write, and that he rebelled against the instruction of the worthy Prinetti, he resolved to give him a severe lesson, and for this purpose apprenticed him to a blacksmith. This chastisement produced the desired effect: the boy, conscious of his folly, and greatly affected by the tears of his mother, whom he had always loved with the utmost tenderness, applied himself to study with a diligence that never flagged.

He studied singing and accompaniment under Angelo Tesei. The time was soon to come when he, at ten years of age, should contribute largely to the support of the family; for Madame Rossini was obliged to quit the stage on account of throat troubles, which necessitated the amputation of the amygdalic glands on each side.

Happily the young Rossini had a charming soprano voice, and was enabled to sing in church choirs. The few francs that he obtained in this manner were of great assistance to his parents. Whilst earning his livelihood he continued his studies with Tesei, and acquired notions of literature in conversation with the engineer Giusti of Bologna, a man highly distinguished for his knowledge and general intelligence.

Without the discipline of a classic education, Rossini was so far instructed as not to be a stranger to science and literature, for he had been careful to collect the grains of knowledge strewn in his path by eminent persons with whom he had come in contact. An able accompanist, the child went from place to place with his father, helping to earn the money of which his parents were so much in need.

With adolescence came the loss of the fine soprano voice, and the boy was of no further service in the choir. In 1807 he entered the Lyceum at Bologna, and studied counterpoint with Father Mattei : he also learned violoncello, and continued the practice of accompanist. However, it does not appear that he profited very much from the dry teachings of his professor. Scholastic studies which address themselves only to the memory, without affecting the mind or touching the heart, inspired the young artist only with disgust. The great dislike which this melodious genius had for the fugue may be dated from this period.

The good Father Mattei would willingly have cultivated the taste of Rossini for church music ; but he cared little for that ; and as soon as he was convinced that he knew enough to write an opera, he ran away, determined to enter the dramatic career towards which his talents as well as his home training inclined him. His mother had sung on the stage, while his father played in the orchestra : he ought to compose an opera.

The information that he had gained from Signor Cavalli, while engaged at the theatre of Sinigaglia, was very useful to the young Rossini at his *début*. Cavalli, who also directed the theatre of " San Mosè " at Venice, proposed to Rossini, then eighteen years old, to put some of his own works upon that stage. Rossini immediately wrote the score and the words of an opera bouffe, in one act, which was performed in the autumn of 1810. For this work he received two hundred francs, the greater part of which he joyfully sent to his parents. He then returned to Bologna, where he composed his cantata of "Didon abandonnée." Rossini never received more than from two hundred to two hundred and fifty francs for an opera ; and therefore, to gain sufficient for his wants and those of his family, he was obliged to multiply his productions in such a manner that he could bring out four or five a year. Such rapid writing would have been a foolish waste of talent for almost any other composer ; but the rich are allowed to be prodigal of their wealth. The genius of Rossini was a soil so generous that there was no fear that the artist would exhaust it in his endeavors to satisfy the requirements of the secondary theatres for which he worked.

Prince Eugène, vice-king of Italy, exempted Rossini from conscription, in consideration of the hopes excited by his happy commencements. This was no small favor, if we consider that it was just the time when France was arming all its children for the great contest of the Empire.

In 1813 a manager named Cera was greatly offended because Rossini had made an engagement with another manager, for he intended that the master should work exclusively for his theatre. Finding that he could not break the contract, and thus prevent Rossini's working for another, he conceived the foolish idea of giving him a bad and troublesome libretto for a text from which to write an opera. By the nature of Rossini's agreement with Cera, he was obliged to write what was given him. The composer revenged himself by writing a bad score to correspond with the text. Among other extravagances, the violins would suddenly stop at each measure in the allegro of the overture, and the violinists bring their bows against the tin shades of the lights.[1] The joke was more than disagreeable to all who were not let into the secret. Of course this opera had but the one unique and very noisy representation. To say the least of it, the composer must have been very sure of himself to have dared such an undertaking. The opera of "Tancredi," written in the same year, was a perfect triumph. All Northern Italy was in excitement over it. Rossini's libretto was made from Voltaire's tragedy. As to the music, it marks a new step in the master's career. The celebrated cavatina in this opera, "Di tanti palpiti," was formerly known in Italy as the "Rice air," because, as the story goes, Rossini composed it in an inn whilst they were cooking rice for him.

In 1816 he brought out "Il Barbiere di Seviglia." The first representation given at Rome excited murmuring, hissing, and general dissatisfaction. Rossini had written the whole of this opera in thirteen days. The first even ing it was given he braved danger, as was the Italian custom ; the second, he did not go to the theatre, but to bed and to sleep. Soon, however, he was awakened by a great noise that seemed to be approaching near his hotel. It proved to be the public of the preceding evening, who, passing from fury to enthusiasm with the mobility of Southern people, had come to find Rossini, and bear him in triumph to the theatre.

There was a revolution in Naples, July, 1820, and Gen. Pepe endeavored to organize resistance to the royal troops by trying to arm the citizens, ordinarily occupied only by pleasure. Rossini, who never troubled himself about politics, thought to escape the national guards. However,

---

[1] The audience were so enraged hat they tore up the benches, and threatened to demolish the theatre.

he was at length obliged to put on the uniform. The officers in command, finding him wanting in the qualities requisite for a soldier, sent him back to his piano. At such a time there was little encouragement for theatricals, and the master composed no more during the year. He went to Rome, where he gave "Mathilde de Sabran," and Paganini directed the orchestra in person.

Soon after Rossini wrote an opera for the Royal Theatre in London, whither he went with his wife, well known as a singer under the name of Mlle. Colbran. He arrived in November, 1823, and during several weeks received every mark of sympathy and attention ; even King George IV. gave him a most gracious reception. However, the contract he had made with the director of the theatre was of no avail, owing to the bad state of its affairs. But this loss to the composer was more than compensated by what he gained in giving concerts and singing lessons, for, like most of the Italian composers, Rossini was a proficient in singing. He was an excellent pianist, incomparable as an accompanist, gifted with a fine barytone voice : he had enthusiastic receptions in the drawing-rooms of the English aristocracy, from whom he realized the greatest pecuniary profits.

Rossini remained some six months in England, then returned to Paris, where he had stopped on his way to London. Nothing could exceed his friendly welcome by the people, who, quite familiar with his music, were delighted to have him in their midst. Without reflecting that the theatre confided to the care of an inexperienced person would be in jeopardy, they made Rossini director of the Italian Opera. Afterwards they appointed him overseer of the king's music and general inspector of singing in France.

In 1829 the master put a seal to his reputation, by a
work, which, among so many masterpieces, will be his most
beautiful title to glory. Who, among the lovers of music,
can fail to see that the opera was " William Tell," performed at the Royal Academy of Music, Aug. 3, 1829.
This opera, written by a man not yet thirty-seven years
old, seemed to open for him a second career, as brilliant,
at least, as that which had just closed. It was said to be
the starting point of a new musical era in the life of the
great artist. But alas! the prophecy of his many admirers
was not to be accomplished. Instead of a long succession
of musical enjoyments from the master they so much
admired, they were forced to be content with what they
already had; for Rossini, satisfied with the glory he had
won and the large fortune his brilliant works had procured,
wrote no more for the stage.

The composer lost the sinecures[1] which he held by the
munificence of Charles X., through the revolution of 1830.
But he reclaimed the retiring pension of six thousand
francs, which had been stipulated in case of his losing his
appointments through unforeseen circumstances. These
unforeseen circumstances were the events of July; and
Rossini, to obtain what he considered his rights, entered
into a law-suit which lasted six years, and terminated in
his favor.

The silence of Rossini has somewhat contributed to
establish the foolish reputation of idleness, which a series
of thirty-seven operas written before he was forty years of
age, proves to be false.

[1] The office of "*Intendant de la Musique du Roi et Inspecteur-général du Chant
en France,*" gave to Rossini the annual income of twenty thousand francs, and of
being pensioned in case he should lose the office by unforeseen circumstances.

As Rossini advanced in years, he imagined he had a nervous attack whenever he
heard music; and as to pianos they were mercilessly banished from his house."

If the author gave up writing for the opera, he did not cease to love music, and scarcely a day passed that he did not compose more or less. But he loved his music as an egotist, for his own pleasure and that of those friends who were happy enough to gain admittance to his musical *soirées.* In 1841 he wrote a " Stabat Mater," and a " Solemn Mass," performed in 1864, several pieces for piano, &c.

After the death of his first wife, Rossini married Mlle. Olympe Pellissier in 1847. He was living in Bologna, where the revolutionary movement which agitated Italy at that time troubled him. Those who should have been proud of the master as their countryman, became sus picious of him on account of his horror of popular sedi tions ; and he felt obliged to go elsewhere. A severe illness detained him for some time at Florence ; then he went back to Paris, and passed the summer at his villa in Passy, where he received artists in the most friendly man ner, thus keeping himself continually surrounded by all the illustrations of wit, talent, and beauty. In 1866 Ros sini wrote a cantata, dedicated to the French people, which was executed by four thousand voices at the Exposi tion universelle.

Our great artist died at Passy, Nov. 13, 1868. By his will he left two prizes to be awarded by the Institute, — one for the best text, the other for the best score. He desired that the score should recommend itself by its melody.

The sweetness of Rossini's melodies has enchanted not only the Roman, but the Teutonic races. "Tell," his richest creation, and the " Barbiere de Sevilla," wonderfully harmonic throughout, full of bubbling mirth and geniality, still prove their vitality whenever performed.

HAUPTMANN.

1794–

MAURICE HAUPTMANN, renowned as a musical theorist, was born in Dresden, Oct. 13, 1794. In his youth he studied mathematics, physics, and chemistry, with a view of becoming an architect. But yielding to his love for music, he devoted himself entirely to its pursuit from his twentieth year. That he might learn to play the violin artistically, he took lessons of Spohr, under whose instruction he wrote some works for the orchestra. In 1812 he received an appointment in the chapel at Dresden. In 1815 he accompanied Prince Repnin to St. Petersburg, Moscow, &c., as music-teacher. Afterwards he found time to devote to study and composition in Pultawa.

In May, 1820, he returned to Dresden; from thence he went to Cassel, where he remained some twenty years, following his calling as a member of the chapel. Among the excellent works that he composed during this period, was the opera "Mathilde."

That he was fully occupied may be seen from the following letter to his friend Hauser, written in 1827, in which he says, "This morning I sent you the opera; since then I have been to rehearsal, given three lessons, taken two meals, and commenced writing a new opera : one can do a great deal. If I have something that I like to do, I am so happy that I wish for nothing but to be left entirely alone and undisturbed where I am ; if, on the contrary, I have nothing to do, I can nowhere feel satisfied." He goes on to criticise the compositions of several musical writers, and finishes his letter with "This is a curious world."

About this time Hauptmann made himself known as one of the most distinguished theorists of our time. Speaking of his pupils he says, " I have some pupils to whom Nature has denied the ability to put three notes together consecutively, and yet these fellows imagine that they can learn to compose. I must say that giving lessons has become a burden to me. I am not stupid enough to give them in the usual manner, and think it the right one, and not clear enough, at least not yet, to base my teaching on a scientific method." Again, " I would like to know why people come from a distance to take lessons of me. I refuse as many as I can, but some will not be refused : they rather wait for a vacancy. Alas ! how rare it is to find a pupil whom it is a pleasure to teach ! "

Whilst in Naples in 1829 Hauptmann had the good fortune to meet the sister of Prince Repnin, with whom he had previously travelled. This lady provided handsome lodgings for him in her hotel on the Chiaja, and paid him every attention. To his friend Hauser he wrote, " It is very strange that a Russian lady of the first rank in the great world, and an unsocial man like myself, can be agreeable to each other, and that she should bestow so much kindness upon him without letting him feel his obligation." The lady also gave him letters of introduction to Boieldieu and Cherubini in Paris.

In 1842 he was appointed cantor and musical director of the St Thomas School, and of the two principal churches in Leipzig. In 1843 he was teacher of counterpoint and fugue in the Leipzig Conservatory of Music.

Hauptmann by his creative talent, which inclines more to the pensive and sentimental than to the brilliant and glittering, as well as by his deep and thorough knowledge, belongs to the most intellectual musicians. Of his less numerous than important works we will mention a grand mass with orchestra, motets, a " Salve Regina," many fine songs, sonatas, &c., and much excellent instrumental music ; among others six sonatas for pianoforte and violin. His chief theoretical work, " Die Natur der Harmonik und Metrik," belongs to the most important of the new musical literature. In 1850 Hauptman took part in the formation of the Bach Society, and in the publication of the works of this great master.

Hauptman says, " A pupil must suit me if he is to learn as he ought, and that seldom happens. Some come to me, as the peasant went to the optician for spectacles, thinking that if he had them he could read. Others are naïve, of a romantic nature : they do not feel right in pure harmony.

The twenty-fifth year of Hauptmann's directorship of music in Leipzig was celebrated Sept. 28, 1868, by a great musical festival.

During the forty-five years in which Hauptmann taught music he had three hundred and seventeen private pupils.

MEYERBEER.
1794–1864.

Occasionally we meet with families of celebrities, so to say ; for instance, that of Jacob Beer, a wealthy Israel-itish banker of Berlin, of whose sons, William, though occupied in banking-business, became a distinguished astronomer ; Michel was celebrated in Germany as a dramatic poet ; and Jacob, the eldest, is the renowned composer, who rendered himself illustrious under the name of Giacomo Meyerbeer, having Italianized his first name, and preceded his surname by that of the banker Meyer, who had, in some way, adopted him, and bequeathed to him a fortune.

Giacomo Meyerbeer was born at Berlin, Sept. 5, 1794. He was a musical prodigy from his most tender years. When only four years old, he would go to the piano, and repeat the airs which the street-organs were playing, making his own accompaniment as he went along. At five years of age he took lessons of Lanska, a pupil of Clementi ; and on the 14th of October, 1800, he appeared in a concert [1] at Berlin. Three years after, the nine-years-old boy was spoken of in the "Musical Gazette" of Leipzig as one of the best pianists of Berlin.

The greatest masters thought it an honor to have the young Meyerbeer for a pupil. Clementi, then Bernard Weber, and finally the celebrated Abbé Vogler, were his teachers.

Charles Weber, Winter, and Gansbacher were fellow-students with Meyerbeer at Vogler's school in Darmstadt. There was great emulation as well as friendship between these young people during the two years they were at school together.

Every morning, after having said mass, the abbé called them together to listen to some theoretical explanation of counter-point ; then he gave each a theme for composition. Meyerbeer soon did honor to the abbé's teaching, by composing an oratorio, "Gott und die Natur," which was successfully performed in presence of the Grand Duke, who bestowed upon him the title of composer to the court. He gave a concert at Berlin the same year with equal success.

---

[1] His parents were so much pleased with his success, that, to remember just how he looked, they had his picture taken in life-size, and in the dress he wore at the concert.

Vogler closed his school, that his pupils might make a tour of Germany. Meyerbeer gave concerts in several cities, and then went to Vienna ; but his courage was somewhat damped by hearing the performance of Hummel. Before appearing again in public, he endeavored to perfect himself in those qualities of the Viennese school which he had not yet learned. For this purpose he worked courageously in perfect retirement for nearly a year. When he again came forward, his playing caused a great sensation. Moschèles has since declared, that, if Meyerbeer had remained a pianist, he could not have been surpassed.

Meyerbeer passed two years in Italy, whither he went, by advice of Salieri, to cultivate his voice. Arriving in Venice just when the enthusiasm of the public was roused by Rossini's "Tancredi," he could not withstand the charm, but set to work immediately to compose operas, *à la Rossini*, for the different Italian theatres. In 1818 he wrote "Romilda e Costanza," for Padua ; "Semiramide," in 1819, for Turin ; "Emma di Resburgo," in 1820, for Venice ; "Margherita d'Anjou," in 1822, for Milan ; "L'Esule di Granada," in 1823, likewise for Milan. Although the works that he composed in Italy had been admired in Germany, he himself received but a very cold reception on his return. In Berlin he was treated as a fugitive, in Vienna as a plagiarist from Rossini. He soon went back to Italy, where he composed "Almanzor," which he could not put upon the stage at the time fixed on account of indisposition. In 1824 he brought out "Il Crociato in Egitto." This opera made the tour of Europe, silenced the malice of some, redoubled the enthusiasm of others, and made him a rival of Rossini.

In 1826 he went to Paris, where he remained for a considerable time without bringing forth any new work.

Meyerbeer married in 1827. He had the misfortune to lose his first two children, after which he became sad and devout. During several years he wrote only a "Stabat," a "Miserere," a "Te Deum," some psalms, and eight of Klopstock's songs.

In 1831 [1] Meyerbeer's "Robert le Diable" was unexpectedly brought out at the grand opera of Paris. This work attracted much attention; for Meyerbeer had abandoned the school of Rossini, and taken a bold and independent stand. [2] His conceptions were characteristic and important: therefore, his composition was richer and broader than any he had before written. So delighted were the French people with this opera, that they did not weary, even though it was performed more than a hundred times. The reputation of Meyerbeer spread from Paris over the whole civilized world. Dr. Veron, who was the director of the opera, tells us, that, on the first evening of the performance of "Robert le Diable," an accident occurred that threw the actors into a state of excitement which well nigh spoiled the play.

After the admirable trio which serves as the *dénoûment* of the work, Levasseur, the artist who personated Bertram, had to jump into a trap alone to redescend to the empire of the dead. Robert, converted by the voice of God and the prayers of Alice, had, on the contrary, to remain upon the earth to marry the Princess Isabel; but Nourrit, the artist who personated Robert, misled by the situation, as well as by the music, threw himself into the trap after Levasseur. Those on the stage thought Nourrit was killed. Mlle. Dorus burst into tears. On the stage,

[1] Cherubini, Rossini, Auber, Mendelssohn, and Hiller were all at work in Paris at this time.

[2] Meyerbeer is considered a chief of a new school.

below the stage, and in the house, three different scenes were passing at the same time. The audience supposed that Robert had to follow Bertram to the abodes of death. On the stage nothing was heard but groanings and lamentations. Fortunately the beds and mattresses prepared for Levasseur's fall had not been removed when Nourrit fell. Levasseur, seeing Nourrit under the stage, asked if any change had been made in the piece. Nourrit, too much in a hurry to go back and set things to rights, did not stop to answer him. When he re-appeared before the audience, leading Mlle. Dorus, who now wept for joy, a shout of applause broke forth from all parts of the house, and the curtain fell.

The managers of the opera were so delighted that they wished a second opera from Meyerbeer, who agreed to furnish the "Huguenots" at a given time. Meanwhile the health of Mme. Meyerbeer was declining, and her physicians recommended a journey to Italy. Then Meyerbeer was obliged to defer his opera, which caused some difficulty between him and the managers. At length the work was announced for Feb. 26, 1836, and when it appeared it excited transports of enthusiasm. But "The Huguenots," awakening the remembrance of religious wars, was adjudged dangerous to the public peace, and its performance in many of the Southern cities was interdicted by the civil authorities. Some time after, D'Halévy's "Charles VI.," supposed to interfere in international relations, had to submit to a similar ostracism.

When Spontini resigned the situation of chapel-master at the court of Berlin in 1832, Meyerbeer succeeded him, and wrote a great number of different melodies and much church music for Frederic William IV. In 1842 he was made königlicher preuszischer general-musikdirectoi [1] On Meyerbeer's return to Paris in 1849, he gave "The Prophet."

The success of this work, at first doubtful, was soon established, and the composer returned to Berlin to fulfil his engagement with the King of Prussia, where, among the works with which he was occupied at this time, we find the "March of the Bavarian Archers," from a poem written by King Louis of Bavaria.

Meyerbeer's health declined towards the end of 1851, and he was obliged to seek repose. A quiet sojourn in Spa, whither he went in 1852, was of great advantage to him.

Up to this time his opera of "Robert" had been per formed in Paris three hundred and thirty-three times; "The Huguenots" two hundred and twenty-two; and "The Prophet" a hundred and twelve. "L'Étoile du Norde" was given Feb. 16, 1854; and the "Pardon de Ploërmel," called also "Dinorah," April 4, 1859. Although these works contain much that is very beautiful, they are inferior to his other works, both in score and text.

It would seem that a man like Meyerbeer, so rich and so celebrated, might be happy. But he was never satisfied with himself while at work; even his masterpieces failed to content him; besides, he was extremely sensitive to criticism. He was as much pleased with admiration and applause as he was grieved by fault-finding.[2]

Certain it is, however, that all the decorations he re-

---

[1] About this time Meyerbeer introduced Jenny Lind to the public of Berlin. He also assisted Spohr.

In 1845 Queen Victoria, who was present at the unveiling of Beethoven's statue, personally presented Meyerbeer with the works of her husband.

[2] In 1860 the Princess of Prussia presented Meyerbeer with an ebony baton, richly ornamented with gold and jewels.

ceived could add nothing to his merit as author of "The Prophet" and "The Huguenots." To receive honors and dignities is one thing, to merit them another.[1]

Meyerbeer died at Paris, May 2, 1864. One ought to have an eloquent pen to paint the consternation with which the world of letters and of arts was seized when the sad words, "*Meyerbeer is dead,*" resounded from place to place. That same morning Rossini had inquired after the health of the sick man, who was equally his friend and his rival. On hearing the sad news he sank down in sorrow, and remained a long time without uttering a word.[2]

When "L'Africaine" appeared as an opera, Scribe and Meyerbeer, its co-laborers, were no more. This noble work may be less popular than the master's other great works, but it will always be appreciated by connoisseurs and artists.

Meyerbeer's mother, Amalia Beer, died in 1855, aged eighty-eight years. She was greatly beloved and respected, not only by her own immediate family and friends, but by artists and all interested in the cultivation of art, for whom her house was ever open, and her hospitable board spread. Her beneficence, patriotism, and generosity had been acknowledged by King Frederick William III., who had decorated her with a "Louisenordnen."

In writing "L'Africaine," love and enthusiasm for his work guided the author's pen ; and so fully was his

---

[1] The University of Zena gave him the diploma of Doctor of Music in 1850.

[2] A sealed document, on which was written, "*To be opened after my death,*" was found in his pocket-book. It contained a wish that small bells should be attached to his hands and feet, and that his body should remain four days in the bed where he died and be carefully watched ; after which it should be taken to Berlin, and buried beside his mother. At the time of Meyerbeer's death his opera of "Robert" had been performed four hundred and seventy times, "The Huguenots" three hundred and ninety-eight times.

heart set upon the completion of this work, that he prayed God not to take him before it was finished.

[Letter to Jules Janin of Paris, dated Oct. 2, 1861.]

Your last letter was addressed to me at Königsberg; but I was in Berlin working, — working away like a young man, despite my seventy years, which somehow certain people, with a peculiar generosity, try to put upon me. As I am not at Königsberg, where I am to arrange for the Court Concert for the eighteenth of this month, I have now leisure to answer your letter, and will immediately confess to you how greatly I was disappointed that you were so little interested in Rameau; and yet Rameau was always the bright star of your French opera, as well as your master in the music. He remained to you after Lulli; and it was he who prepared the way for the Chevalier Gluck: therefore his family have a right to expect assistance from the Parisians, who on several occasions have cared for the descendants of Racine and the grandchildren of the great Corneille. If I had been in Paris, I certainly would have given two hundred francs for a seat; and I take this opportunity to beg you to hand that sum to the poor family, who cannot fail to be unhappy in their disappointment. At the same time I send you a power of attorney for M. Guyot, by which I renounce all claims to the parts of my operas which may be represented at the benefit for the celebrated and unfortunate Rameau family. Why will you not come to Königsberg at the festival? Why, in other words, are you not in Berlin? What splendid music we have in preparation! As to myself, it is not only a source of pleasure to me, but I feel it a duty, in the position I hold, to compose a Grand March, to be performed at Königsberg while the royal procession passes from the castle into the church, where the ceremony of crowning is to take place. I will even compose a hymn, to be executed on the day that our king and master returns to his good Berlin. Besides, I have promised to write an overture for the great concert of the four nations, which the directors of the London exhibition intend to give at the opening of the same, next spring, in the Crystal Palace. All this keeps me back: it has robbed me of my autumn, and will also take a good part of next spring; but with the help of God, dear friend, I hope we shall see each other again next year, free from all cares, in the charming little town of Spa, listening to the babbling of its waters, and the rustling of its old gray oaks.

Truly your friend,   MEYERBEER.

Once when a friend begged Meyerbeer to be more careful of himself, to take some rest, he answered smiling, " If I should leave work I should rob myself of my greatest pleasure, for I am so accustomed to work that it has become a necessity." Notwithstanding that he was troubled by weak eyes, he read all the news of the day, and kept himself well posted in arts, science, and politics.

MOSCHELES.

1794–1870.

THE distinguished pianoforte player, and celebrated composer for that instrument, was the son of an Israelitish merchant of Prague, where he was born May 30, 1794. Notwithstanding the pressure of business, his father found leisure to devote to music, of which he was passionately fond. It was his earnest wish that one of his children should become a thoroughbred musician ; but he little dreamed of the talent of the child, who, standing beside his eldest sister whilst she took her music-lesson, learned faster than she did. One day, tired of seeing his sister's unskilful performance, the little fellow cried out, " Oh, dear, how stupid ! I could do it better myself." " Try," said the teacher, putting him on the stool. After that he took lessons regularly, and made rapid progress.

In those days, when parents discussed the French Revolution in presence of their children, playing soldier was the favorite game of the boys ; and Ignace, our young hero, often ran from his piano to fulfil his duties as captain of a company. When the military band performed parade music in front of the guard-house, he was sure to be on hand, and ready to hold their music for them. At seven years of age he had what he afterwards called a

Beethoven fever, and even attempted to play the " Sonate pathétique " of the great master.

His father, seeing the necessity of strict discipline and regular training for his gifted son, took him to Dionys Weber, saying, " I want to find out if my boy has such genuine talent that you can make a really good musician of him."

After hearing what the child considered his best piece, "Beethoven's Sonate pathétique," the teacher said, " Candidly speaking, the boy is on the wrong track ; but he has talent, and I could make something of him if you would hand him over to me for three years, and follow out my plan to the letter. The first year he must play nothing but Mozart ; the second, Clementi ; and the third, Bach, but only that, — not a note as yet of Beethoven ; and if he persists in using the circulating libraries, I have done with him forever." The father agreed to all these terms, and on his way home enforced upon the mind of his son that it was in his power to bring credit, not only to himself, but to all the family.

One day Mr. Moscheles took Ignace to the theatre as a reward for diligence in his studies. The boy, delighted with a funeral march played in the opera, played it correctly from beginning to end when he got home ; at which the astonished father shed tears of joy, and looked forward with pleasure to the time when he should hear his boy's first composition. But, alas ! death severed the tie which bound the hearts of father and son so closely in unison. Ignace was but fourteen years old when he lost this best and dearest of fathers. Soon after his mother, contrary to the advice of relatives, sent him to Vienna to continue his musical studies and earn his own living.[1]

[1] The widow and her five young children were left completely unprov'ded for

At Vienna he was kindly received into the family circle of friends, and allowed to join in their musical parties : he soon made himself known, and formed acquaintances in the circles of distinguished musicians. Meanwhile he studied assiduously with the chapel-master Albrechtsberger, who gave him a written testimonial of his approbation. He became acquainted with Salieri, who treated him in a very friendly manner, and gave him a free pass to all the theatres of Vienna.

In 1814 Moscheles first heard Meyerbeer, with whose masterly playing he was delighted. At this time the liberation of Germany was exciting the hearts of the Viennese poets and musicians; who vied with each other in celebrating the event. Spohr wrote his "Befreites Deutschland ;" Hummel celebrated the return of the Kaiser ; Moscheles wrote the "Entry into Paris," and afterwards a sonata, entitled "The Return of the Kaiser," and various other pieces, among which was the "Sonata mélancholique," thought to be one of his best: he was then in his twenty-first year. He became acquainted with Beethoven, and commenced arranging "Fidelio" for the piano.

Moscheles in his diary says, "When I came early in the morning to Beethoven, he was still lying in bed ; he happened to be in remarkably good spirits, jumped up immediately, and placed himself, just as he was, at the window, with the view of examining the "Fidelio" numbers which I had arranged. Naturally a crowd of boys collected under the window, when he roared out, 'Now, what do these confounded boys want ?' I laughed, and pointed to his own figure. 'Yes, yes ; you are quite right,' he said, and hastily put on a dressing-gown."

Early in 1815 the Countess Hardegg sent for Moscheles,

and begged him to write something to be played at a concert on Ash Wednesday, for the charitable institutions of Vienna. "Write something as quickly as you can, and let it be brilliant," she said. He commenced writing Jan. 29, and by Feb. 5 had finished the famous "Alexander Variations," which won him so much fame.

In 1816 Moscheles gave a concert in his native city, Prague, the proceeds of which, twenty-four hundred florins, were given to the poor.

Returning to Vienna, he resumed his former pursuits, and by dint of hard study and practice he steadily improved in finish and execution ; so that his playing was by many preferred to that of Hummel, whose "touch was said to be as soft as velvet, whilst his running passages were as perfect as a string of pearls." Moscheles captivated his hearers with his dashing bravura and youthful enthusiasm ; but there was not the least personal rivalry between the two artists themselves. Whilst Moscheles recognized the merits of others, he used to say, "We musicians, whatever we may be, are mere satellites of the great Beethoven, the dazzling luminary."

At Karlsbad he made the acquaintance of Schumann, to whom he afterwards dedicated a sonata.

The Countess Hardegg and other influential admirers of our young artist had prepared a grand tour for him on his return to Vienna, by furnishing him with letters of introduction to every court he might visit, to every art celebrity, as well as to many highly influential citizens of the different cities through which he should pass. This readily explains Moscheles's success ; and when we add that his manners were modest and unassuming, his presence agreeable, his disposition kind and affectionate, we do not wonder that he was everywhere a welcome guest.

Moscheles found life in Leipzig extremely pleasant, was successful with his concerts, and made many friends. A fit of sickness confined him to his chamber for a month, in Dresden : as soon as he was restored to health he introduced himself to the artist world. He next visited Munich, and presented his letters of introduction to Prince Eugène of Leuchtenberg and the court. The old King Max was much pleased with, and very kind to him : as a token of his regard, he presented the artist with a diamond ring. The prince also presented him with a pin, having the letter E set in diamonds on an enamelled ground.

Moscheles next played at Augsburg, before the ex-Queen Hortense. Then he gave several concerts in Holland. In 1821 he went to Paris, where he met his friend Spohr at the house of Baron Poiféré de Cère. "The baron gave morning parties every Sunday, where the aristocracy of artists, as well as the great world of Paris, were numerously represented."

Moscheles and Spohr both played in public, and each shared in a brotherly way the applause of the appreciative audiences. The former steadily devoted his morning hours to pianoforte practice and composition, after which, according to his diary, he plunged cheerfully into the joys and delights of the great capital. He was constantly receiving "invitations to dinners, balls, and all sorts of *fêtes*." His great success in Paris enabled him to assist his mother and sisters, on whom he was able to bestow constant and beneficent care ever after. Going from Calais to Dover in a heavy storm, Moscheles was very sick. The steward supposing him to be a courier, because his packet of music was stamped [1] "Despatches," with the Imperial

[1] This had been done at the Austrian Embassy, that he might travel free from tax and detention.

seal, exclaimed, "For shame! a courier, constantly cross-
ing and recrossing the channel, and so seasick!"

It is very pleasing to see how appreciative Moscheles is
of talent and skill of other pianoforte players: he writes
of Cramer, "His interpretations of Mozart are like
breathings 'from the sweet south.' He is exceedingly
intellectual and entertaining." Then in his characteristic
humorous way, he goes on to remark, "He is one of the
most inveterate snuff-takers. Good housekeepers maintain that after every visit of the great master, the floor
must be cleansed of the snuff he has spilled; whilst I, as a
pianoforte player, cannot forgive him for disfiguring his
aristocratic, long, thin fingers, with their beautifully shaped
nails, by the use of it, and often clogging the action of the
keys." About the 20th of June, Moscheles "took an unwilling leave of the London art-world, but was delighted
to get away from the London atmosphere."

He next made a musical tour with Lafont, giving concerts which were brilliantly successful. Returned to
Paris, he was in constant requisition until the end of the
season, when he accepted the pressing invitations of
friends to return to London : there he found J. B. Cramer
on the point of giving his yearly concert. Moscheles
hastily wrote his allegro of the well known "*Hommage à
Handel*" as a finale to Cramer's sonata. To hear Moscheles and "Glorious John" playing together in a composition on which both had worked was, as the newspapers
said, "an unrivalled treat and an unprecedented attraction." Towards the end of the year, when the London
Academy of Music sent him his diploma as honorary
member of the society, he inserted the following note in
his diary : "I feel more and more at home in England,
for people there evidently wish to show me respect and
friendship. I feel deeply grateful for this."

Like others of his countrymen, he found some difficulty in learning the English language. One day at the table of his friends, the Barlows, he was asked at dessert which fruit of those on the table he would prefer, to which he answered ingenuously, " Some sneers ;" at which the company laughed. He had found, in his phrase-book, " Not to care a fig," meant " To sneer at a person ;" and wishing for figs, thought he had chosen the right word. Among his pupils in London was a lady of sixty, who was very talkative and very hospitable, obliging him to lunch with her every time he went to give the lesson. As to her playing, he " could hardly persuade her to hazard her gouty little fingers on a piece of modern music." Frequently his conscience would not allow him to accept the guinea which she, every time, handed him, neatly wrapped up in paper.

Sir George Smart was always ready to assist Moscheles, who found him to be one of those rare beings, who, in spite of all sorts of business, find time to help everybody. In August, Moscheles went to Paris. Soon after his arrival, a box containing a snuff-box presented to him by the Duchess of Berry, a silver coffee-service, twelve spoons, an antique ring, a Venetian chair, and other articles valuable to him as *souvenirs*, was stolen from his room, and never recovered.

Arrangements had been made to give him a concert at Spa, whither he went ; but the lady who had offered the use of her piano refused to send it, because, as she said, she had been told that Moscheles played with his feet.

Again in Vienna he visited Beethoven in company with his brother, who was very anxious to see the great master. Knowing his dislike to strangers he said to Beethoven, " May I be allowed to introduce my brother to you ? " To which Beethoven replied, "Where, then, is he?" "Below," was the answer. "What! below?" cried he with some vehemence, then rushed down stairs, seized the astonished young man by the arm, and almost dragged him up into the middle of the room, exclaiming, "Am I so barbarously rude and unapproachable?" After which outburst, he was very kind and friendly.

In 1824 Moscheles was dangerously ill at his mother's house in Prague. After four months' confinement to the house, he was called upon to give a concert in presence of their Majesties, who had just arrived in the city. To do this he roused himself to action, and thus celebrated his return to health by a splendid concert.

In the autumn he made the acquaintance of the Mendelssohn family, who became his dearest friends. With Felix, then a boy of fourteen, he was perfectly charmed, considered him a phenomenon, and predicted that he would become a great master. The pleasure of the acquaintance was mutual, and the oftener Moscheles visited the family, the heartier was his welcome. The parents of Felix begged Moscheles to give him some lessons ; but he refused, for he felt that the boy needed no instruction from him. However, after being urged by Mrs. Mendelssohn, he consented, and from that time became very intimate in the family : scarcely a day passed during his stay in Berlin that he was not either with Felix, or at the house of his parents, who treated him like a son.

In 1825 Moscheles met with Charlotte Embdem ; and after a short acquaintance they were married, March 1.

The death of Carl Maria von Weber, which took place at the residence of Sir George Smart, was a great affliction to Moscheles, whose sympathies had been largely drawn upon by the suffering of this brother artist and much beloved countryman

Moscheles was heartily welcomed at Vienna, whither he went with his wife after the London season. "They never failed to attend the levees of his former patroness, Frau von E——, which took place daily between four and six, the interval between dinner and theatre. The old lady, painted, rouged, and reclining on her luxurious sofa, received company. Abbés, poets, savants, &c., met at these receptions, where the last new thing in politics, or Vienna gossip, was · discussed by officials and statesmen. Ladies appeared in evening dress. The conversation was carried on in rather poor French, and the atmosphere generally seemed artificial. In 1828 Moscheles and his wife were invited to breakfast with Sir Walter Scott. 'He opened the door himself,' says Moscheles, 'and welcomed us heartily. He was suffering from gout, and walked with a stick. His conversation was extremely animated and delightful. The amiability and sweetness of his manners quite charmed us.' Afterwards they had a party, Sir Walter and Sontag being among their guests. That night Sontag had two worshippers, Sir Walter and Clementi, who were both in ecstasy. They shook each other by the hand, and vied with each other in attentions to Sontag.

"The poet, musician, and songstress were, of course, the great attraction of the evening.

"In 1829 Fetis joined Moscheles in sketching the plan for the 'Méthode des Méthodes,' in the joint publication of which Fetis's skill as a linguist was of the greatest service to Moscheles, as he translated into excellent French his friend's musical treatise on the study and higher branches of pianoforte playing."

The 10th of November he gave a concert in Copenhagen, where he cleared six hundred and forty-one thalers. Besides, he received a present of a gold enamelled snuff-box from his Majesty the king, a diamond ring from Prince Christian, a gold chain from a lady, and all sorts of complimentary messages from the court.

Of Paganini, who made his appearance in London about this time, Moscheles says, "Paganini often comes to us. We receive him well, although I suspect he is rather too sweet to be genuine."

The impression made by Paganini at his first concert was overwhelming. The crowd in the opera house was wild with excitement. He had to play nearly every thing twice over, and was not only greeted with vehement clapping of hands, but every lady leaned forward out of her box to wave her handkerchief at him. People in the pit stood up on the benches shouting, "Hurrah! Bravo!" No other artist ever made such an impression on the public.

"On the 31st December, 1833, Moscheles writes in his diary, 'On reckoning, I find that I have given this year 1,457 lessons, of which 1,328 were paid, 129 gratis. Of the latter those I gave to Litolff, who is making rapid strides, were the most interesting.' Henry Litolff, a boy of ten years of age, had been introduced to Moscheles as a poor, clever, but rather neglected child. Moscheles immediately recognized his talent, and commenced teaching him." In 1835 Litolff published many of his early and very promising compositions.

While in London, in 1836, Malibran was a constant visitor at Moscheles's house, where the children, of whom she was very fond, claimed her constant attention. She would sit on the floor with them, and paint pictures to their heart's delight. The little silk bag, in which she brought paint-box, paper, and pencils, had a wonderful attraction for them, and never were they happier than when pulling out its contents. "Indeed the whole family, whilst loving her as a true and noble woman, were in raptures about her language, painting, and music.

Thalberg a former pupil of Moscheles, "now returned as a master." Ole Bull also visited them. After this his first visit, he came from time to time to get his host to play for him.

In 1837 Moscheles got up a series of pianoforte concerts, in which he introduced the music of Sebastian Bach and other old composers. This was quite a novelty, as the English were accustomed to, and fond of, light Italian music. However, Moscheles succeeded so far as to bring out Beethoven's "Ninth Symphony" with good success.

In a letter to a relative in reference to the symphony, Moscheles writes in high spirits, saying, "Wealthy England has enriched herself by this additional treasure, and I rejoice that I have been permitted to disinter it."

Thalberg enjoyed extraordinary success in London : his playing with Moscheles was a real triumph. In the month of May, there were a host of talented musicians in the city, all visiting and wishing to exchange music with Moscheles.

Our distinguished artist, having well prepared himself by the study of ancient and modern music, commenced a series of historical concerts in 1838. His intention was to begin with the old masters, and gradually lead his audience up to his own time, that they might have an opportunity to compare and draw their own conclusions. The concerts were successful, and the newspapers loud in praise of the undertaking.

What with composing, giving concerts, and being so much in company, teaching was becoming very tiresome to him. His father-in-law advised him to double the price of his lessons, and thus diminish their number; to which he replied, "I can't make up my mind to such a step; for people might well accuse me of selfishness, and that, too, in a country to which I am mainly indebted for my present position."

In 1839 we find Chopin and Moscheles playing at St. Cloud, in presence of the royal family. "Chopin's enthusiasm, I think," says Moscheles, "must have kindled that of his hearers, who overwhelmed us both with compliments. Chopin played another solo as charmingly as before, and met with the same reception. I then improvised on some of Mozart's sweetest airs, and finally dashed away at the ' *Zauberflöte* ' overture. Better than all the words of praise which flow so glibly from the lips of princes, was the king's close attention during the entire evening. Chopin and I revelled like brothers in the tri umph achieved by the individual talent of each : there was no tinge of jealousy on either side. At last, after enjoying some refreshment, we left the palace at 11.30, this time only under a shower of compliments, for the rain had ceased, and the night was clear." Shortly after, Moscheles received a valuable dressing-case, having the words, "Donné par le Roi Louis-Philippe," engraved upon it.

It might not be amiss for those of our readers who think that their progress in music depends on the number of lessons they take, to know what so good a teacher as Moscheles thought. "Any one who has heard and studied a great deal that is good," he says, "ought to need no teacher to spur him on. The student should always bear in mind the greatest models, and emulate them, playing a great deal with accompaniment; he should become more and more familiar with masterpieces, and enter earnestly into a sense of their beauties : thus the gradual development the pupil attains will place him above the common run of amateurs."

As before stated, Moscheles had been indefatigable in bringing Beethoven's works before the English public. A quotation from "The Times" of May 4, proves his great success. "Artists and amateurs now are glad to own that Beethoven's Ninth Symphony is as much remarkable for majesty and grandeur as for simplicity. For this recognition we are in a great measure indebted to Moscheles, who conducted the work with great care and conscientiousness. As a conductor he surpasses almost all our musicians ; for whenever he swings his baton, he leads the orchestra, whereas others are led by it. Nothing would so much tend to elevate the character of these concerts as the permanent appointment of Moscheles as a conductor : he is one who inspires the orchestra with a respect due to him, and would always lead it onwards to success." At this time Liszt and Moscheles frequently played together ; and Liszt was a welcome visitor at the house of his brother artist, where brilliant conversation and fine playing distinguished him as a man of genius. The commencement of the year 1842 was very sad for Moscheles, whose wife and son were lying ill of scarlet-fever, when he received news of his mother's death. His feelings find expression in the following lines : "This blow has almost stunned me. Never was a son loved more affectionately. Never has a son more heartily responded to such love than I did. This gap must remain unfilled." During this saddest of winters he had to study and rehearse Spohr's Symphony for the Philharmonic concert.

At the time of the great Hamburg fire, Moscheles got up

a concert, the profits of which, six hundred and forty-three pounds, were given to the sufferers. All that Moscheles asked was one thousand marks[1] to distribute among families selected by himself. "Afterwards the City of Hamburg presented him with a medal, made of the molten bronze of the church-bells. It bore this inscription, 'Hamburg thanks.'"

The Leipzig Conservatory was inaugurated April 10; and Mendelssohn, who was at its head, tried to persuade Moscheles to join him. The latter, worn out with lesson-giving, was strongly inclined to accept his friend's invitation, and devote himself only to the education of young artists.

A young man who had toiled assiduously over and learned about a dozen pieces, now appeared before the London public as a youthful prodigy, and excited much admiration by his wonderful powers of execution. In trying over some "scale pieces" with Moscheles, he was so often at fault that Clara, Moscheles's little daughter, ran up to her mamma, calling out, "Mamma, hasn't Mr. —— learned the scales?"

In 1844 Moscheles set out for Vienna, accompanied by his wife and daughter. They stopped at Frankfort, and gave a concert to an over-crowded house. Mrs. Moscheles wrote to a friend from Munich, where her husband was intending to give a concert, "Here the feet of Fanny Elssler are in opposition to Moscheles's hands. It is impossible to secure band or public, as she is forever dancing."

Moscheles was so much in demand at Vienna, that he was forced to prolong his visit, and allow his wife and daughter to go on to Hamburg. After the Archduchess

---

[1] A mark is about twenty-four cents.

Sophia's concert, at which he played, she sent him sixty ducats; which he refused, saying he would prefer a souvenir if she wished to make him a present. She then sent him three diamond studs. Moscheles attended the musical festival in Bonn, August, 1845. He wrote to his wife that at the hotel where he put up were all the crowned heads of music, all art judges, German and French reviewers, English reporters; also "Listz, the absolute monarch, by his princely gifts, outshining all else." Gentlemen and ladies, with armies of porters and band-boxes, all trying to find a shelter.

Beethoven's statue was unveiled Aug. 12, in presence of the King and Queen of Prussia, Queen Victoria and Prince Albert, with a numerous suite. At five o'clock a grand concert was given. The last day of the festival, there was a banquet at the "Stern," at which the crowd was immense. Healths were drunk, and speeches made. Spohr proposed the health of the Queen of England; Liszt that of Prince Albert, and went on to say that, " Here all nations are come together to pay honor to the master. May they live and prosper, — the Dutch, the English, the Viennese, who had made a pilgrimage hither!" Upon this Chelard rose in a violent passion, and accused Liszt of forgetting the French. A tumult ensued, the contending parties becoming boisterous and violent. The landlord thought to stop the noise by making the band play as loudly as possible. Finally Moscheles, who had remained neutral, deafened by the noise, made his escape.

Early in 1846 he received the formal offer of his appointment at the Leipzig Conservatory, and a pressing invitation from Mendelssohn to come. After mature deliberation with his wife, and fully discussing all the pros and cons, he determined to accept, and wrote to his friend accord-

ingly. Mendelssohn was not long in returning the expres
sions of his joy. "When you come," he writes, "I'll
have some houses painted rose-color; but your arrival
alone will give a rose-colored tinge to the old place."

Although unwilling to part with Moscheles, his judicious
friends approved of the steps he had taken, as it would
give him "some repose after so many laborious years."

During the summer months, however, he was more
busy than ever. An extract from his diary will show to
what extent his energies were taxed : —

"I usually get to bed at about one or two o'clock.
Thank Heaven, my constitution seems made of iron, otherwise I could not stand the night and day work. Yesterday, or rather this morning, I saw the sun rise at four
o'clock, as I was going to bed. It is now eight o'clock,
and we are up, and writing. Our party last night began
with music, and ended with dancing. I, old as I am,
tripped it lightly with the youngsters. To-day I have six
lessons ; and at five o'clock I must be in the Freemasons'
Hall. To-morrow, besides the lessons, I have to conduct
a concert a *mile long* for a pupil."

About this time his daughter Emily married Mr. Roche,
a professor of French literature, with whom she had long
been acquainted.

Moscheles once comfortably settled at Leipzig, every
artist passing through the city made a point of calling
upon him ; and he, with his usual kindness, listened to every
thing they had to tell him about their music, often showing
them how this and that must be played to give it correct
expression.

The death of Mendelssohn, in 1847, caused a general
mourning in Leipzig. Moscheles was with him when he
breathed his last. After the funeral ceremonies, which

were grand and impressive, Moscheles, though "impressed with a dreary sense of isolation at the loss of his art-colleague" and dear friend, resumed his duties in the Conservatory, feeling that it was now his duty to do the work of two. It was in the conscientious performance of this duty that he derived some comfort in his deep sorrow. Nor did he allow the progress of art, as far as he was concerned, to be interrupted by the troubles of 1848 and 1849. In December he made great exertions to get up a concert for a blind singer, but was unsuccessful.

That the political state of Germany depressed the spirits of Moscheles, there can be no doubt, though he says, "People are desponding; but I cling fast to my art, and lean upon 'Frau Musica' for support." At the request of Sontag, Moscheles wrote something for her to sing when she was in Leipzig, in 1852. The people, as usual, could think of nothing but Sontag whilst she was in their midst; and, when she left for Dresden, Moscheles said, "All Leipzig is · mad about her. People think and talk of nothing else. They nearly forget to start the railway trains, and to wind up the church clocks."

Moscheles, Berloiz, and Liszt dined with the Dowager Grand-Duchess of Weimar. In the evening, they all went to the opera, and then to Liszt's, where art was fully and freely discussed.[1]

In 1856 our artist was ill. Restless from loss of sleep, he endeavored to quiet his nerves, and divert his mind by composition. His "Humoristische Variationen" was the result.

Moscheles spent his holidays in Paris in the summer of ·1860. He visited Rossini at his residence in Passy. This

---

[1] Moscheles considered himself the connecting link between the old and the new school.

great master complained of the pianoforte players of the time ; said they maltreated their instrument. "They not only thump the piano, but the arm-chair, and even the floor." However, he was pleased with Moscheles' style, and raised him to the kingship of pianists, to which Moscheles modestly replied, "Whatever I am is due to the old school, the old master Clementi." A long and interesting conversation,[1] then the kiss and the blessing, and the two parted. After Moscheles returned to Leipzig, he received many kind messages from Rossini.

Moscheles, generous and forbearing as he always had been and always was to all brother-artists, could not quite agree with some of them in their new-fangled ideas ; for he says, "I know many think me old-fashioned ; but the more I consider the tendency of modern taste, and the abrupt and glaring contrasts indulged in by many composers of the present day, the more strenuously will I uphold that which I know to be sound art, and side with those who can appreciate a Haydn's playfulness, a Mozart's sweetness, and a Beethoven's surpassing grandeur. What antidotes have we for morbid moanings and overwrought effects ! In Gounod," he continues, "I hail a real composer. His 'Faust' is a fresh, interesting work, with a copious flow of melody, and lovely instrumentation."

In 1866, after the excitement of a London season, Moscheles rejoiced to be with his family, and surrounded by his grandchildren, for whom he composed "Familien-leben," and several other little pieces.

In December, 1869, he began to show symptoms of de-cline, and suffered from loss of sleep and restlessness.

---

[1] Speaking of German music, Rossini said, "I take Beethoven twice a week, Haydn four times, and Mozart every day. Mozart is always adorable. It is because he went to Italy when he was very young, at a time when they still sang well there."

The 1st of March, 1870, was the forty-fifth anniversary of his wedding-day; and he made every effort to take part in the home festival. He played with his daughter and two friends, and the next day insisted on going to a rehearsal. This was to be his last effort.

On the 10th of March, 1870, he joined the dear ones who had gone on before.

MARSCHNER.

1795-.

HENRY MARSCHNER was born at Zittau, 1795. He entered the choir of the children of the gymnasium, and profited so well by the instruction he received under Schneider, the director, that the organist of Bautzen offered him a place in the choir of his church. But Marschner, preferring harmony to Greek and Latin, returned to Zittau, where he began to study composition unassisted. He wrote every thing that came to mind, — songs, motets, piano music, &c. About the same time he wrote a ballet, "La Fière Paysanne." In 1812 he went to Prague, and thence to Leipzig, where Schicht by his instruction rendered him valuable assistance. " While here he became acquainted with Beethoven, Kotzeluch, and Klein of Presburg. In 1821 he went to Dresden. The operas that he composed whilst in this city gained him a high reputation; and here, in company with Weber and Morlacchi, he became director of the Dresden Opera. "

" He married Mlle. Marianne Wohlbruck, a celebrated singer, in 1826, and removed to Berlin, where his wife had most brilliant success on the stage. In 1827 he brought out ' Le Vampire ' at Leipzig. This was the most celebrated of his works."

In 1830 he was called to Hanover as chapel-master to the king.

Fetis says of this composer, " His melodies are expressive ; but his manner of writing is negligent, and he often abuses the use of transitions. Still the author of ' Le Vampire,' ' Le Templier,' and ' Hans Heiling,' will leave no common name in the history of art."

LÖWE.

1796–1870.

JOHANN KARL GOTTFRIED LÖWE was born Nov. 30, 1796, at Löbejün, near Halle. He received his first instruction from his father, who was the cantor. Afterwards he was sent to school at Köthen, then to the gymnasium of the Waisenhause in Halle. Here the development of his musical talents was guided by Türk, director of music at the university. Löwe not only studied singing, and the theory of music, &c., but theology and philosophy likewise ; thus uniting the artistic with the higher and scientific attainments. He lived in Dresden in 1819–1820, became acquainted with Carl Maria von Weber, who was ever after a very dear friend. At the end of 1820 he went to Stettin as cantor at St. Jacob's, and instructor of the tone art at the gymnasium. The next year he was advanced to the general directorship of the same. Whilst in this position he worked energetically for the improvement of the music of which he had charge, and established a singing society. Many thanks are due him for the formation of thorough and able pupils.

His ballads and songs are well known ; yes, many of them have become almost popular. About a hundred and twenty-five works which appeared one after another prove his versatility of talent. His songs suffice to keep his name in grateful remembrance.

SCHUBERT.

1797–1828.

On the 9th of October, 1808, a child of eleven years, with wild, staring eyes, and hair curled like that of a negro, dressed in a peasant's blouse, presented himself at the Conservatory of Vienna for examination. There were ironical whisperings and stifled laughter among the crowd of aspirants. One asked the other from whence that odd-looking,[1] homely little creature came, and who he was. But the surprise became general, when the child readily answered all questions propounded, and solved all difficulties proposed to him, drawing upon himself the warmest felicitations of Salieri, president of the jury of admission.

The name of the young aspirant received at the Conservatory on that day was Franz Schubert.

He was born at Vienna, Jan. 31, 1797.[2] His was a family of teachers, since his father and his three brothers were all professors. We can imagine, by the actual situation of school-teachers in Austria at the present time, what must have been their position some seventy years ago. A teacher in that country has seldom been able to procure a comfortable living in compensation for his labors, and is, therefore, generally poor. Such was the case with the family Schubert. But music reigned in their

---

[1] His face was round, forehead low, nose stubby, hair short and curly.

[2] There is a small gray tablet on the house in which he was born, bearing the inscription, "Franz Schubert's Geburtshaus." Of his eighteen brothers and sisters, but few lived to grow up.

humble dwelling, and nothing more was needed to make these teachers forget the fatigues of the day and the anxieties of the morrow. In the evening the father and his three eldest sons performed the trios or quartets of Beethoven. Franz, the youngest, who had received lessons from his father, took part in these concerts, and distinguished himself as much by the correctness with which he played as by the delicacy of his musical perceptions.[1] At ten years of age he was the admiration of his master, the old Holzer, who was surprised to find that he had nothing to teach to a child whose instinct went beyond instruction. At an early age, thanks to his fine soprano voice, he became soloist in the choir of a church. He was a member of the Conservatory, as we have already remarked; and we must add, that, in a short time from his admission, he figured in the school as violinist, and from time to time as leader of the music, when the teacher had occasion to be absent. Schubert studied composition; but, too poor to purchase a sufficient quantity of ruled paper,[2] he could not have written down many of his musical ideas without the aid of his friend, Joseph de Spaun, who afterward became one of his most faithful protectors. A letter that he wrote to one of his brothers may not be out of place while speaking of the destitute situation of our young artist.

"Let me tell you immediately what I have most at heart. I am right to the point; for I hate preambles. I have long reflected on my situation: as a whole, it is good; but it could be better. You know by experience, that it would be pleasant to have some white bread and

---

[1] It has been said that "Schubert entered upon music as a prince enters upon his dominions. What others toiled for, he won with little effort. Melody flowed from him like perfume from a rose: harmony was the native atmosphere he breathed."

[2] When but thirteen he consumed an enormous quantity of music-paper.

apples to eat between a middling sort of dinner and a very light supper. The desire to have them is becoming imperious. The few groschen that father gave me are gone : now, what am I to do ?

" *There is no shame in asking*, says St. Matthew. Could you get a few kreutzers for me ? Nothing would make me happier. Listen to him who implores, and remember your affectionate brother,

" FRANZ." [1]

Schubert studied with the court organist and with Salieri. Sometimes this latter wished to make him set Italian words to music, which produced a lively discussion between the master and the pupil, whose patriotism decided him in favor of his own language.[2]

Franz left the Conservatory, and went home in 1813, when his voice began to change. He accepted the situation of assistant teacher, rather than be a soldier. But teaching was very trying to his fine, delicate, and nervous organization ; and the paternal fireside had lost its charm in the death of his mother, whom he tenderly loved. His father married again, and Franz left home to give himself up exclusively to the cultivation of music. Although his music is everywhere known, Schubert never visited foreign countries ; but he travelled through Austria in company with his friend Vogel, the singer. Like the " minnesingers " of olden times, they visited different cities and towns, and were received and *fêted* everywhere, thanks to the songs of the one, and the beautiful voice of the other. Schubert, mild, gentle, without ambition, and without

[1] When this letter was written, Schubert was in a free school, where poor students were boarded as well as taught.

[2] Notwithstanding that Schubert refused to take any more lessons of Salieri, he was always grateful to him for his kindness and his instruction, whilst Salieri continued to love and watch over him with affectionate interest.

desires, lived exclusively for art, and gave himself up unreservedly to the lively sentiments of his nature, whilst he never had the least ability to change his music-papers into bank-notes. But publishers did good business with him, and why not? Had he not an inexhaustible source of enjoyment in his vivid imagination, in the transports with which the works of Haydn, Mozart, and Beethoven, inspired him, and in familiar intercourse with such minds as could understand and appreciate him? He sang: he was happy. Why should he trouble himself about money matters? A little more, a little less, what difference would it make?

The Viennese composer could say, " My songs and I are one." What a noble and touching image of the author do these songs present! How they show him to us with his sweet melancholy, lightly impregnated with mysticism![1] With all due respect to Schiller and Goethe,[2] let us say that it is lucky for their poetry that he adapted it to his melodies so full of strength, and grand in character. Both these poets could have done without him, it is true; but did not Schubert preserve the name of his friend Mayrhofer,[3] — a name that we should scarcely know at the present time, but for the great musician?

It is much to be regretted that an artist like Schubert should have passed away so soon. Probably the extraordinary excitement caused by his musical labors preyed upon his naturally robust constitution. He was literally

---

[1] "The important elements of Schubert's character were a love of truth and a marked hatred of jealousy, tenderness with firmness, sincerity, and affection, sociability, modesty, frankness, and a deep tinge of melancholy."

[2] Strange to say that Goethe did not even acknowledge the fifty of his songs which Schubert set to music, and sent to him.

[3] Mayrhofer, the poet, was one of Schubert's most intimate friends. "He was constantly writing poetry, which Schubert was constantly setting to music."

killed by inspiration. Schubert died at the early age of thirty-one years, of the fever by which he had produced his master-works. Laboring under physical sufferings, he worked with redoubled zeal, as if engaged in a contest for speed with death, of whose cold approach he was aware. But this continued fever of production soon exhausted him. He died Nov. 19, 1828, in the arms of his brother Ferdinand,[1] a year after Beethoven. It was Schubert's wish to be buried in the cemetery of Wahring, by the side of the composer whom he best loved.[2] He was so poor at his death,[3] that his friends were obliged to get up two concerts to pay his funeral expenses, and erect a monument.

Schindler tells us, that, when the great Beethoven was sick, some one presented him with a collection of about sixty of Schubert's songs, mostly in manuscript, to amuse him. They were fitting to his taste and genius, and afforded him much gratification : he recognized and appreciated the talent of the author, whom he ever after held in great esteem.

The great master, who, until then had known only some half-dozen of Schubert's songs, was surprised at their number, and could scarcely believe that Schubert, at his age, had written six hundred. Not their number alone, but their intrinsic value, struck him with admiration. "Truly," said he, "there must be a divine spark in this Schubert." He wished to see Schubert's piano music and his operas; but his disease made such rapid progress, that his wishes were not realized. He prophesied a brilliant

[1] Ten years after the composer's death, Schumann found his Ninth Symphony among some old papers in Ferdinand Schubert's house in Vienna.

[2] Beneath his bust is the following inscription : " Music buried here a rich possession and yet fairer hopes."

[3] " This rich prince of song left only a few coats, several handkerchiefs, and some old music.'

career for this artist, and regretted that he had not known him before.

The Count of Spaun had been a very generous protector to Schubert : it was he who assisted him in 1819, about the time that he brought out " Die Zwillinge," which merited more attention than it at first received.

Although Schubert was carried off in the flower of his age, he has left a very large number of works of all kinds ; but he excels in his beautiful songs, so much celebrated for their originality.

The number of his works is about one thousand, inclusive of the six hundred songs above mentioned. Schubert's theatrical music appeared just at the time when Rossini's music was in vogue, and therefore its lack of success. Of the fifteen operas of Schubert, only the " Enchanted Harp " and " Rosamond " were put upon the stage during his lifetime. Of his lyric works, the " Domestic War," an operette in one act, was put upon the stage in 1861 ; " Alfonso " was given at Weimar in 1854 ; and " Fierabras," which is considered the best dramatic work of Schubert, has never been put upon the stage.

His church-music, which is still performed at Vienna, is in great repute. He wrote six masses, two stabats, many offertories, and the great " Hallelujah " of Klopstock. One of his best symphonies was performed at Leipzig, under the direction of Mendelssohn, with great success. The music that Schubert composed for the piano brings to mind Beethoven's manner. The Fantasia, &c., dedicated to the Countess Esterhazy,[1] are brilliant works.

---

[1] The family Esterhazy were very kind to Schubert, whose music they highly appreciated. Unfortunately, however, he fell in love with Caroline, the youngest daughter, who, though she could not reciprocate his affection, continued to be a kind friend. " Had he not been so wedded to art, he would probably have been inconsolable as it was, there is no knowing how deeply his sensitive nature suffered from this disappointment in early love."

Many of his choral compositions have become popular in Germany.

When we reflect upon the vast number of pieces that Schubert wrote in about a dozen years, we are filled with astonishment at his prodigious facility. Naturally attracted by the genius of Goethe and Schiller, he set the greater part of their detached poetry to music. He was also very fond of Gallic poetry.

Schubert's nature was so impressionable, that what he read, what passed under his notice, changing scenery, &c., immediately rebounded within him; so that he found a note corresponding in force and truth to whatever presented itself.

No writer has gone farther in adapting the art of sound to the most delicate sentiments of the human soul. Schubert is the poet of music. Compared with him, other composers seem to have written in prose. In his works, the imagination is never isolated : it is always accompanied by sentiment. Thus it often is with ardent and tender souls, who passionately love nature, solitary walks on the borders of lakes, in the deep woods, or on the mountain heights : even the noise of the reeds invites to melancholy reveries ; and the pure mountain air does not allow the heart to beat for vulgar affections.

Schubert is not only one of the greatest musicians of Germany, but he is the melodious and faithful interpreter of all human sufferings, through the union of his musical inspiration with the deepest sentiments of the soul. Even his " Barcarolle " and the " Serenade," though written in a light and easy manner, are somewhat serious and melancholy. We feel that those who sing them are persons who, in other circumstances of their life, will also sing " Ave Maria," " The Young Mother," perhaps " Marguerite," and certainly the "Adieu." Schubert is the singer of grief.[1]

The letter which Schubert wrote to a dear friend in 1824 shows how despondent he was at times.

"You are so good and kind, you will forgive me much which others would take ill of me : in a word, I feel myself the most wretched and unhappy being in the world. Imagine a man whose health will never come right again, and who in his despair grows restless, and makes things worse, — a man whose brilliant hopes have all come to nought, to whom the happiness of love and friendship offers nothing but sorrow and bitterness, whom the feeling, the inspiring feeling at least, of the beautiful, threatens to abandon forever, and ask yourself whether such a one must not be miserable. Every night, when I go to sleep, I hope that I may never wake again ; and every morning renews the grief of yesterday. My affairs are going badly : we have never any money."

Schubert was poorly paid for the "Erl King ;" but the publisher realized a handsome sum at first, and thousands have since been made happy by it. Two years after Schubert's death, Madame Schröder Devrient sang it to Goethe, who was delighted with it.

---

[1] The titles Schubert gave to the compositions he wrote between the ages of eleven and sixteen seem like "prophetic shadows ;" for example, "A Complaint," "Hagar's Lament," "The Parricide," and "A Corpse Fantasia." The year 1815 is marked as the most prolific year of his life ; in it he produced nearly a hundred songs, half a dozen operas and operettes, symphonies, church-music, and chamber-music. Among these were some of his finest songs. The most popular of Schubert's works, the "Erl King," was composed in 1816. It is said that when Goethe's poem of the "Erl König" was shown to him, he read it over two or three times, and became so fascinated with it, that he immediately set it to music, so hurriedly indeed, that the very notes seem to tumble over one another. However, upon examining his writing, he, on a sudden, became disgusted with it, and threw it away among a pile of waste paper. Some days after, a friend withdrew the manuscript from the waste paper, played, and sang it Schubert pronounced it a fine song, but did not at first recognize it as his own.

" Schubert's masses and psalms possess all the breadth and sweetness of his secular works. The Twenty-third Psalm, for female voices, might be sung by a chorus of angels."

His songs have been divided into seven classes, viz., " Religious," " Supernatural," " Symbolical," " Classical," " Descriptive," " Songs of Meditation," " Songs of Passion."

MERCADANTE.

1797–1872.

SAVERIO MERCADANTE,[1] was born at Altamura, in the province of Bari, in 1797. At twelve years of age he entered the royal music-school of San Sebastiano, at Naples, then under the direction of Zingarelli, whose favorite pupil he soon became. He studied violin and flute, acquired the talent of a *virtuoso*, and soon published several compositions for these two instruments. He was, first, violinist, then leader of the orchestra, of the Conservatory. Obliged to work for his living, he was often more precipitate than careful in his compositions. In 1818 he wrote a cantata for the Theatre Del Fondo, in Naples, which pleased so much, that he received an order for the opera " L'Apoteosi d'Ercole " for the theatre of San Carlo, and " Violenza e Costanza " for the new theatre in Naples. His success increased with each new work, and he had the rare pleasure of seeing all the Italian theatres open to him.

He was called to Rome in 1820, where he brought out two works with great success ; but an opera which he offered at Bologna in 1821 was coldly received. However, he soon made up for this slight drawback by his " Elisa e

1 This composer is one of those who for the last half-century have filled Italy with their name and their works.

Claudio," performed at Milan in 1821. The score, the best that he had written until that time, raised him for the moment, by his too enthusiastic admirers, to the rank of Rossini.

This triumph was followed by reverses. Foui works, which he composed rapidly, were of little or no account. But Mercadante was not easily discouraged. His "Didone," given in 1823, was a brilliant triumph. After this he went to Vienna, where some of his first works were performed. While there, he rapidly composed "Doralice," "Le Nozze de Telemaco ed Antiope," and "Il Podestà di Burgos." On his return to Naples, the musical critics were very severe, accusing him of taking too little time for his compositions. However, success smiled upon him at Turin and at Venice in 1826, when he brought out "Nitocri" and" Donna Caritea."

In 1827 the manager of the Italian Theatre in Madrid proposed to Mercadante an engagement for seven years, with a salary of two thousand piastres yearly, on condition of having two new operas written especially for him. The artist accepted ; but, for some reason best known to himself, he returned to Italy at the end of the first year. However, he went there again, and remained until the close of the year 1829. Among his works performed in that city were "La Testa di Bronzo," and "Rappressaglia," an opera bouffe, which obtained great success. During a journey that he afterwards made in Italy, he recruited Italian singers for the theatre at Cadiz ; then he went to direct the music at Madrid, when he brought out "La Testa di Bronzo."

Mercadante returned to Naples in 1831, where he produced "Zaïra, and, the following year, "I Normanni in Parigi," which was successfully performed at Venice.

In the beginning of the year 1833, he accepted the situa‐
tion of chapel‐master of the Cathedral of Novara. But
this did not hinder him from working for the theatre,
bringing out "The Count of Essex," which, however, did
not succeed. The drama of "The Brigands," that fol‐
lowed, had been composed for Paris, and was performed
there in 1836, under the direction of Mercadante himself,
but with doubtful success, notwithstanding the eminent
artists who interpreted the work. "Il Sermone," a lyric
drama in four acts, has kept its own better, and had more
success in Italy, than any other of Mercadante's works.
The piece is an imitation of Victor Hugo's "Angelo."
The score is remarkable for the brilliancy of its instru‐
mentation, the skilful arrangement of its harmony, and that
of the voice parts. The most important part of the first
act is a beautiful andante for three voices. In the second
act is a charming chorus for women. This opera was
given with great success in 1858.

In 1839, at the Carnival season, Mercadante had an
attack of acute ophthalmia, which made him almost blind.
He retired to Novara, where he dictated his music, playing
the piano. He brought out "The Two Illustrious Rivals"
at Venice, which was received with great enthusiasm.
Through his reputation, and real scientific knowledge, he
was chosen to fill the office of director of the Conservatory
of Naples in 1840, where, during a space of thirty years, he
rendered great service by his science of harmony, and his
thorough knowledge of church‐music.

In 1842, after he had composed "Gabriella di Vergy,"
he went to Paris, to have "La Vestale" performed; but,
notwithstanding its beauties, it did not succeed.

In 1856 he was elected member of the Academy of Fine
Arts in Paris. After "La Vestale," he wrote a great

number of operas, which had more or less success. Mercadante's masses and motets, like the most of his other works, appear to be written for the singers, independent of the subject and the thought. However, he was an excellent teacher, and formed a great number of pupils for singing and composition.

He died in 1872. A few years before his death, he was completely blind.

DONIZETTI.

1798–1848.

DONIZETTI, endowed with real sensibility, and marvellous facility united with consummate talent in the art of writing, gave himself up to his natural inspiration for music. Taken as a whole, with his qualities and his faults, he is the most distinguished composer, after the incomparable Rossini, of which Italy can boast; and he knew best how to console musical Europe for the silence which the author of "William Tell" chose to keep. If we reflect upon the terrible blow which deprived him of reason before taking his life, we do not fail to recognize that Providence afforded him very little time to make himself equal to the princes of art; and yet he has given us four or five masterworks.

Gaëtano Donizetti was born at Bergamo, Sept. 25, 1798. His father, although possessing but a moderate fortune, and having a large family of children, did not fail to give Gaëtano a good classic education. Entering upon the stage of life, the young Gaëtano had to choose between three very different careers, — the bar, which the will of his father indicated; architecture, to which his taste for drawing seemed to fit him ; and music, towards which a secret voice, the voice of destiny, impelled him.   Fate had decided that he should be a composer ; and music over-powered her two potent rivals.   In 1815 his father sent him to Bologna, that he might have the benefit of the instruction of Pilotti and Father Mattei.   After three years' study, he returned to Bergamo with a goodly number of compositions.   Then his father tried to dissuade him from writing for the theatre, and proposed that he should give his undivided attention to sacred music as the highest branch of his profession.   But Donizetti had no inclina-tion for such heights of musical science, though he wrote two or three masses to gratify his father, after which he determined to write operas, and operas only.

Rather than do that for which he had not the least taste, and annoyed by his father's persistence, the hasty young man chose to enlist as a soldier, thinking to find opportunities, in the leisure of a garrison life, for his beloved music.   While at Venice, whither his regiment had been sent, he wrote his first operas, " Enrico di Borgogna," and " Il Falegname di Livonia," which were put upon the stage, and so far successful, that they procured him friends by whose influence he was freed from military service.

He now commenced writing with a facility which aston-ished even the Italians, a nation accustomed to the wonders of improvisation.   In the short space of ten years, he wrote twenty-eight operas, among which were " Olivo e Pasquale," " Le Convenienze Teatrali," " Il Bor-gomestro di Saardam," " Gianni di Calais," " L'Esule di Roma," " Il Castello di Kenilworth," " Imelda de' Lam-bertazzi."   Donizetti was so poorly paid for his composi-tions, that he was really obliged to write as much as possible in order to gain a livelihood : therefore we need

not be surprised that he did not always wait for inspiration, and that crude ideas often fell from his pen. It was
not until 1831 that a visible improvement was manifest in
his works,[1] and that the individuality of the composer
shone forth. Until this time he had only been the more
or less happy follower of Rossini ; now he traced out a
path for himself, outside of that which his glorious predecessor followed, and showed us his own power in the opera
of "Anna Bolena," which was brought out at Milan, and
gained him great credit in Italy. In 1832 he composed,
among other things, "L'Elisire d'Amore," an opera bouffe,
likewise a good work, which he is said to have composed
in fifteen days.[2] Then followed, in rapid succession, "Il
Furioso," "Parisina," "Torquato Tasso," and "Lucrezia
Borgia ; " in 1834, "Gemma di Vergi." Donizetti then
went to Paris, where he brought out "Marino Faliero," in
1835,[3] but it did not receive merited appreciation beside
Bellini's "I Puritani." However, he was fully compensated by the favor with which "Lucia di Lammermoor,"
written also in 1835, was received at Naples, where he was
appointed to a professorship in the Royal Musical School.

The death of Bellini, and the silence of Rossini, left the
author of "Lucia" without a rival. The directors of
Paris turned their eyes to the only Italian master then
in the field ; and Donizetti, whose scores were having
brilliant success, put the first opera which he had really
composed for the French upon the stage in 1840. This
was "La Fille du Régiment," a delightful opera in two
acts. The history is that of a poor child, abandoned upon

[1] In this year he brought out "Anna Bolena" at Milan.
[2] Donizetti married a Roman lady in 1833.
[3] "His wife, to whom he was fondly attached, died of cholera in 1835. Their two
children died in infancy. It is supposed that he worked as he did at that time to
drown his sorrow, and rid himself of the remembrance of his former happiness."

the field of battle, taken by a brave and good man, Sergeant Sulpice, and adopted by his regiment. Madame Sontag, the well-known singer, had left the stage on her marriage with Count Rossi : but reverses of fortune induced her to return ; and this opera afforded a good opportunity for her re-appearance.

In 1841 Donizetti wrote " Maria Padilla," for the theatre in Milan. In 1842 he brought out "Linda di Chamounix," in Vienna, which was received with great enthusiasm, and gained for him the distinguished title of Hofkapellmeister.

In 1843 Donizetti returned to Paris with the opera " Don Pasquale." At its rehearsal, the musicians of the orchestra presaged its fall ; and the managers of the theatre appeared to be of the same opinion. However, they were mistaken ; for its success was complete.

At this point the task of the biographer becomes very sad. He has no longer to speak of dramatic success, but of the sure and unconquerable progress of a disease which attacked the mind of the artist before exhausting his body. Donizetti, an incessant worker, overseer of his operas on twenty different stages, had to suffer the penalty which all must suffer who overtax their brain. That which made his glory caused his ruin, viz., the excessive tension of creative activity, the uneasiness of genius. If he could have been persuaded to take absolute rest, he might have driven away, at least for a time, the effects of the sad disease that had warned him in 1843. But how can a man to whom labor has become an actual want be condemned to rest ? On the contrary, the composer worked with a zeal which made it seem as if he anticipated the coming of the scourge which was in a short time to deprive him of all power.

It is reported, that, during one of the rehearsals of "Don Sebastien," Donizetti was heard to say to one of his friends, "Don Sebastien" will be the death of me. He said the truth. But when such a worker, with such a genius, has to lay his pen aside, it is because his hand refuses to wield it. In 1844 he gave an opera at Naples, the bad success of which had an injurious effect upon his health. Then he went to Vienna, where his duties as chapel-master required his presence ; but he could no longer attend to the court music, undermined as he was by the nervous affection that was daily becoming more alarming. On his return to Paris, in 1845, he set himself to work with renewed ardor. His friends visited him as usual ; and several of them, in listening to his conversation, supposed that his health and faculties were perfectly restored.

In the mean time, the composer was attending to a new score, and to the remodelling of one of his youthful operas, which the Italian Theatre was upon the eve of accepting. He applied himself severely to this double task, when this strain of work brought on the finishing stroke. He was attacked by paralysis on the 17th of August, and lost his beautiful mind,[1] — a mind of which he had made such valuable use. In January, 1846, he was placed in an insane asylum at Ivry, where he received all the succor which science could bestow. In vain the celebrated Dr. Blanche strove to cure : the insanity of Donizetti defied all the resources of art. Then it was hoped that his native air, the mild influence of the Italian climate, might have some miraculous power over him. His nephew and a faithful servant took him to Bergamo

---

[1] He was insane during 1844-47. He wrote the entire score of an opera in thirty hours. It is no wonder that exciting, "constant, and rapid composition should have affected his brain."

in 1848.   But Donizetti returned to the city of his birth to die.[1]   He expired April 8, 1848, in the arms of his brother.   The inhabitants of the Peninsula were then at war with the Austrians ; and, by a strange coincidence, the bells that sounded the knell of the great composer mingled their lugubrious notes with the sounds of the cannon fired to celebrate the victory of Goïto.

Two posthumous works of Donizetti have been performed at Paris, — "Elizabeth," an opera in three acts, the subject of which is the affecting history, related by Mme. Cottin, of a young girl who went from the centre of Siberia to St. Petersburg to beg the pardon of her exiled father.   This work met a warm reception by the public. The other work is a comic opera in one act, which was given at Paris in 1860.

Clément says, "The partisans of future music who have not respected Rossini will not fail to attack Donizetti. Those who have treated Rossini with irreverence would like to give us a languishing *mélopée*, entirely orchestral and descriptive, in place of those touching airs, duos, and trios, which, after having enchanted us on the stage, still charm us in the concert and drawing rooms.[2]   But we leave theories while we appreciate and admire the gifts of genius and of a fine artistic organization, without being influenced by the wisdom of the so-called musicians of the future."

Donizetti's best works sparkle with piquant and gracefully florid melodies, such as suit and please the different kinds of voices.

[1] The composer was a warm, kind-hearted, and generous man.   He wrote the operette "Il Campanello" for the benefit of the poor singers of a theatre in Naples.

[2] Donizetti wrote sixty-four operas, besides a mass of other music, such as cantatas, ariettas, duets, church-music, &c., in the short space of twenty-six years.

HALÉVY.

1799–1862.

IF, in France, a contemporary of Louis XIV., an admirer of Racine, could return to us, and, full of the remembrance of his earthly career under that renowned sovereign, he should wish to find the nobly pathetic, the elevated inspiration, the majestic arrangements of the olden times, upon a modern stage, we would not take him to the French Theatre, but to the opera on the day in which one of Halévy's works was given.

Fromental Halévy belonged to that Israelitish race, which, but recently emancipated, has rapidly taken prominent places in arts and sciences. The patience of this race, its domestic qualities, and its own tolerance, enable it to understand and appreciate the benefits of civil equality. Thus it is with the great composer whose life we are about to sketch, and who, with a mind naturally elevated and religious, wrote as much for the Catholic as for the Jewish worship.

Born at Paris, May 27, 1799, he manifested great love of music while yet in his most tender years. He was sent to the Conservatory, and entered the solfeggio class at the age of ten years. In 1810 he studied the piano; then Cherubini gave him five years' instruction in counterpoint. The future author of the "Jewess" was hardly twenty when the institute awarded him the grand prize for the composition of a cantata. The young laureate received a government pension, dwelt at Rome for two years, and during the time employed himself assiduously in the development of his talent. Returning to France, he had to contend with the difficulties of a debutant, which **were** not a few, even though he had received the prize at Rome. After several years, in which all his undertakings seemed fruitless, he almost gave up the idea of bringing out an opera. It was not until 1827 that he became known to the public through an opera in one act: this was soon followed by many others, in which the master had scattered many brilliant gems; but no one for a moment supposed that he would at some future day rival the favorite Rossini.

Halévy's advance to glory was signalized by the "Jewess," which surpasses all his other works by its grand, passionate, and touching inspiration. It was performed Feb. 23, 1835, with unusually lavish and luxurious decorations and costumes. The managers of the opera expended one hundred and fifty thousand francs in putting it on the stage; and they were useless expenses, for the work did not require so much magnificence in order to obtain the unanimous applause its merits demanded.

Yet the envious and the powerless did not fail in their usual attacks. They declaimed against the magisterial work with which the composer had enriched the lyric repertory, attributing the success of the opera to the splendid manner in which it was put upon the stage. Halévy replied to their attacks by another opera, in three acts, "L'Eclair," which was performed the same year, and still increased the reputation of its author. It is so graceful, light, and expressive, that it may be considered the best that the master has written in this sort of comic opera, and has never been taken from the repertory.

Halévy left the theatre for about two years, then he returned with an opera in five acts; but, unfortunately, this score, though worked out with the utmost care, was connected with a dull and sad, rather than dramatic poem,

which proved a drawback to its success. The failure of
"Treize" and of "Schérif" was owing to the same cause.
It is very rare that bold originality is accepted without
resistance. Involuntarily one endeavors to put himself
upon his guard against an innovator, though forced to
surrender afterwards. In the present case, the *habitués*
of the comic opera could but acknowledge that the harmonic combinations of both these operas were rich and
powerful beyond what they were accustomed to hear.

In 1841 the artist made a brilliant stroke with the
"Reine de Chypre." Here the poem is not wanting in
literary merit, and the score is brilliant. It is said that
one of the singers, every time he came to the passage, —

> "Ce mortel qu'on remarque
> Tient-il
> Plus que nous de la Parque
> Le fil?"

whether accidentally or intentionally, fixed his eyes upon
the proscenium-box, which was generally occupied by the
notabilities of politics and of finance. As several of these
personages died during the first run of the "Reine de
Chypre," superstitious people imagined that the singer
was bewitched, and consequently avoided that box.

The opera of "Charles VI." soon followed. Political
circumstances, of which we are unable to judge, for a
long time prevented the repetition of this opera. It is sad
to think that the admirers of Halévy were condemned to
wait for a war to break out between England and France,
before they could be permitted to hear that magnificent
score again.

"Le Val d'Andorre," a lyric drama performed in 1848,
is filled with heart-rending scenes. If the gayety of the
recruiter is amusing enough, the despair of poor Rosa

when her betrothed is taken by conscription, the conflict of her emotions between love and duty, her uneasiness and remorse in consequence of a theft she has committed, fill us with painful impressions that are not dissipated until the young girl is again under the care of her mother.

In 1849 Halévy brought out some scenes from "Prometheus in Chains," the music for which he had written from a translation by his brother. In this composition the artist proposed to reproduce the presumed effects of the enharmonic style of the Greeks, — a very bold attempt, which did not succeed, for want of proper stringed instruments.

The master was very kindly received by the inhabitants of London in the year 1850, when his Italian opera, "The Tempest," was performed at the Queen's Theatre. The subject is taken from Shakspeare. Balfe directed the orchestra. The success of this opera caused Lablache to write the following, —

> "The Tempest of Halévy
> Differs from other tempests :
> These rain hail ;
> That rains gold."

In 1854 Halévy, who had entered the Institute in 1836, was elected secretary of the Academy of Fine Arts. These new duties gave him an opportunity to show that he knew how to use his pen to write other things than music. In his eulogiums of great men, he displayed much literary ability. But to be able to appreciate foreign artists as a specialty could not have been a difficult task for him, whose house was a sort of museum, where the masterpieces of artists of different nations were well represented. Statuary and painting were, with melody, his favorite guests. However, in the midst of the labors imposed

upon him by his colleagues, Halévy did not forget the
theatre. He produced a number of operas, all of which
were favorably received. The author of the " Jewess "
astonished his friends by the vigor of his moral faculties
when the change in his countenance, and the perceptive
decrease of his strength, caused them very justifiable
anxiety. The physicians advised his dwelling at the
south. The Parisians at Nice received the illustrious
invalid with all the regard due to his glory, and the sympathy that his position inspired. Not a Sunday passed
while he was in Nice, that the band of the garrison did
not perform some of the beautiful airs of his operas on
the public promenade, — a touching homage, as honorable
for him who was the object of it as for those whose
thoughtfulness prompted it.

Alas! neither the solicitude of the whole populace, nor
the anxious and tender cares of a family who adored its
head, could prolong his life. Halévy died at Nice, March
17, 1862. He had always preferred conversing upon literature and philosophy; but, when he drew near his end,
he seemed to choose the expressions and figures which
recalled the art he loved so well. One evening he tried to
take a book that lay upon a table a little beyond his
reach. " Can I do nothing now *in tune?* " he said to his
daughter, as she handed him the book. Even on the
morning of his death, he made a more unexpected, odd,
and touching application of the musical language so dear
and so familiar to him. He was seated upon a couch,
and wished to stretch himself, and place his head upon the
cushion; but he could not do it unassisted. His daughters
came. " Lay me down like a *gamut*," he said. They
understood his wants, and moved him softly, slowly, and
as if in measure. At each movement, he said, smiling,

do, re, mi, fa, sol, la, until his head was lain upon the cushion.   These notes served him for the last time : they were
the last he uttered.

At the present time we can place Halévy in the first
rank of those who have charmed, elevated, and consoled
humanity by their art, thus fulfilling their glorious mission.
Halévy said that music is an art that God has given us, in
which the voices of all nations may unite their prayers in
one harmonious rhythm.

An extract from the great critic Sainte-Beuve may not
be out of place here : —

" Halévy had a natural gift for writing, which he cultivated and perfected by study, by a taste for reading, that
he always gratified in the intervals of labor, in his study,
in public conveyances, everywhere, in fine, when he had a
minute to spare.   He could isolate himself completely in
the midst of the various noises of the family, or the conversation of the drawing-room, if he had no part in it.   He
wrote music, poetry, and prose, and he read with imperturbable attention, while people were around him talking.

" He possessed the instinct of languages ; was familiar
with German, Italian, English, and Latin ; knew something
of Hebrew and Greek.   He was conversant with etymolo-
gy, and had a perfect passion for dictionaries.   It was
often difficult for him to find a word ; for on opening the
dictionary somewhere near the word for which he was
looking, if his eye chanced to fall upon some other, no
matter what, he stopped to read that, then another, and
another, until he sometimes forgot the word which he
sought.   It is singular that this estimable man, so fully
occupied, should at times have nourished some secret
sadness.   Whatever the hidden wound might be, none, not
even his most intimate friends, knew what it was.   He

never made any complaint. Halévy's nature was rich, open, and communicative. He was well organized, accessible to the sweets of sociability and family joys ; in fine, he had, as one may say, too many strings to his bow to be very unhappy for any length of time.

"To define him practically, I would say he was a bee that had not lodged himself completely in his hive, but was seeking to make honey also elsewhere.

"Had Halévy lived, he would, without doubt, have been named to the French Academy. M. Villemain touched upon the subject one day. Halévy's face lighted up for a moment ; but the expression of pleasure immediately disappeared : he feared it might be prejudicial to his well-beloved elder brother."

"La Juive," "Guido," "La Reine de Chypre," "Charles VI.," are real lyric tragedies, marked with the seal of ineffaceable beauties. Some less perfect productions, more easy to be understood by the crowd, have enjoyed greater popularity ; but the suffrage of connoisseurs is the only one which interests a conscientious artist, and Halévy obtained a good share of that. We do not think we are mistaken in saying that the popularity of Halévy will increase as musical education becomes more generally diffused.

BELLINI.

1802–1835.

It has often been asked whether talent is a gratuitous gift, or the fruit of long study ; but no satisfactory answer can be given to such a question ; for in most cases the human mind is like a soil, more or less fertile. Study is

the plough which works the soil ; and the master is the
laborer who guides it in the furrows.   One thing, however,
is very certain ; and that is, that, among artists, some owe
most to labor, and others to nature.   Bellini ranks among
the last ; for nature had richly endowed him.

Vincenzo Bellini was born at Catania in Sicily, Nov. 3,
1802.   He early displayed great musical talents, and
received a good musical education.   Although the Conservatory of Naples was then considered the best place in
the world for learning to write music, Bellini profited little
from the instruction he there received.   His nervous and
tender organization, and his peculiarities of character, disinclined him from the hard discipline of classic study.   It
was no easy matter for him to learn the method of instrumentation, although he wrote fifteen symphonies, three
masses, and a great number of pieces for flute, clarinet,
and piano.   However, his true vocation manifested itself
in his dramatic music.   In 1824 he wrote " Adelson and
Bianca " for the college theatre, and in 1826 " Bianca and
Fernando " for the Theatre San Carlo.   The king, who was
present at this latter representation, displayed the greatest
enthusiasm for the young artist.   As is often the case in
the history of arts, the people wanted something new, and,
beginning to be tired of Rossini's music, were pleased with
that of Bellini, even if it were less perfect.   Besides, it
seemed that some good genius had presided over the birth
of Bellini, and had taken care to smooth life's way for
him.[1]

At the outset, he conquered the lyric stage of Southern

---

[1] Bellini was affable, honest, sincere, modest, and affectionate.   Favored by
nature with noble and regular features, a delicate complexion, large, clear blue eyes,
and abundance of light hair, he could not fail to find favor in the eyes of all lovers
cf the beautiful and the good.

Italy. Then when called to Milan, as if fortune watched over him, on leaving Naples he met the poet whose inspiration was best suited to his music. We all know, that, for an opera to be good, words and music must harmonize, composer and poet must sympathize in ideas and feelings. For want of this necessary union, many a good score has failed to please. Therefore Bellini was fortunate in meeting with Felice Romani,[1] a writer whose sweet and melancholy verses agreed so well with his music. Their first work was "Il Pirata," an opera in two acts, performed at the Theatre of La Scala in Milan, during the winter of 1827. It was represented at the Italian Theatre in Paris, 1832, where it was well received, and brought Bellini into good repute. This very original work soon made the tour of Europe. "La Straniera," put upon the stage of Milan in 1828, was equally successful with "Il Pirata;" and Bellini could say with Lulli, "I am persuaded that my music pleases; for I hear it everywhere among the populace."

In 1830 "I Capuleti ed i Montecchi" was represented at Venice. The succession of tender, pathetic, and terrible scenes in this well-known Shakspearian play could not be fully carried out by Bellini, who lost as much in the tragic and funereal as he gained in the tender and melancholy parts.

The productions of which we have spoken are not of the sort that immortalize their authors. Although several of them gained popular favor, and were quite in vogue, they were not calculated for lasting success, or braving the wear of time. However, in the year 1831, Bellini pro-

---

[1] Romani was professor of belles-lettres for fifteen years in his native city of Geneva. He was much in vogue with the celebrated musicians of his time, and wrote for Rossini, Mercadante, Donizetti, &c.

duced two operas which sealed his reputation, and preserved his name among artists. They were "La Sonnambula" and "La Norma." The first, brought out in Milan, 1831, displayed the measure of his faculties; for it showed the tenderness and delicacy of this melodic genius.

In the "Sonnambula," the instrumentation is somewhat neglected; but the melody is effective. The elegiac part is touching; and all the scenes in the work are interesting, although the general coloring is rather monotonous. Bellini did not, like Rossini, possess the double privilege of excelling in the *genre* bouffe and the *genre* serious at the same time. Madame Pasta, who took the part of Sonnambula, also took that of Norma. There is little doubt but that Bellini had the image of the great tragedian present to his mind's eye while writing these, his best of scores. In this subject the composer sought no local color: he did better in giving it an original, strange, and picturesque character, without changing its nationality.

The opinion of those who consider Norma as Bellini's *chef-d'œuvre* is confirmed by himself. One day, when he was in Paris, a lady asked him which of his operas he considered the best. The question was embarrassing, and his answer evasive. The lady persisted, "But if you were out at sea with all your scores, and should be shipwrecked"— "Ah!" he cried, without allowing her to finish, "I would leave all the rest, and try to save 'Norma.'"

In 1834 he wrote "I Puritani"[1] for the Italian Theatre in Paris, — an opera which was much admired on account of its dramatic truthfulness, choice instrumentation, and carefulness in the arrangement and finish of single parts.

---

[1] The order of the Legion of Honor was awarded to the composer after "I Puritani" was brought out.

It was brought out by a splendid troop, viz., Grisi, Rubini,[1] Tamburini, and Lablache. The managers of the grand opera of Paris, and those of the opera of Naples, each desired a score ; and Bellini retired to a country-seat at Puteaux, near Paris, that he might write them more at his leisure. However, he was soon seized by an intestinal malady, which carried him off Sept. 23, 1835, in his thirty-third year.

From what has already been said of the works of Bellini, it is easy to have a general idea of the character of his music. The great difference between him and Rossini is, that the latter amplified his pieces, whilst Bellini made short, melodic, and concentrated phrases, which the public easily understood.

Bellini was not a genuis in the strict sense of the word. Though excellent in the *cantabile*, thanks to his sensibility, he failed in grand scenes. The finale of some of his pieces is noisy without being dramatic, and in this respect he was the precursor of Verdi.

Bellini's death was a great loss, not only in the musical world, but to the crowd of admirers who had learned to appreciate his character. This eminent composer was the spoiled child of fortune, and we can but praise him for his simplicity and modesty even in the height of success. He knew nothing of those intrigues, which, for many artists, are but auxiliaries to their talent. Finally he made himself

---

[1] Great singers though they were, Bellini was not disposed to allow them to sing his music as they liked, as is proved by the following anecdote.

The celebrated Rubini, rehearsing Gualtiero with the *maestro*, failed to produce the desired effect, whereupon the latter, losing his patience, exclaimed, 'You put no life into your music. Show some feeling. Don't you know what love is?" Then, changing his tone, he continued, " Don't you know that your voice is a gold-mine that has not been fully explored? You are an excellent artist ; but that is not sufficient. You must forget yourself, and represent Gualtiero. Let's try again." They did so ; and Rubini sang to the entire satisfaction of the composer.

beloved at a time when he had glory enough to be only admired.

"Bellini, naturally melancholy, became more so in consequence of disappointment in love. The father of the lady to whom he offered himself, a Neapolitan judge, objected to Bellini's social position. Afterwards, however, when Bellini became known as the celebrated composer, the judge wished to make amends ; but Bellini was too proud to listen to him. Soon after the young lady, who really loved Bellini, died of a broken heart ; and Bellini never recovered from the shock produced by her death."

LORTZING.

1803–1851.

Gustav Albert Lortzing was born at Berlin, Oct. 23, 1803. His parents educated him for the stage. In 1812 he performed children's parts ; yet his inclination led him to prefer music, which he had studied in his course of preparation for an actor. 1819–22 he performed at Dusseldorf and Aachen. In 1824 he wrote his first opera, " Ali-pascha von Janina," which he brought out at the Court Theatre in Detmold. From Detmold, he went to the theatre at Leipzig in 1833, where he won the respect of the public as a man, and their applause as an artist.

His opera " Czar and Zimmermann " was performed in all the German theatres within six months of its first appearance.

Besides the above mentioned, Lortzing wrote many other operas, all of which were successful. His vaudevilles and detached pieces, particularly for flute and piano, on which instruments he was an excellent performer, are everywhere admired. He died at Berlin, 1851.

BERLIOZ.

1803-1869.

HECTOR BERLIOZ was born at La-Côte-Saint-André in the department of l'Isère, Dec. 11, 1803. His father, a physician, intending to have him follow the same career, sent him to Paris to prepare for it. But the young disciple of Æsculapius, whose taste was for music and nothing else, soon gave up the course of the faculty, preferring that of the Conservatory. His father, disappointed and angry, left him to provide for himself. He then engaged to sing in the choruses of a minor theatre, besides which he gave lessons on the flute and violin. In short, he left his medical studies for those of composition under Reicha. Very soon his artistic nature, inimical to restraint, began to manifest itself; and he left his teacher, resolving to follow his own course, although his knowledge of the art of writing was very limited. At that time, just previous to 1830, every thing was in a feverish state of excitement. A wind of intellectual renovation pervaded society. The dramatic world was divided into two parties by the quarrels of the classic and the romantic. The painter Delacroix, braving the anathemas of the school of David, introduced unheard-of boldness of color and movement into his paintings. How, then, could music escape the universal change? Berlioz was verily the man of his times when he undertook a musical revolution; for there was a revolution in politics, literature, philosophy, and religion. His first essay, when he was twenty-two years old, was a mass with orchestra, executed at the churches of St. Roch and St. Eustache. It pleased neither performers nor listeners, who declared it to be wholly unintelligible. However, Berlioz was not to be discouraged by the opinion of others ; for, according to his idea, music needed renovating, and he knew, at least, how to commence the renovation.

Berlioz, who had re-entered the Conservatory since 1826, obtained the first prize for composition in 1830, for a *cantata*, the subject of which was " Sardanapalus."

Soon after, he was sent to Italy to pursue his studies as government stipendiary ; but living in Italy did not modify his æsthetic ideas ; and the two productions that he carried to Rome — viz., an overture to " King Lear," and a symphony entitled " Le Rétour à la Vie "— fully displayed the energy of his reformatory tendencies.[1]

Berlioz, who wrote musical criticisms, paid those who attacked him, in their own coin. He had published several articles upon the symphonies of Beethoven ; and he wrote successively for several papers, which did not prevent his writing a great many works, all of which excited the musical public either for or against him, according to their various standpoints, but left no one entirely indifferent.

If the romantic composer met with more ill than good will in his own country, he was more than compensated by the admiration which musical Germany professed for him. In 1841, while making the tour of Germany, he was kindly received at Leipzig by Mendelssohn,[2] with whom he was somewhat acquainted ; and the two artists are said to have exchanged their conductors' bâtons as keepsakes.

[1] About this time he married Miss Smithson, an English actress.

[2] "Dear Berlioz, I thank you heartily for your pleasant letter, and am rejoiced that you still remember our old friendship in R me. I shall never forget it in my life, and shall be glad to talk it over with you. Every thing that I can do to make your stay in Leipzig agreeable to you, I shall make 't equally my duty and pleasure to do. I believe I can assure you that you will be happy here, and be satisfied with artists and the public. I charge you to come as soon as you can leave Weimar. I shall rejoice to give you my hand, and to bid you welcome to Germany. I shall always be your own Felix Mendelssohn Bartholdy."

During his stay in Austria, Berlioz wrote the "Damnation of Faust,"[1] a sort of oratorio, afterwards performed at the Opera Comique, Paris. This work, the words of which as well as the music were written by Berlioz, tested the musical ability of the master, and the result of his theories. It was in vain that the master did his best to rid himself of the rules of composition, which had been fully established by the princes of art during the last three centuries: he could neither free himself always nor entirely from the effect of his musical education. Protest as much as he would, he was always sure to find himself on the grand route, and in good company, in spite of his theories.

"The Damnation of Faust" was too full of oddities to succeed with the French public.[2] Offered to the *dilettanti* of Vienna in 1866, it excited wild admiration. A curious anecdote shows to what excess of musical enthusiasm some Germans may be wrought. At the end of the concert in which Berlioz himself had led the orchestra, a very enthusiastic amateur seized the conductor's bâton, which he hid under his coat. Berlioz perceived the theft, stopped the man, and said, "Ah, sir! I am willing to give you my bâton, but I do not wish you to take it." The amateur was obliged to confess, and give up the coveted object. Berlioz then presented it to him, saying, "Now, sir, have the goodness to accept it." Our musical genius marched off triumphantly, twice happy in having the bâton, and having it from the hand of the artist himself. Age and experience have the virtue of smoothing and softening down. Berlioz did not escape. "L'Enfance du Christ" gave signs of a return to received method, and

[1] Then followed "L'Enfance du Christ," a "Te Deum" for two choirs in 1856, "Beatrice et Bénédict," 1862, "Les Troyens à Carthage," 1864, &c

[2] Though French by birth, Berlioz was quite German in taste

was appreciated by his contemporaries, because so much better understood than his other music. Still greater was the change in the "Trojans," an opera in five acts, of which Berlioz wrote the words himself. It was represented Nov. 4, 1863. In this work are found the traces of the system of imitative and literary work to which Berlioz applied himself with so much ardor; but the score is appreciated as a beautiful, original, and conscientious work should be. Let us add, that on account of the simplicity and grandeur of the situations, of which the Æneid furnished the subject, the presenting it upon the lyric stage was a delicate and bold undertaking ; and it required much taste and judgment to personate the characters as engraved upon the mind of the college student : however, our composer succeeded in this also. He was certainly no ordinary artist who dared to expose himself to the ostracisms of directors and the astonishment of the public, rather than go out of his own way. He had great qualities that excited admiration, united to a character which commands esteem. Besides the articles he wrote for journals, he left quite a number of works on music, together with a great variety of musical compositions. He was a member of the Academy of Fine Arts from 1856.

Berlioz is thought by some writers to be one of the first musical geniuses of his time, by others as having fine taste and good understanding, with a peculiar weakness concerning his own talents. Yet all parties agree in acknowledging him to be an able composer as well as a good writer. He was the author of " Voyage Musical en Allemagne et en Italie," " Les Soirées de l'Orchestre," " Les Grotesques de la Musique," " A Travers Chant,' and " Traité d'Instrumentation."

He died in 1869, aged sixty-six years.

LACHNER.

1804–.

FRANZ LACHNER was born in 1804 at Rain in Bavaria. His father, an organist, perceiving that the little Franz manifested great musical gifts, had him early instructed in music. He sent him to Nuremberg and to Munich, where he studied composition with Winter. Afterwards he went to Vienna, and became acquainted with the most prominent artists of the city, among whom was the Abbé Stadler, whose counsels were of great service to him. He read all the best works pertaining to music ; so that "to the talent of a skilful executant on the organ, piano, and violin, he added the merits of great erudition."

In 1835 a prize was offered at Vienna for the best symphony : it was awarded to Lachner for his "Sinfonia Passionata." In the same year he was appointed chapel-master to the King of Bavaria. Among Lachner's principal works are, "The Four Ages of Man," an oratorio "Moïse," also an oratorio, and several symphonies.

COSTA.

1804–.

MICHAEL COSTA, the Italian composer, was born at Naples, February, 1804. When very young, he was sent to the Conservatory of his native city, under the celebrated Tritto. He made his *début* by a cantata "L'Imagine," and by "Il Delitto punito," after which he entered one of the small Italian theatres as composer and director of the orchestra. His first work, "Malvina," performed at St. Carlc in 1828, was unsuccessful. Costa then went to

England, and assisted at the Birmingham Festival. In 1831 he was appointed leader of the orchestra of the Royal Theatre, in place of Bochsa. From 1831 to 1833 he brought three ballets upon the stage, viz., "Kenilworth," "Une Heure à Naples," and "Sir Huon." In January, 1837, our artist attempted to bring out his "Malvina" again, under the title of "Malek-Adel," at the Theatre des Italiens, in Paris. But in spite of the efforts of Lablache, Rubini, Tamburini, and Grisi, it met with no better success: however, it was afterwards performed in London. June 29, 1844, Costa put his "Don Carlos" upon the stage. This work, considered his masterpiece, had complete success.

A disagreement arising between Costa and the director of the Queen's Theatre, the former helped to establish a second Italian opera-house at Covent Garden. He became leader of the orchestra, and identified himself with the new opera. He was followed by many of the musicians of the Queen's Theatre, and sustained by them in the contest which arose between the two parties. In 1856 he brought out his oratorio "Eli," at the Birmingham Festival: its success was immense. Thereupon his admirers, among whom was Lord Willoughby, presented him with a magnificent piece of silver. In 1864 a new oratorio, "Naaman," also performed at Birmingham, was received with like favor. In 1869 Costa was knighted by the queen. He directed nearly all the musical festivals in England, was leader of the Royal Italian Opera, and director of the Royal Concerts.

HERZ.
1806-.

HENRI HERZ, the celebrated pianist, was born at Vienna in 1806. He studied at Coblentz, under his father's guidance. He played in public when he was but eight years old ; and, before he was nine, he composed his first sonata for the piano. In 1816 he obtained the first prize at the Conservatory in Paris, after which his reputation grew rapidly. In 1818 he published "L'Air Tyrolien varié," and the "Rondo alla Cosacca." His great success dates from his acquaintance with Moscheles, whose influence tended to improve his manner of playing. His works for piano were in great demand ; and publishers paid more for his manuscripts than for those of any other composer for the piano. They were reprinted in Belgium, Germany, England, Italy, and afterwards in America. The best of the hundred works which he has published are his three concertos for piano with orchestra ; a trio for piano, violin, and violoncello ; "Rondo brilliant," dedicated to Moscheles ; fantasia (for four hands) in "Guillaume Tell ;" variations on "Norma," &c. He has also written a method for pianoforte. In 1831 Herz gave concerts in Germany, and in 1834 in England, with good success. In 1846–47 Herz gave concerts in America. The music of Herz attracts by its brilliancy, polish, and elegance.

BALFE.
1808–1870.

MICHAEL WILLIAM BALFE was born in Dublin, May 15, 1808. His father, — a good violinist, and passionate lover of music, — delighted to discover in his little son Michael an aptitude for his favorite pursuit, did not fail to teach him the rudiments of music as early as possible.

At the age of seven the boy composed a polacca for a band, which was duly performed. The executants could hardly believe that it was the composition of a little child.

For six years from the period when he gave indisputable proofs of the genius born in him, young Balfe studied assiduously.

His father died in 1823 ; and the boy of fifteen was left as the stay and protector of his widowed mother and her little family.

Michael felt the pressing necessity of immediate exertion; but what was he to do ? Go to London ? Yes : there he would find an open field for his talent. Whilst ruminating upon the possibility of getting there, his eye rested on a play-bill, notifying the public that Mr. Horn, the celebrated singer, was to appear for the last time, that evening, previous to his departure for England. " What if he would take me with him ? " thought the boy ; and away he ran to the stage-door, sent his name to Mr. Horn, was admitted to his dressing-room. " Mad as the thought might seem that had thus worked itself into action, there was method in it, nevertheless ; for children are close reasoners, even in their childish dreams." Questioned as to the cause of his visit, he answered in such a straightforward manner, that the kind-hearted singer did not hesitate to accede to his proposition ; and the next morning Michael William was on his way to the goal of his ambition. Although Mrs. Balfe had bound her son to Horn for seven years, he usually gave the lad perfect liberty of action, only contenting himself by taking the part of adviser and friend. He introduced Michael into good society, and afforded him every opportunity for study and improvement.

Balfe's fame as a youthful prodigy having preceded him, it was not long before he obtained a situation in the Oratorio Concerts ; and, when these concerts were finished, he entered the orchestra of Drury Lane, the di-

rector of which was the well-known Tom Cooke. Mr.
Cooke soon discovered the ability of Balfe, and took
advantage of it in allowing him to direct the orchestra
from time to time. It was a matter of surprise to many,
that the members of the orchestra were willing to be
guided by a mere boy. Meanwhile Balfe made rapid
progress in his studies with Mr. Horn, father of the gentleman who had so kindly befriended him. His original
and sparkling compositions met the approval of his
teacher.

About this time a sham maestro undertook the task of
producing a new score for an old opera in a limited time.
He was acquainted with our enterprising boy, and conceived the idea of turning the work over to him. Michael,
dazzled by the brilliant offer of ten pounds cash, to be
paid on delivery, set himself to work right earnestly. At
the end of a week the score was written. Then came the
re-action that follows overwork and loss of sleep. Balfe
felt the need of relaxation, and, at the suggestion of his
comrades, set out for "a spree." Of course his ten
pounds were soon squandered; but he had the satisfaction
of receiving the obsequious attentions of those who wished
to come in for a share.

When Balfe discovered that his voice was a fine baritone, he determined to cultivate it. After a year's hard
study, he tried his fortune as an actor and singer; but this
was not his forte.

One day he was introduced to a rich Italian count,
named Mazzara, who turned deadly pale at seeing him,
and seemed on the point of fainting. Recovering himself,
however, he explained that the marvellous resemblance of
young Balfe to an only son whom he had recently lost
had given him a sudden shock. Afterwards Balfe in-

dulged the company with his own compositions; and the Italian count was so charmed by his music, as well as by the frankness and openness of his manners, that he offered to take him to Rome, and provide for his musical studies, — an offer which the young student did not hesitate to accept.

The count stopped at Paris, and introduced Balfe to Cherubini, who was much pleased with his playing and singing : before they parted, the master begged Balfe to call upon him at any time that he might need his advice or instruction.

While in Rome, Balfe studied with Federici : when the master left for Milan, Balfe followed. Among the letters of introduction given him by the count was one to Glossop, an English impressario who had taken upon himself the burden of managing " La Scala " in Milan, and "St. Carlo" in Naples. This gentleman gave Balfe an opportunity of winning the applause of the Milanese in "La Pérouse." "Success at 'La Scala' is success indeed:" so thought Balfe, and longed for another opportunity to gain public favor. But the difficulty of obtaining a libretto prevented any further attempt on his part. Soon, however, he resolved to go to Paris, and put himself under Cherubini's instruction. No sooner thought than done. He went to Cherubini, who received him kindly, and invited him to meet Rossini and wife at dinner. Through Rossini, Balfe made an engagement to sing at " Les Italiens " for three years, receiving fifteen thousand francs for the first, twenty thousand for the second, and twenty-five thousand for the third year.

At Palermo, whither he went at the expiration of his engagement, he became acquainted with the celebrated singer, Miss Lina Roser, who was afterwards his loving, faithful, and devoted wife.

In 1836 Balfe put the "Maid of Artois" upon the stage in London : through Malibran, it brought into the treasury £5,690 ;[1] that is, about £355 per night.

Apropos of Malibran. Balfe wished to improve the *rondo finale*, but Malibran objected. "You are crazy," she said : "it is the most brilliant piece in the opera." Nevertheless, the author was set upon improvement. He went home very tired, threw himself upon a sofa, and slept soundly until midnight, when he arose much refreshed. Then, seating himself at the piano, he found what had been hidden in his brain. In a few minutes the *finale* was written, and he was satisfied.

Next morning he hastened to Malibran's residence. She was in bed, and would not be disturbed. Balfe played the rondo to her husband, who suggested that a small cottage-piano should be carried into his wife's chamber. They did so ; and Malibran was forced to listen in spite of herself, although she loudly protested, and " declared that both the disturbers of her peace were cracked." However, after hearing a few bars, she listened with great attention, then, bursting into exclamations of admiration, she promised to sing it at the rehearsal that very forenoon. A speech of Balfe's will suffice to show his unsuccessful attempt to establish a " National Opera " in London, 1841.

"Ladies and gentlemen, about two hours ago I received a note from Mr. John Barnett, whose pupil Miss Gould is, stating that he could not allow her to appear at this theatre any longer. She being the third who has left this establishment, I am not able to find a substitute for the time being. Had I known that she would not sing, in season to notify you, I would have done so. This is the

---

[1] It had a run of sixteen nights.

last night of the English Opera House, or, at least, the last under my reign. [Cries of 'No.'] The fact is, there are no funds to carry it on, and I am already burdened with five or six hundred pounds' debt through it. I have done all that I could do. I brought my opera of 'Keolanthe' gratis, for which Madame Vestris offered me three hundred guineas, if I would have it brought out at her theatre. I had another opera ready cast and studied; but I was not able to produce it in consequence of the secession of Mr. Philips. [Cries of 'Shame.'] I am only sorry that I ever was such a fool as to take the management of an English theatre. In future I shall appear before you only as a composer."

Balfe, discouraged, but not disheartened, went to Paris, where, by the advice of Erard, who kindly offered the use of his spacious rooms, he gave a concert, the programme of which was made up of his own compositions. The concert-room was crowded : friends came for Balfe's sake ; enemies to criticise ; but the mass to make fun of English music. However, the concert was a complete success ; and Balfe went home, not only delighted with the approbation he had received, but with the more substantial filling of his pockets.

A few days after, Scribe proposed to write a comic opera with him, which proposition he joyfully accepted ; and " Le Puits d'Amour " was the happy result of their collaboration.

Balfe's first appearance as conductor of the orchestra of her Majesty's Theatre, in 1846, was greeted most enthusiastically. The masterly ability of Balfe, and the exceptional charm of Jenny Lind's voice and genius, were great attractions to this theatre. Our composer maintained his post as conductor in the most satisfactory manner for seven years.

In 1849 Balfe visited Berlin, whither he had been invited by the crown-prince, who introduced him at court, and took him to spend an evening at Charlottenburg, where he had the pleasure of hearing the band perform some of his own compositions.

In 1859 Balfe took a second journey to St. Petersburg with his daughter, who afterwards married the English ambassador at the Russian court, Sir John F. Crampton.

In 1864 Balfe gave up his London house, and retired to his country estate, where he became gentleman farmer. An entry in his diary this same year reads thus, "What a wonderful woman my darling wife is! What a beautiful place she has made of this! I could scarcely believe my eyes, every thing is so lovely and so comfortable."

In 1868 Balfe had a bronchial affection, which alarmed his family, but did not prevent his going to Paris and London, and interesting himself in all that was going on in the musical world. He was very much depressed, however, by the death of his oldest and favorite daughter, and, feeling weak and suffering, he longed to be at home. He went to his final rest, Oct. 19, 1870.

Twenty-seven operas, three cantatas, and numerous songs, display his merits as a composer.

MENDELSSOHN–BARTHOLDY.

1809–1847.

FELIX MENDELSSOHN was the grandson of an Israel-itish philosopher, and son of a rich banker of Hamburg, where he was born Feb. 3, 1809. His father Abraham was a learned man, and a passionate lover of the fine arts. He had abjured Judaism, and become a Lutheran. One of his sisters, wife of Frederic Schlegel the distinguished poet, was converted to Catholicism. The uncles of Felix were distinguished writers ; and when we add that his mother, a daughter of Bartholdy the banker, was a gifted, graceful, and high-spirited woman, it is easy to conceive that such surroundings must have been favorable to the development of the faculties of a naturally gifted youth. The family Mendelssohn removed to Berlin when Felix was three years old. In his eighth year he played the piano with wonderful facility, and at the same time he could write the harmony to a given base, thanks to the good instruction of his teacher Berger.[1] At the age of sixteen he had gone through a literary and scientific course, and could read Greek and Latin tolerably well. Whilst still young, he published in Berlin a translation of "Adrienne" of Terence into German verse. He spoke English, French, and Italian fluently, painted well, was a fine cavalier, and an amateur in fencing and swimming. Notwithstanding all the time the above intellectual and gymnastic exercises had occupied, he was none the less skilful on the piano, executing the most difficult compositions, even the fugues of Bach, with expression and delicacy.

Zelter,[2] his professor in harmony, took him to Weimar in 1821, and presented him to Goethe,[3] who was much surprised at the execution and improvisation of this young musician of twelve years, and ever after took great interest in his progress. Mendelssohn was fifteen when he became acquainted with Madam Bigot, a remarkably fine pianist,

---

[1] And the teachings of his mother, from whom he had his first music-lessons.

[2] "Zelter considered Mendelssohn his best scholar at the age of twelve years. His letters to Goethe are evidences of his interest in the lad."

[3] Mendelssohn corresponded with Goethe, who always expressed his admiration of his " cheerful, affectionate, and interesting letters."

who gave him much useful advice, which he treasured up
with affectionate remembrance. About this time he received lessons from Cherubini. During the same year, and
before he was quite fifteen, he brought out " Die Hochzeit
des Camacho," an opera in two acts, at Berlin ; but, as its
success seemed doubtful, he immediately withdrew it.
His talents were not recognized in the city of his youth.

In 1829 he went to England. With the education of a
gentleman, fine manners, excellent qualities, and an agreeable face, it was no wonder that the drawing-rooms of the
élite were everywhere opened to the young artist. His
first symphony performed at a concert in London gained
him great applause. Then he went to Scotland, where,
inspired by the poetic landscapes of this country, he composed the "Hebrides,"[1] an overture for a concert. Thence
he returned to Germany, and afterwards to Rome, where
he remained some six months. Finally, after having seen
most of the Italian cities, he went to Paris the following
December.

During his stay in Rome, he visited the museums,
palaces, &c., and was everywhere received with urbanity,
and even with the most flattering cordiality. He heard
the music of the Sistine Chapel, the works of Palestrina,
of Vittoria, of Allegri, without their interfering in the least
with his own individuality, as he was in the habit of bringing all to an absolute and determined ideal. For this
reason, his Italian correspondence bears the imprint of
uneasiness and discontent.

" He preferred the cold sky and the pines of the North
to charming scenes in the midst of landscapes bathed in

---

[1] Mendelssohn's sisters asked him to tell them about the Hebrides. "It cannot
be told, only played," he said. And, placing himself at the piano, played the theme,
which grew into the overture.

the glowing rays of the sun and azure light. He acknowl-edges that religious ceremonies affected him in spite of himself; yet he speaks of them with sarcasm and irony."

We will go away from that Italy which he seems not to have understood, though he brought from it the Psalms of Luther set to music, and one of his finest symphonies. We must remember, likewise, that, whilst in Italy, he associated mostly with foreigners, to whom his talents were an introduction : among them were the sculptor Thorwaldsen and the painter Leopold Robert. He became acquainted with the family Vernet, whom he charmed by his impro-visations. Horace Vernet painted the portrait of Men-delssohn, which was sent to his mother.

About this time he wrote the overture of the "Hebrides," his first Song without Words, "Walpurgis Nacht," overture in C, symphony in A major, Capriccios, and the overture to the "Märchen of the Schönen Melusina." "In 1833 he was invited to assume the direction of the annual Musical Festival at Dusseldorf. With his visit to Dus-seldorf begins a new epoch in our composer's life. The first stage in his career was his boyhood in his father's house; the second was the time devoted to travel ; and this, of which we now speak, was the third, that which was to put his genius, power, and learning to the test."

In answer to a letter from Moscheles, his former teacher and faithful friend, he thanks him in the heartiest manner for his favorable opinion, and jokingly adds, "Your praise is better than three orders of nobility."

Whilst in Dusseldorf, he was offered the directorship of the Singing Academy, which he accepted for three years, and associated himself with the poet Immermann in several musical enterprises, but without satisfactory results. The criticisms made of Mendelssohn's music at the time annoyed and imbittered him. Some writers attribute his irritability entirely to his extreme self-love; but it was, without doubt, caused chiefly by his mental labors,[1] for he over-taxed himself to such a degree, that he was obliged to sleep for hours in order to recuperate. Called to the great musical festival of the Pentecost at Aix-la-Chapelle in 1834, he was so much displeased at being obliged to alternate with Ries[2] in directing, that he is said to have treated him unkindly.[3] Soon after, he resigned his position at Dusseldorf, and went to Leipzig to finish his oratorio of "Paul,"[4] and direct the concerts of that city. In 1836 the title of Doctor of Philosophy and Fine Arts was conferred upon him. In 1837 he married Cecelia Jeanrenaud, a charming young woman, daughter of a minister of the Reformed Church in Frankfort-on-the-Main.[5]

In 1841 Mendelssohn went to Berlin at the call of the King of Prussia, who gave him charge of the general directorship of his music. While in this city he set

[1] We copy the following from an account of Mendelssohn's life while in Paris, which shows how little rest he gave himself: "Monday, Rothschild's; Tuesday, Société des Beaux Arts; Wednesday, my octet at Madame Kiéné's; Friday, a concert at Erard's; Sunday, a concert at Leo's." We read of his going to Frankfort to rest, that is, to give up directing, and betake himself to composing. In his last sickness, he used to say to his wife, when she urged him to rest, "Let me work a little longer: the time for rest will soon be here." The impulse to labor was the law of his nature.

[2] Ries, born 1784, at Bonn, had lived many years in London, where he was much esteemed by a large circle of friends. He was an excellent piano-forte player, and a good composer.

[3] Notwithstanding, Mendelssohn was careful, considerate, and kind to artists, even though they differed from him upon musical points. When Liszt first made his appearance in Leipzig, Mendelssohn made a party for him, to which he invited the musical people of the city, that they might hear him perform.

[4] The years 1837 and 1838 might be called the St. Paul years; for this oratorio was sung fifty times in forty German cities within one year and a half.

[5] Mendelssohn was very happy with this gentle, amiable, and affectionate woman, although her name is so seldom mentioned in any reminiscence of him which has as yet appeared.

Racine's "Chorus of Athalie" to music, and finished the musical part of Shakspeare's "Midsummer Night's Dream," the overture of which he had written in 1829. He also wrote church choruses with orchestra, and psalms with accompaniments; but, though busy, he was not happy in Berlin:[1] he preferred Leipzig, where he was better appreciated, and more admired.

The "Hymn of Praise," a great symphony cantata, was sung in Leipzig at the fourth centennial celebration of the invention of printing. This cantata is thought by some to be Mendelssohn's greatest work.

If he never wished to see Paris again, he felt differently towards England, whither he went seven times from 1832 to 1846. During this period his grand oratorio, "Elijah," was first performed under his own direction, with the most gratifying success. Revised and refined, as was the composer's custom, "Elijah" was given a second time at the Festival of Birmingham, in the month of April, 1847, to the great delight of the English nobility and all lovers of good music. The queen honored the occasion by her presence.[2]

---

[1] The oratorio of "St. Paul" was brought out, at the request of the king, in Berlin, Nov. 28, 1844.

"It was said in England and Berlin that Mendelssohn was too exacting and irritable to be a good conductor; but this was never said in Leipzig. No doubt, when out of a sympathetic atmosphere, when contending at his desk with the obstinacy of Berliners, who looked upon him as an interloper, and the stupidity of the English players, many of whom thought him an upstart, he failed to conciliate the orchestra, or to conquer its defects. Yet it is acknowledged that he wrought wonders in England with the most stubborn material. Devrient, his friend and admirer, speaks of his conducting, under favorable circumstances, as perfect." It would be a matter of difficulty to decide in what quality Mendelssohn excelled the most, — whether as composer, pianist, organist, or conductor of an orchestra.

[2] "He had so many callers while living in Hobart Place, that his old servant said 'Ach! me almost run down, dere be so many visit.'"

Lampadius says, "Her Majesty, who, as well as her husband, was a great friend of art, and herself a skilful musician, received the distinguished German in her own

Soon after his return to Leipzig, he determined to pass the summer at Vevay, and went to Frankfort to meet his wife and children. There he heard of the death of a sister, Madam Hansel,[1] whom he tenderly loved. She was a highly gifted woman, and an excellent pianist. His grief at the loss of this sister was very poignant. In hopes of turning his attention, the family set out on their journey as soon as possible. They went to Baden, and from thence to Interlachen,[2] where he remained until the next September. The little church of a village situated on the Lake of Brientz [3] keeps in grateful remembrance the beautiful improvisation which he performed upon the organ a few days before his departure, and which was the last of its kind for him. He wished to go to Fribourg to try Mooser's famous organ; but the approach of winter prevented him. He returned to Leipzig, and resumed his former occupations.

In the mean time he composed an operette for his own family, entitled "Heimkehr aus der Fremde," or "Return from among Strangers." Mendelssohn intended to

sitting-room, Prince Albert being the only one present besides herself. As he entered, she asked his pardon for the somewhat disorderly appearance of the apartment, and began to re-arrange the articles with her own hands, in which Mendelssohn gallantly offered his assistance. Some parrots, whose cages hung in the room, she herself carried into the next apartment, in which Mendelssohn helped her also. She then requested her guest to play something; and afterwards she sang some songs of his, which she had sung at a court concert soon after the attack upon her person. She was not wholly satisfied, however, with her own performance, and said pleasantly to Mendelssohn, 'I can do better; ask Lablache if I cannot; but I am afraid of you.' This anecdote was related by Mendelssohn himself. He used often to speak afterwards of the graciousness of the English queen."

[1] "Mendelssohn never got over the death of this his beloved sister Fanny."

[2] While at Interlachen, he worked hard at the education of his children, and at the unfinished "Lorelei," and the unfinished "Christus."

[3] "The church was situated in an out-of-the-way place, and almost hidden from view by the ivy, moss, and maiden-hair with which it was covered, and the organ was but a very poor instrument; yet Mendelssohn brought from it such tones of power and grandeur as astonished the two or three listening friends '"

have it performed at the fortieth anniversary of his mother's marriage. It was executed for the first time in public at the theatre of the grand opera of Berlin, during the year 1851.

This was one of the last of this master's productions. He now became a prey to a singular melancholy, which was naturally painful to those about him : he seemed as if pre-occupying himself for his approaching end. However, he continued to work, and even with redoubled activity, until Oct. 9, 1847, when he was taken suddenly ill at the house of a friend whither he had gone to accompany the performance of some parts of his "Elijah."[1] He was carried home; and, under energetic treatment, he soon revived, regained strength, made his usual tours on foot or on horseback, and was preparing to go to Vienna to direct the performance of his last oratorio, when he had a second attack of apoplexy (Oct. 28), and a third on the 3d of November, to which he succumbed the following day at nine o'clock, P.M., aged thirty-eight years. All Leipzig attended his funeral. All Germany mourned the loss of the artist and the patriot; for never did a more devoted heart beat in a German breast. Mendelssohn was one of the most intelligent musicians of our times.[2] He was learned in arts and sciences, and gifted with great penetration and delicacy of observation.

Not only his oratorios,[3] but his chamber music, have

[1] The "Elijah" was the death of our great artist. "There can be little doubt that the excitement and incessant toil incident upon so great an undertaking helped to shatter a frame already enfeebled by excessive mental exertion."

[2] "Educated with an almost Spartan rigor, early brought into contact with every department of human knowledge, and associating constantly with his elders, Mendelssohn, nevertheless, retained throughout his life the simplicity and impulsiveness of a child; yet his career is full of manly energy, enlightened enthusiasm, and the severest devotion to the highest forms of art."

[3] Next to "The Messiah," the "Elijah" is the most popular oratorio in England; and in it Mendelssohn asserts his claim to join hands with Händel, Mozart, and Beethoven.'

gained for him great celebrity. His piano music, and songs without words, are everywhere known, and justly admired; but it is in his overtures that the composer raises himself to the most elevated conceptions which unite in an instrumental coloring filled with original and new thoughts.

It has been said that heat and light are wanting in Mendelsschn's compositions: perhaps, if he had not been so exclusively German, he might have been a little modified by coming in contact with the French and Italian schools. And also, that, "however extended his mortal span might have been, his fine talents would, in all probability, have continued to unfold, and discover fresh beauties.

" He used his wealth as the means of giving his talents the more exclusively to his art. He did not compose in order to live ; but he lived in order to compose."

"An occurrence at the Birmingham Festival throws a clear light on Mendelssohn's presence of mind, and on his faculty of instant concentration. On the last day, among other things, Händel's " Anthem " was given. The concert was already going on, when it was discovered that the short recitative which precedes the " Coronation Hymn," and which the public had in the printed text, was lacking in the voice parts. The directors were perplexed. Mendelssohn, who was sitting in an ante-room of the hall, heard of it, and said, 'Wait, I will help you.' He sat down directly at a table, and composed the music for the recitative and the orchestral accompaniment in about half an hour. It was at once transcribed, and given without any rehearsal, and went very finely."

CHOPIN.

1810-1849.

IT seems to have been the province of Chopin to express the complaint of suffering Poland's soul in the language of his art. Perhaps the immense success which this artist enjoyed was as much owing to the sad condition of Poland at the time he first appeared in Paris, as to his own real merit.

Frederick Francis Chopin was born Feb. 8, 1810, at Zelazowa-Wola, near Warsaw. He was a very frail and delicate child, requiring constant attention. There was nothing under the envelope of the puny little one to indicate in the slightest degree any remarkable intelligence. He gained strength slowly; was a quiet, thoughtful, and interesting child, with a sweet disposition; and was patient under suffering. He manifested no particular aptitude for study, until he commenced music. His first teacher was an old Bohemian, named Zywny, a passionate admirer of Bach's works, and who had the care of young Chopin's musical instruction from his ninth to his sixteenth year. In 1820 he became acquainted with Madame Catalani, who was probably the first to perceive in him the bud of promise.[1]

The prince Radziwill, admiring the ability, skill, and gracefulness of execution of the youth, became his protector. As Chopin belonged to a family whose means were insufficient to give him a good musical education, the prince sent his young *protégé* to one of the best schools in Warsaw, and furnished the necessary means for his studies.

---

[1] Madame Catalani presented the boy with a watch in token of her affection. At that time, probably, such a gift was of more account to a boy than at present.

Chopin acquired those distinguished manners which after-wards contributed so much to his prestige among the young nobility of Poland with whom he studied. His character, which was amiable and mild, and his politeness, which did not exclude a certain sort of calculation, en-abled him to win the affection of his comrades, particu-larly one young nobleman, who several times took him home to his mother's house to pass a vacation. This highly cultivated lady introduced the young musician into an aristocratic society, where he became familiar with etiquette and *bon ton*, whilst displaying his precocious talent. Chopin learned the theory of harmony, and the principles of composition, at the age of sixteen, under the direction of Elsner, principal of the Conservatory of War-saw. Soon after, he visited Berlin, Dresden, and Prague, to perfect his musical education by hearing the distin-guished musicians of those cities. Desirous of making his way in the world, he went to Vienna in 1829, and made his first appearance, Sept. 11, in a concert given by an artist then in vogue. According to Liszt's biography, neither on that occasion, nor in the concerts that he after-ward gave, did Chopin obtain the success he had a just right to anticipate.[1] However, the "Leipzig Musical Gazette," in its November number of 1829, renders full justice to the brilliant qualities of the young pianist, in calling him "a master of the first rank," &c.

Chopin left Vienna in 1831. On account of the disasters that were falling upon his country, he resolved to establish

[1] " Liszt had been before him ; and he found those large audiences, whose ears had been so lately stunned with the thunder of cascades and hurricanes, wholly unprepared to listen to the murmuring of the waterfall, or the sighing of the midnight wind. The genius of Chopin could never cope with the masses. 'I am not suited for concert-giving,' he said to Liszt. 'The public intimidate me : their breath stifles me. *You* are destined for it ; for, when you do not gain your public, you have the force to assault, to overwhelm, to compel them.' "

himself in London ; but, passing through Paris on his way, he stopped there, and became its guest to the end of his life.

The first time the Parisians were invited to listen to the Polish virtuoso was at the house of Pleyel, the pianoforte maker. Most of the artists who composed Chopin's auditory recognized his exceptional manner, and did not hesitate to assign an honorable rank to the productions he had performed before them. However, there were a few, as is always the case, who protested against his playing. Field declared that Chopin's was *Un talent de chambre de malade.* Kalkbrenner, likewise, found something to criticise. However, Chopin could judge better for himself than any one else could. He saw that what was fine and delicate would produce little effect in a concert : therefore he reserved his playing for drawing-rooms. Not receiving the applause he expected when he gave his concerts in the " Salle des Italiens," he separated himself. from that time forth, from the masses, feeling perfectly satisfied with the suffrages which he obtained from the most refined and the most aristocratic of Paris. Noble families among the Polish emigrants received him with the sympathy due to a compatriot, and the consideration due to an artist of rare talent. This was his society during the first years of his sojourn in Paris : among such people he felt at home ; for they could appreciate the national character of compositions which breathed the genius of Sobieski's people.

Unlike some other distinguished musicians, Chopin was not averse to teaching. A superior musician, of elegant manners, he could not fail to have a large number of pupils, especially among the ladies. To take lessons of Chopin became a sort of infatuation, a fashion. While giving his lessons, the professor conquered his melancholy, and appeared to take pleasure in forming pupils who imitated his style, and would play none other than his music

In 1837 his health, always feeble, was much impaired. Phthisic was making alarming progress with him ; and his physicians advised him to pass the winter in Majorca.[1]

The delightful climate of this southern isle exercised a salutary influence upon Chopin while there ; but, on his return to France, the show of returning health disappeared, and from 1840 till the time of his death, the unfortunate musician led a miserable life of continued suffering.[2] In 1846 the slightest walk, the going up a few stairs, brought on fits of suffocation.

During the troubles of 1848, he visited England and Scotland.[3] This journey, which he had taken contrary to the advice of his friends, was fatal to him ; for the ovations that he everywhere received made him forget the care which his health required. He played at a ball given in London in aid of the banished Poles, and this was his last appearance before the public.

He returned to France, his adopted country, where he died Oct. 17, 1849. His corpse, dressed in ball-costume, was put into a coffin filled with roses ; and, to crown this sad parade, a solemn service was ordered in the Church of the Madeleine, where Mozart's Requiem was sung ; Signor Lablache, Madame Viardot, and Madame Castellan taking part, whilst Mons. Wely presided at the organ.

[1] Thither he went in company of Madame Sand, who nursed him carefully until his health was seemingly restored.

[2] Chopin's sufferings were mental as well as physical. We are told that "the dream of his life was union with Madame Sand in marriage." When she refused his offer, he said, " All the cords that bound me to life are broken."

[3] He had a flattering reception in England, was presented to the queen, and played at many private concerts gotten up among the nobility and gentry *especially for him.*

Chopin lies in the cemetery Père la Chaise, between Cherubini and Bellini.

"Although Chopin lived in France, his music is not French. His country, ever uppermost in his thoughts, gives coloring to all his compositions." He united the brilliant qualities of the pianist to the sensibility of the artist, and the imagination of the musician. The rhythm of his music cannot be proposed for a model : it is too capricious, too odd, though the general effect pleases by its vivid elegance, and the charming part which the author has drawn from the resources of his instrument.[1]

This composer's best works, those which are most natural and fresh, are his shorter pieces, such as mazurkas, waltzes, nocturnes, polonaises, impromptus, and the like. In larger works, such as concertos, sonatas, &c., he is irregular and diffusive.

DAVID.

1810–.

"Felicien David was born 1810, at Cadenet, near Aix, in France. At an early age he exhibited a taste for music, and was educated in a college of the Jesuits. His compositions of 1830 were full of original inspiration ; but he did not compose any thing calculated to make him renowned until 1838 and 1839. His great work is 'The Desert,' which has been widely celebrated."

SCHUMANN, ROBERT.

1810–1856.

Robert Schumann was born at Zwickau, in Saxony, June 8, 1810. He was the son of a bookseller, and the

---

[1] These remarks apply particularly to the piece entitled " Fantasie Impromptu."

youngest of five children. He acquired the elementary knowledge of the German schools, where music is always on the programme of studies, without displaying any manifestation of talent. Any one who marked the zeal with which the child played soldier might have supposed that he was destined to figure in the wars which were exciting all Europe at that time, rather than to be one of the leaders of the great song-writers of Germany. When he was ten years old, he chanced to hear the celebrated pianist Moscheles, and was seized with an extraordinary love for music; and from that time his career in life was decided. He applied himself zealously to the study of the piano, and practised so much, that he injured one of the fingers of his right hand. Although his knowledge of harmony was very superficial, he attempted composition. His father, struck with the inclination for music so manifest in his son, begged Weber to take charge of his musical education. But for some reason, which is unknown, the project did not succeed; and Robert recommenced the ordinary course of study at the Gymnasium of Zwickau. However, guided by his fancy and his instinct, he continued his music as before.

Like many other artists, Schumann had a strong predilection for literature. Byron and Jean-Paul [1] were his favorites; but, unfortunately, the reading of the latter infused into his dreamy imagination that morbid sentimentality which finally brought the musician to his unhappy end. Schumann's father died in August, 1826, after which his mother obliged him to give up the study of music, and turn to that of law. It would have been impossible to

---

[1] In a letter to his friend Rosen, he says, "If the whole world would read Jean-Paul, it would be decidedly better, but more unhappy. He has often reduced me to the verge of despair; but the rainbow of peace always floats softly above the tears, and the heart is wonderfully exalted and transfigured."

ask a greater sacrifice ; yet the son obeyed his mother, in so far that he passed through the University of Leipzig and that of Heidelberg. Philosophy suited him much better than law ; for he was fond of speculative studies : so he gave himself up to it with considerable ardor ; yet music continued to be the constant object of his affections. At Leipzig he found an opportunity to study with Wieck ; and in this way he lost no time. But at Heidelberg, where he led the life of a careless student, it was otherwise. Meanwhile he went to Italy, and his enthusiasm for music revived.

After some years' contest with his mother and his tutor, Schumann, who had interested Wieck in his cause, obtained permission of his mother to give up the study of law, and become the pupil of that able artist, of whom he had already received some instruction.[1] Ever since he had heard the grand performance of Moscheles, he could think of nothing but being a great pianist. It was his ambition to surpass all other virtuosos ; and, in order to do this, he undertook to practise in a way of his own, which he carefully concealed from every one ; but the result was entirely different from that which he had anti-

[1] Wieck received the student into his family ; and it was in this way that he became acquainted with Clara, whom he afterwards married.

"It was a habit of Schumann to collect Wieck's children in his room at twilight, and frighten them by the recital of the most horrible ghost-stories of his own invention. Then he would shut the door, and appear suddenly, by the light of a spirit-lamp, as a spectre in a fur coat turned inside out, exciting universal terror. The children were very fond of him ; the tricksy side of his nature having a peculiar charm for them."

Schumann worked hard all day : in the evening, he met his friends at a restaurant, where he spent several hours. Generally he was silent, apparently passive, so much so, that people least acquainted with him supposed that the beer, and not his friends, attracted him. When he went home at night, he wrote the events of the day in his note-book, counted his ready money, and closed his day's work by recording the musical ideas that had come to him during the evening : this he played over, and extemporized a while before retiring.

cipated. His method of operation was to use only four fingers of the right hand, whilst the third was bound by a chord. The inactivity forced upon this finger soon paralyzed, first that finger, then the whole hand; so that Schumann had to give up the hope of ever being a pianist: however, he consoled himself with the study of harmony and counterpoint, determined upon making a name as a composer. His first works were variations for the piano, published in 1831, under the pseudonyme of d'Abegg, likewise a symphony performed in 1832, but not published, sonatas in F sharp minor, and G minor, and a fantasia in C major.

The influence that Schumann exercised upon art in Germany was principally due to his works as a critic. He was naturally an adversary to classic shackles, and was contending with "The Musical Gazette of Leipzig," when he commenced a journal, entitled "Neue Zeitschrift für Musik." [1] This paper, of which he was the chief editor, and which numbered among its contributors val-

---

[1] In 1833 Schumann was attacked by a fit of violent mental excitement, which greatly alarmed his friends.

The year 1834 was, to use Schumann's own words, "the most remarkable of his life."

"At the close of 1833 a number of musicians, mostly young, met in Leipzig every evening, apparently by accident at first, for social purposes, but no less for an exchange of ideas on the art which was meat and drink to them, — music. It cannot be said that the universal state of Germany was then very pleasant. Rossini still ruled the stage; Herz and Hünten were sole lords of the piano. And yet but a few years had elapsed since Beethoven, M. C. von Weber, and Franz Schubert were with us. To be sure, Mendelssohn's star was in the ascendant, and wonderful things were reported of a Pole, Chopin by name; but they exercised no real influence till later. One day the young hot heads thought, 'Why do we look idly on? Let's take hold, and make things better; let's restore the poetry of art to her ancient honor.' By this we see what was the first motive for establishing 'The New Journal for Music.'"

Schumann's silence and strange conduct at friends' houses was patiently borne by them; for instance, he would walk into a room, unannounced, bow, pucker up his lips as if to whistle, take off his hat, open the piano, strike a few chords, close it, and disappear without speaking.

iant and bold writers, appeared April 3, 1834. Whilst severely criticising the masters' pieces then in vogue, Schumann did his utmost to exalt Schubert, and gain for him a just appreciation among the Germans.[1] However, it was happy for the enthusiastic editor, that, in his own compositions, he was not always faithful to the theories that he extolled in the articles of his journal.

On the 12th of September, 1840,[2] our artist married Clara Wieck, daughter of his former teacher, who, however, did not countenance the union until Schumann had been received as Doctor of Philosophy at the University of Jena. One peculiarity curious to observe, and which is revealed to us by Schumann himself, is the influence that opposition to his marriage had upon his music. "There certainly is something in my compositions," he says, "which tells of the contests that Clara cost me."

During this, one of the most active years of his life,[3] he gave up composing exclusively for the piano, and wrote his songs,[4] which, fine as they were, were by some critics considered much inferior to those of Schubert, Weber, Mendelssohn, and of Spohr.

In 1843 he was appointed professor in the Conserva-

[1] That he succeeded in his honest endeavor, there is not the slightest possibility of doubt.

[2] Schumann's compositions in 1840 were entirely opposite in character to his earlier efforts. They were exclusively lyric. A rich stream of song gushed from his poetic soul; and this year is justly called "the year of song." He wrote a hundred and thirty-eight different songs during the year.

[3] He set many of Burns's and Heine's poems to music. His songs, like those of Schubert, whom he admired, have a character of their own.

"Schumann was in thought and action a free-thinker. His views of life and the world, based on true religious feelings, were pervaded by a deep moral fervor. He once said, if a man knows the Bible, Shakspeare, and Goethe, and has taken them into himself, he needs no more."

[4] He is said to have composed about one hundred and thirty songs, and music for songs, during the year 1840. Besides this, he studied the modern classic composers with the utmost diligence.

tory of Leipzig, which situation, not proving agreeable, he soon relinquished. In 1844 he and his wife made a musical tour through Russia ;[1] and, on their return, they removed from Leipzig to Dresden. The nervous excitements which had troubled Schumann more or less since 1833 became so frequent and severe as to impair his mental faculties. In 1845 he was obliged to lay aside his studies for a while, until his nerves were quieted. No sooner was he in some degree restored, than he recommenced his labors with indefatigable assiduity. He studied counterpoint, and wrote a symphony in C Major, &c., after which he finished his opera, "Genoveva." He had counted much upon this opera, which was performed three times in Leipzig, and only once in Weimar. About this time he was director of the "Liedertafel and Chorgesangvereins" in Dresden, whereby he was enabled to bring out many of his richest works.

In 1850 he took his family to Dusseldorf, where he succeeded Hiller as musical director. His compositions of this period are a symphony in E Major, and "Der Rose Pilgerfahrt," also some overtures to "Julius Cæsar," to "Hermann and Dorothea," to the "Brant von Messina," and much other ballad, choral, and orchestral music.

In 1853 and 1854 that which had been considered as a nervous excitement became insanity. His friends were in despair when the master expressed his firm belief in Spiritualism, and declared that he was in relation with Schubert and Mendelssohn, who both came to him to dictate his melodies. On the 7th of February, 1854, Schumann suddenly left his house at midnight, and threw himself into the Rhine. His clothing kept him above

[1] They were well received, and kindly treated by the emperor and empress, to whom Clara sang and played several times. She also gave four concerts.

water ; so that he was saved from drowning. But, if his life was spared, his reason was not. The remainder of his days was passed at a lunatic asylum in Enderich, in the neighborhood of Bonn, where he died July 29, 1856.

Madame Clara Schumann, born Wieck, a very talented pianist, devoted herself to propagating the renown of her husband, with an energy, perseverance, and sentiment of conjugal piety truly admirable. The greatest praise that can be given Robert Schumann is, that he inspired such deep and lasting affection. She caused her husband's compositions to be performed in all the large cities of Europe.

Schumann's " Concertos for Two Pianos " are more noisy than pleasing ; but his cantata, " Paradise and the Peri," is an admirable work, and justly praised. The compositions that the artist was pleased to call " Children's Scenes," display more artistic sense, and more maturity, than his orchestral works.

HILLER.

1811-.

FERDINAND HILLER, a distinguished composer and pianist, was born at Frankfort-on-the-Main, Oct. 24, 1811, of well-to-do parents. At an early age he was placed under the instruction of Hoffman, Schmitt, and Vollweiler, and afterwards under that of Hummel, with whom he lived at Weimar for two years, where his natural taste for music was fostered with the greatest care. Hiller appeared in public for the first time when only twelve years of age. His first composition was a quartet for the piano, viol, violin, and cello which was published at Vienna when he was seventeen. During his seven-years' residence in Paris, he worked assiduously for the promotion of the solid music of Bach and Beethoven. In the winter of 1836 he led the Sicilian Society of his native city, after which he went to Milan, and brought out his opera " Romilde." In 1839 his oratorio, " The Destruction of Jerusalem," was performed in Leipzig with great success. In 1841 Hiller married an Italian lady, and lived in Frankfort for a time. In 1844 he removed to Dresden, where he directed the Gewandhaus-concerts, and brought out two operas, the " Dream of Christmas Night," and " Conrad, the last Hohenstaufe." In 1847 he accepted the position of musical director at Dusseldorf. Three years after, he was appointed chapel-master at Cologne. In 1851 he directed the Italian opera in Paris. In 1852 he gave his symphony, " In the Open Air," at one of the concerts of the Philharmonic Society in London. Hiller was the friend of Mendelssohn, and one of the best composers of his day. As a pianist and composer, he was remarkable for purity of style. His " Destruction of Jerusalem " merits a place beside the oratorios of Mendelssohn. " His compositions consist chiefly of symphonies and concert overtures, with pieces and studies for the piano."

LISZT.

1811-.

FRANZ LISZT, the greatest pianist, and, next to Paganini, the greatest virtuoso, of modern times, was born the 22d October, 1811, at Raiding, a Hungarian village near Pesth. His father, an accountant in Prince Esterhazy's house, cultivated music as an amateur, but with so much talent that the prince frequently employed him in his chapel. In this way Adam Liszt made the acquaintance of Haydn, who died in 1809, two years before the birth of Franz. When the child was six years old, he retained the theme, and was able to sing the principal melodies, of a concerto of Ries, which he heard his father play upon the piano. Such evidence of a musical gift induced his parents to put him to the study of the piano. While very young he read the " René " of Châteaubriand, which, without doubt, had great influence in casting over him that shade of melancholy by which he has since been characterized. Indeed, there is no difficulty in understanding that such a work as " René " would make a deep impression upon the imagination of the young pianist, who read and re-read it during six months, and often with tearful eyes.

If there are simple, truthful natures like Mozart's, that are not misled by youthful glory, there are more frequently those in which infant prodigies, or those supposed to be such, become presumptuous through public applause ; and this presumption is very apt to follow them through life.

It was under such unfortunate auspices that Liszt commenced his career. At the age of nine years he played for the first time in public, and excited general astonishment. Prince Esterhazy was so delighted with his rendering of a concerto of Ries, to which he improvised a fantasia, that he openly caressed the boy, and afterwards made him a present of fifty ducats. At Presburg, where the young artist went with his family, he soon gained the favor of the Counts Amadé and Szapary. These gentlemen, with the view of assisting in his musical education, agreed to allow him six hundred florins a year for six years. While in Vienna he astonished his professor, the celebrated Czerny. This excellent artist, who had under

.aken to teach him, was not a little surprised to see him execute Clementi's sonatas with facility. It was rarely that works of such composers even as Beethoven and Hummel offered too great difficulties for the precocious youth. The day on which Hummel's concerto in *si minor* was published, Liszt, who chanced to be at the editor's, played it at first sight. This musical feat produced a great sensation throughout the city ; and the little Franz soon became the lion of Viennese drawing-rooms. Czerny himself could not refrain from the general enthusiasm. He refused the three hundred florins stipulated for lessons, saying that he was but too well paid by the success of his pupil. Liszt studied carefully eighteen months, besides having some advice from Salieri in regard to composition. Then he gave his first concert. The audience, composed of the *élite* of the aristocracy and arts, were united in the opinion that the career of the young musician would be brilliant. We next find him performing to admiring audiences in all the cities through which he passed on his route to Paris.

It was the desire of Adam Liszt to place his son at the Conservatory, where he could study counterpoint with Cherubini. But, notwithstanding the good recommendations of M. Metternich, this project could not be carried into effect, since, according to the rules of the Conservatory, the candidate must be French. But the Parisians, who dote on whatever or whomsoever affords amusement, were less exclusive to the young stranger than was the great music school. They not only patronized all the concerts which he gave in their city in 1823, but they made him the ornament of the most aristocratic drawing-rooms. The beautiful Duchesses of Faubourg Saint-Germain, astonished by the nimbleness of his fingering, and his childish grace, showed him marked attention. All were fully satisfied with him. They looked forward to the time when he should revive the glorious image of Mozart.

But, with all this success and flattery, Liszt was not idle; besides, his father was determined to keep him in continual practice: so he obliged him to play twelve fugues of Bach daily, and to change them from one key to another. This course of practice was only interrupted by a journey to London in May, 1824. On his return to Paris, he renewed his studies, and began to compose. In 1825 he went again to England, where his concerts yielded a golden harvest.

Since his sonatas and fantasias were well received, it may be asked why he did not limit himself to that in which he might hope to excel. Simply because he was stimulated by the paternal ambition of Adam Liszt, and under a pressure that well agreed with his secret pretensions. Liszt thought himself capable of composing operas. His "Don Sancho" was brought out Oct. 17, 1825. The generous public were unwilling to criticise the bewitching virtuoso too severely. Accompanied by his father and family, he left Paris the following February, and visited all the principal cities of France, receiving the warmest applause wherever he went.

The poor success of "Don Sancho" proved the need Liszt had of a better knowledge of composition : therefore he determined to finish a course of lessons he had commenced with Reicha ; but, soon after, a sort of mysticism took possession of him, and, for the moment at least, drove out his love, — music. His father, alarmed at what seemed to be the enfeebling of the boy's health, or, it may be, troubled by the thought that such a meditative turn would prove injurious to the speculations he had in view, endeavored to divert his attention by taking him to the baths of Boulogne. But Adam Liszt was no longer to guide and direct the course of his son : he died at Boulogne.

Left to himself, freed from the iron yoke that had opposed his aspirations until the present time, Liszt did not at first take advantage of the liberty so suddenly and sadly acquired, except so far as to give himself up entirely to his melancholy and religious instincts. After a severe illness, he became more and more religious, attending churches, and all the exercises of a rigorous disciple : from this severe Catholic devotion, he suddenly turned to the St. Simonians ; and then he became an ardent republican, as we see by an unpublished revolutionary symphony composed after the events of 1830.

The talent of Liszt as a performer, so remarkable in early youth, again shone forth with a splendor that would have defied all comparison, had Chopin not existed. The two rivals had each his own kind of merit. Pure, discreet, and, withal, endowed with a delicate and original charm, the Polish artist never saw his success go outside the limits of the circle that enclosed the *beau monde.* On the contrary, the Hungarian artist governed souls longing for powerful emotions, and ears avaricious of noise, mostly by the impetuosity of his performance, and the strength of his acoustic efforts. Entering a hall to which he had been invited to play, he threw his gloves to a lackey, put back his long hair with a gesture of pride, and took his seat in a manner peculiar to himself. The performance commenced : he ran his feverish hands over the key-board, while his eyes wandered around, and the perspiration pearled his brow.

More than once whilst executing pieces from Beethoven, Weber, and Hummel, he took it into his head to substitute

his own improvisations for the inspirations of these masters ; and these improvisations drew forth rounds of
applause from a brilliant but ignorant audience. Afterwards, such kind of success weighed upon his conscience
as an artist. He himself freely expressed this in the following lines : " I then executed the works of the masters,
both in public and in private ; and I acknowledge, to my
shame, that in order to obtain the bravos of the hearers,
always slow to understand beautiful things in their august
simplicity, I made no scruple in altering the movement,
and making changes : yes, I even went so far as to add
passages which gained the applause of the illiterate, but
came near leading me into a false way."

Liszt lived quietly in Geneva for about two years, then
returned to Paris, where he began to rival Thalberg.
From 1835 to 1848 he made a musical tour through
Europe, and was everywhere received with an enthusiasm
bordering on delirium. The students of Berlin unhar-
nessed his horses, and absolutely wished to draw his carriage. His fellow-citizens of Pesth awarded him a sword.
(What should he do with it ?) In Russia he was regarded
as a supernatural being. At his first concert in St.
Petersburg, he made fifty thousand francs,[1] a sum which
one might. be tempted to consider exaggerated, if the
admirers of Liszt were not capable of believing whatever
might be said in his favor.

But the generosity and liberality of the celebrated pianist
frequently emptied the purse that his talent had filled.
Very few unfortunate people came within his notice without receiving his aid ; and none ever appealed to his charity
in vain. Whilst aiding the unfortunate, he gave proofs of

---

[1] " Liszt acquired a large fortune, at times having three hundred pounds a month ;
but he eventually lost a great deal by speculation."

disinterested zeal for the memory of Beethoven. When the project of erecting a statue at Bonn in memory of Beethoven was started, Liszt, not content with sending a large sum to the committee on subscriptions, used his utmost endeavors that the inauguration of the monument should be an artistic *fête* worthy of the immortal sympho· nist whom they wished to honor. He wrote a cantata for the occasion, and directed the rehearsals himself, giving up, for the time, engagements that would have yielded him large sums. Such devotion is worthy of the gratitude and respect of all lovers of Beethoven's music.

When the revolution of 1848 broke out, Liszt was chapel-master at the court of Weimar, which position he had held for several years, although he had travelled almost continually, and therefore resided but a short time in that city. After the 24th of February, Liszt performed the functions devolving on the chapel-master ; and through him Weimar became a sort of musical fireside, able to compete with any in Germany.

About this time Wagner re-appeared upon the scene of action. He had been exiled for his participation in revo· lutionary matters, of which Germany was then the theatre : the music of the future seemed enveloped in the disgrace of its founder. Just at this time, when every thing appeared to conspire against it, Liszt brought it into fashion. He entered into its service with a zeal and activity which should merit all praise. It was a source of great joy to Wagner, when he heard that his " Tannhäuser " and " Lohengrinn " were before the public.

A great fault in Liszt's works is, that no one can perform them but himself. Tormented by the idea that the piano was insufficient to express all his inspirations, he thought of some instrument which would combine the piano and organ. The manufacturer, Alexander, endeavored to satisfy his wants by inventing the piano-melodeon, or, as it is sometimes called, the piano-Liszt.

The religious tendency which had marked the early youth of Liszt again manifested itself in his soul so filled with contrasts. Tired of human vanities, the artist entered into holy orders immediately after a journey to Rome. He seems now to occupy himself only with sacred music. M. Emile Ollivier is married to one of Liszt's daughters.

Among the most interesting productions of Liszt is the arrangement of Schubert's melodies. One of his masses, executed at St. Eustache, was thought to be noisy and unpleasant by some of his most devoted admirers. As regards memory, power in fingering, and ability to play at sight, Liszt has hardly an equal.[1]

THOMAS, AMBROISE.

1811–.

THE French composer, Ambroise Thomas, was born at Metz, Aug. 5, 1811. It may well be said that he learned the notes of music as soon as he learned his alphabet; for his father, who was a professor of music, taught him solfeggio when he was but four years old. At the age of seven he began to learn to play upon the violin and the piano. He was admitted to the Conservatory in Paris, 1828, where he studied first under Zimmermann and Kalk-

[1] The principal works of Liszt are his oratorios of "Christ" and "St. Elizabeth," two symphonies, Goethe's "Fest-March" and "Preludes," then his "Ronde des Lutins," in which the composer seems to make a show of his splendid performance of all imaginable difficulties.

"Liszt is the owner of the instrument on which Beethoven played; and in 1853 he purchased the old harpsichord formerly belonging to Beethoven, which was offered for sale in Weimar, where Liszt now resides."

brenner, and then under Dourlen, Barbereau, and Leseur. In 1829 he obtained the first prize for piano ; in 1830 the first prize for harmony ; and in 1832 the Roman prize for composition, which allowed him to go to Italy as a stipendiary of the government.

The young laureate passed three years in Italy, during which time he lived mostly at Rome and Naples. From thence he went to Vienna, and returned to Paris in 1836. The fruit of his sojourn in Italy was a requiem.

"La Double Echelle," a comic opera in one act, represented in 1837, was the first step in the brilliant career of this composer. Soon followed many other light scores, which were well received ; but " Mina," a comic opera in three acts, represented in 1843, contributed much to increase the esteem of the musicians for the talents of Thomas. The overture is a *chef-d'œuvre* of instrumentation ; and the melodies throughout the work are very charming.

The great success of " Caïd," an opera bouffe given in 1849, began the popular celebrity of the composer. This work has continued to be admired for more than twenty years. A score which keeps the audience laughing seldom fails to please the less cultivated and the most numerous portion of the public. The only thing about it to be regretted is, that there is a school of this style. A composer of talent like Ambroise Thomas, gifted with a poetic imagination, did wrong to authorize by his example these operettes, which are multiplying in our day to the prejudice of art and taste.

With these exceptions, we do not hesitate to acknowledge that the author, in this production, has shown himself to be a man of genius and a good musician. The overture is sprightly and original ; and the finale is a master-piece of musical comedy.

It was to be feared that Thomas, dazzled by the reception given to the score of " Caïd," would remain for a long time a wanderer from the path that had been so favorably open to his style of talent, as well as his fine and delicate perceptions ; for there is something so exciting in applause, even of the illiterate, that strong heads are apt to succumb to it.   But a genuine artist, endowed with exquisite sensibility and real originality, ought never to be satisfied with success among the mediocrity.   Character and qualities will show themselves ; and so " Mignon," one among the last of Thomas's works, reveals that which is in our artist.

The " Songe d'une Nuit d'Eté," represented April 20, 1850, is a work of high inspiration, but not so much in favor as " Mignon."   After the " Songe " comes " Le Secret de la Reine," a lyric drama in three acts.   The legend of the Man with the Iron Mask is the foundation of this sombre text, more appropriate to the strongly accentuated manner of Verdi than to the vaporous charm that characterizes the music of Ambroise Thomas.

In 1851 the composer was called to take Spontini's place in the Institute.   For a long time the author of " Mina " had proved himself admirably fitted to occupy a place in the Academy.   He proved it again in writing " La Tonelli," a comic opera in two acts, performed in 1853.   The new academician sought the suffrage of connoisseurs, and he obtained it ; so that he felt fully indemnified for the indifference with which the crowd received this scientific and tasteful production.

" Pysche," which appeared soon after, had but little success, thanks to the *maladresse* of the *librettiste*.   There is certainly much wit and many well-turned verses in the text ; but the comic element is too prominent ; and the ridiculous persons who surround Psyche throw all the poetry of the graceful fable of antiquity into the shade, and prevent the hearer from paying attention to the ravishing melodies of the lovers, and the sweet and fresh chorus of the nymphs in the second act. The comedy perfectly distracts one. Only sensitive and delicate minds can comprehend the musical beauties of "Pysche," and realize a feast in the performance of this opera. Another objection to this opera is, that the feminine roles predominate, even to the exclusion of the tenor.

The "Carnival of Venice," a comic opera brought out the same year, was expressly composed to show the wonderful flexibility of Mme. Cabal's voice. Very few singers can take the part of Sylvia, who sings a violin concerto from beginning to end, under the title of "Ariette without Words."

After having kept himself from the stage six years, the eminent composer gave "Mignon," a comic opera in three acts, Nov. 17, 1866. The brilliant success of this opera was a sort of compensation to the composer for the time lost through indisposition. The author of the libretto, inspired by Ary Scheffer's painting, as well as by Goethe's recital, treated this difficult subject most happily. In it Thomas found the picturesque and poetic element so suited to his taste. His melodic phrase well expresses the appearance of the personages of Mignon, of Philine, and of Wilhelm Meister; whilst his harmony happily paints their character, and the depths of their sentiments.

Mignon is a *chef-d'œuvre* of taste, grace, and poetry. Every thing is good in this work; and, in spite of a certain indifference of the press, the disdain of some sectarians, and the false pretences of many of the partisans of lyric buffoonery its success, first seen in the well-filled choice seats, radiated through the parterre and the amphi-theatre.

The subject, in itself interesting, has been developed and completed by a very pathetic scene in the third act A scene remarkable in a literary point of view, and treated by the musician with continued inspiration, is that in which Mignon recalls to Wilhelm the only remembrance she has of her childhood. The poetic composition of Ary Scheffer, "Mignon regretting her Country," wonderfully inspired the composer, whom the poet has well aided by the following touching lines: —

> "Connais-tu le pays où fleurit l'oranger,
> Le pays des fruits d'or et des roses vermeilles,
> Où la brise est plus douce et l'oiseau plus léger
> Où dans tout saison butinent les abeilles ?
> Où rayonne et sourit comme un bienfait de Dieu,
> Un éternel printemps sous un ciel toujours bleu ?
> Hélas ! que ne puis-je te suivre
> Vers ce rivage heureux d'où le sort m'exila.
> C'est là que je voudrais vivre,
> Aimer et mourir — C'est là ! "

When Wilhelm says, "Adieu, Mignon! Courage!" the melody is touching, — speaking, so to say, — hardly sur-passed by the sympathetic duet between the two unfortu-nate persons, ignorant of what they are. The cradle of Lothaire, the gentle romance of Wilhelm, the prayer of Mignon, give character and part to each separate person-age in the drama. There are few works in which the characters have been so faithfully drawn, and so artistically finished by the musicians.

The last of Thomas's operas is "Hamlet," performed at the Grand Opera, March 9, 1868. This very successful work adds to the glory of the artist.

Besides the compositions above cited, the author wrote "La Gipsy," "Le Panier fleuri," "Carline," "Le Roman d'Elvire," a requiem, several church pieces, songs, &c. His "Le Tyrol" was listened to with pleasure at the Exposition universelle, 1867.

TAUBERT.

1811–.

WILHELM TAUBERT, a distinguished composer, was born at Berlin in 1811. His teachers were Berger and B. Klein. He was chapel-master at the Royal Opera in Berlin for a number of years. His operetta called "Die Kirmese," produced in that city in 1832, was well received, as was "Blue Beard," a romantic opera. His "Kinderlieder" are much esteemed. Taubert was the author of Jenny Lind's "Birdling" song.

THALBERG.

1812–1871.

THALBERG was one of the most remarkable pianists of this century. Sigismund Thalberg was born at Geneva, Jan. 7, 1812. He was the son of Count Dietrichstein, and at an early age received musical instruction from Hummel and Mittag.[1] When fifteen years old he began to play before amateurs, whose suffrage he easily obtained.

In 1828, when sixteen, he published [2] variations upon the themes of the "Euryante" of Weber. When older the composer treated the first productions of his youth with disdain : however, it is not difficult to find, in these first

[1] Thalberg was very young when taken to Vienna, and placed under the instruction of these teachers. His precision in fingering was remarkable for a child of his age.

[2] He studied the theory of music with Simon Sechter.

essays, gems of the character by which his style is distinguished.

In 1830 the artist commenced his first musical tour
through various cities of Germany ; and the newspapers,
classic trumpeters of fame, began to make his feats of
skill known to the musical world.

He had composed a concerto for piano and orchestra,
which he performed during his peregrinations ; but this
attempt in a kind of music unsuited to his talent did not
prove successful.   The piano was emphatically his instrument, and he well deserves to be placed among its masters.

In 1834 Thalberg was attached to the Austrian court, as
pianist of the imperial chamber.   He accompanied the
Emperor Ferdinand to Toeplitz, where he delighted the
sovereigns there assembled, and was laden with compliments and presents.[1]

After he had gone through and received the applause
of nearly all Europe, Thalberg unwisely followed the
advice of imprudent friends, and brought his operas
" Florinde " and " Christine " upon the stage, where these
attempts met with poor success.   But fortune, though un-
faithful on the stage, never ceased her favors elsewhere.

Thalberg visited America at different times, and the
concerts he gave in the United States and in Brazil were
very productive.   The artist bought an estate near
Naples, where he had a vineyard, and made a wine of
fine quality, which yielded him a handsome income.   Our
celebrated pianist did not disdain to submit the wines of
this vineyard to the jury of the Exposition universelle of
1867.   Among Thalberg's productions were excellent

---

[1] The wife of the composer, whom he married in 1845, was a daughter of Lablache
the singer, and widow of the painter Bouchot.

pieces for the piano.[1] His studies for the same are much
esteemed by many teachers, and have formed able pupils.
He died April 27, 1871.

FLOTOW.

1812–.

FLOTOW is a gentlemen who cultivates music with talent and success. Not that he may be considered among
the number of inspired artists, whose lips, like those of
the prophet Isaiah, have been touched with heavenly fire ;
but he has taste, great refinement, and a good method.
He knows how to frame an elegant idea in an agreeable
orchestration. What more is necessary if one aspires to
shine only among stars of the second magnitude in the
musical galaxy?

Count Frederic de Flotow was born in feudal Mecklen-
burg-Schwerin, at Teutendorf, an old patrimonial estate,
on the 27th of April, 1812. Young noblemen in Germany
have no choice between the career of arms, or diplomacy.
Flotow's father was commander of a squadron in the Prussian service, and he looked forward to making his son
Frederic an ambassador.

When the lad was sixteen years old he was sent to Paris,
a visit to that city being considered necessary for foreigners of distinguished families. But the taste of the
youth not inclining him to feel anxious about gratifying
his father's ambition, led him to take advantage of his stay
in Paris for the study of composition with Reicha, who
had discovered an improved method of instruction. On

---

[1] Thalberg wrote a concerto, a sonata, nocturnes, many pieces for piano, and
fantasias, besides the two operas, &c.,which have already been mentioned

his return to his family after the revolution of July, when he was about nineteen, he wrote his first essays. Order being re-established in France, Flotow returned to Paris, appearing to limit his artistic pretensions to being heard by private societies. The opera of " Pierre et Catharine," his *début*, was performed by amateurs before it was brought out at the court of Mecklenburg. Then came " Rob Roy," an opera taken from Sir Walter Scott, and performed in a château near Paris ; and the " Duchesse de Guise," performed in 1840 for the benefit of the Poles. All the nobility of Paris were present at this last perform-ance, in which Mme. de Lagrange made her first appear-ance upon the stage.

Flotow did not really begin to make himself known to the public until 1839, when, in connection with Pilati, he gave " Le Naufrage de la Méduse." It was performed at Hamburg in 1846, under the name of " Die Matrosen " ("The Sailors"). " L'Esclave de Camoëns," represented in 1843, did not meet with merited success. The libretto is very interesting : it shows us the poet of the " Lusiad " proscribed, and dying of hunger. An Indian slave, whom he has with him, sings at the corners of the streets in the evening to nourish her master. The King of Portugal, ashamed of his ill-will towards Camoëns, pardons the poet, who in gratitude to the slave, his humble benefactress, marries her.

This composer, who never lost a good opportunity, remodelled the music of an opera by Niedermeyer, which had succeeded in Paris in 1837. It was played under the title of " Stradella," and received with marked favor throughout the principal cities of Germany. On hearing it, the Duke of Mecklenburg, conferred upon Flotow the title of Chamberlain, to which he afterwards added that of director of the ducal music. "L'Ame en Peine," a work put on the stage in Paris, 1846, had only an ephemeral existence, notwithstanding that in point of style, of dramatic conception, and of instrumentation, it is the most remarkable of Flotow's works.

If the composer had written no other than the works above mentioned, he would not have passed beyond the line of musical amateurs. In reality, there is little or no difficulty for a man of fortune and good social position to find a manager willing to bring out his works ; and less still to obtain the applauses of politeness from a suitably composed audience. All this, however, has nothing to do with art. But in 1847 Flotow received sincere applause and unalloyed success. In 1843 he had composed a ballet, "Lady Henrietta," in three acts. This ballet he remodelled, and brought out an opera, which was performed at Vienna in 1847, under the name of "Martha." The libretto, originally German, has been translated into French and Italian. In the German version, the action passes under the reign of Queen Anne ; the Italian places it in the fifteenth century ; and the French brings it nearer to our time. The sub-title of the work, "Der Markt zu Richmond" indicates the subject.

The composer has introduced a charming Irish melody into this opera, "The Last Rose of Summer."[1] Without the music, perhaps the pleasant poetry would scarcely be heeded by the multitude of careless readers. Thanks to the Irish melody, and its being made popular by the arrangement of Flotow, thanks to its interpretation by the most renowned singers of Europe, those stanzas have been applauded not only in the original, but in the languages into which they are translated.

[1] From the Irish Melodies of Thomas Moore

"Martha," the best known of Flotow's operas, has had wonderful success in Germany. However, we must not fail to remark, that, as regards harmony, it is far from perfect. But the work has great beauties, is well conducted, and the interest is sustained throughout. The charming manner in which Mme. Ronzeau (Nilsson) interpreted "Martha" at the Lyric Theatre, will long be remembered. Among other works given by Flotow are "Pianella," performed May 11, 1860. "Evening Songs," "Des Rêveries," overtures, romances, songs, trios for piano, violin, and violoncello, &c. But he who was the happy composer of "Martha" ought to be satisfied.

We give different versions of the, —

LAST ROSE OF SUMMER.
[The original.]

"'Tis the last rose of summer,
    Left blooming alone ;
All her lovely companions
    Are faded and gone ;
No flower of her kindred,
    No rosebud, is nigh
To reflect back her blushes,
    Or give sigh for sigh.

I'll not leave thee, thou lone one,
    To pine on the stem ;
Since the lovely are sleeping,
    Go, sleep thou with them.
Thus kindly I scatter
    Thy leaves o'er the bed
Where thy mates of the garden
    Lie scentless and dead.

So soon may I follow
    When friendships decay,
And from love's shining circle
    The gems drop away.

When true hearts lie withered,
    And fond ones are flown,
Oh ! who would inhabit
    This bleak world alone ?

[German version.]

Letzte Rose, wie wagst du
    So einsam hier blüh'n ?
Deine freundlichen Schwestern
    Sind längst schon, längst dahin.
Keine Blüthe haucht Balsam
    Mit labendem Duft,
Keine Blättchen mehr flattern
    In stürmischer Lüft.

Warum blüh'st du so traurig
    Im Garten allein ?
Sollst im Tod mit den Schwestern
    Mit den Schwestern vereinigt sein ;
D'rum pflück ich, o' Rose,
    Vom Stamme, dich ab,
Sollst ruh'n mir am Herzen,
    Und mit mir, ja, mit mir im Grab.

[Italian version]

Quì sola, vergin rosa,
    Come puoi tu fiorir ?
Ancora mezzo ascosa,
    E presso già morir ;
Non ha per te rugiade,
    Già colta sei dal gel ;
Il capo tuo già cade,
    Chino sul verde stel !

Perchè sola, ignorata
    Languir nel tuo giardin ?
Dal vento tormentata,
    In preda a un rio destin ?

> Sul cespite tremante
> Ti colgo, giovin fior !
> Su questo core amante
> Così morrai d'amor !

[French version.]

> Seule ici, fraiche rose,
> Comment peux-tu fleurir ?
> Alors qu'a peine éclose,
> Tu vis tes sœurs mourir,
> En ces lieux ne s'étale
> Que le deuil des hivers !
> Et la brise n'exhale
> Nul parfum dans les airs.

> Pourquoi seule ignorée,
> Languir dans ce jardin.
> L'aquilon t'a frappée,
> Ne fuis plus ton destin !
> Sur ta tige tremblante
> Laisse-moi te ceuiller,
> Et, d'amour palpitante,
> Sur mon cœur viens mourir.

WAGNER.

1813–.

RICHARD WAGNER,[1] the most distinguished musical composer of the future, was born at Leipzig, May 22, 1813. His father, a city official, died when he was but ten months old. His mother afterwards married the actor and painter Louis Geyer ; and he, having obtained an engagement in the theatre at Dresden, removed thither with his family.

The young Wagner was destined by his father-in-law to become a painter, but Geyer died before the boy had attained his seventh year.

1 " Wagner, the high priest of the so-called music of the future."

This event wrought a great change in the course of the child's education. He took lessons on the piano; but being unwilling to submit to the teachings of his professor, he gave it up, and, seized with a passion for poetry, he set himself to writing a tragedy.[1] Hearing one of Beethoven's symphonies, his natural love for music was roused, and he declared that he would be a musician.

He learned composition and harmony while studying philosophy and æsthetics at the university.[2] His first work, an overture, was performed at Leipzig, at the concert of the *Gewandhaus.* At the age of nineteen he wrote a symphony, which had tolerable good success. This symphony cost him so much labor, that he saw the necessity of studying fugue and counterpoint, which he had heretofore despised.[3]

These studies occupied him in the winter of 1834, while at Würzburg, whither he had gone for his health, which in 1835 was so far re-established that he accepted the situation of leader of the orchestra in the theatre of Magdeburg.

For this theatre he wrote "The Novice of Palermo," which had but one representation. The young composer was so vexed with the failure of his opera, that he broke his engagement at the theatre, and went to Königsberg to occupy a similar position. But he, who aspired to eclipse all contemporaneous artists, suffered considerable mortification in being obliged to direct the works of others while waiting to bring forward his own. He made but a short

[1] He was then at the school of Nicolaï in Leipzig.

[2] It is said that his family were much opposed to his devoting so much of his time to music.

[3] Never was a person more indefatigable in the study of Beethoven's works than Wagner. At this period of his life they seemed to occupy his day thoughts and night dreams.

sojourn in Königsberg, then went to Riga, where he had been offered the baton of chapel-master. But this time he did not go alone : a talented actress had not hesitated to give her heart and hand to, and share with him whatever might befall, "for better or for worse."

The troubles that Wagner had experienced at Königsberg, recommenced at Riga. He was continually obliged to contend with the ennui of an employment ill-suited to his ambition. Suddenly convinced that Paris was the only place in which his talent would be understood and admired as it ought to be, he applied himself arduously to the composition of a new opera for that city.

. "Rienzi," a romance of Sir Bulwer Lytton, furnished the subject for his opera. When he had sketched the score, and prepared the music for two acts, sanguine of success, he embarked for France, accompanied by his wife. The vessel in which our voyagers were, was wrecked on the coast of Norway, a circumstance that furnished him with ideas for another opera, viz., "The Phantom Vessel." For want of means to continue their journey, they were obliged to remain four weeks at Boulogne-sur-mer. Meeting Meyerbeer, Wagner made his projects known to him ; and he, after looking over the score, gave the young man several letters of introduction to musicians, and others interested in art. With these letters in his portfolio, the young master innocently imagined that he now had the open sesame to as many doors ; but experience soon undeceived him.

He had been mistaken in believing that he, a stranger and unknown, could force his way into the theatres in a trice. The director of the Academy of Music refused to get up the work.[1] The director of the Renaissance was

[1] The opera was in five acts, and altogether on too vast a scale for the generality of theatres.

more obliging to the composer ; but unfortunately he failed just as they were preparing for rehearsal. At this juncture, Wagner was happy to find a friend in Maurice Schlesinger, editor of the music, and proprietor of "The Musical Gazette," who employed him in writing articles for that paper.

Wagner had now passed two years in Paris, during which time he had been driven by necessity to arrange operas for the piano and other instruments, instead of bringing out his own compositions.[1] It was very hard, after so many dreams of glory and fortune. With the idea of being able to overthrow even the princes of music, how bitterly he must have felt the task of merely arranging their works. Happily he was never discouraged : he attended to the business furnished by Schlesinger, and worked upon a new opera, "Der Fliegende Holländer."

Meanwhile "Rienzi" was to be brought out at Dresden. No sooner had Wagner heard the news, than his only thought was to leave Paris, and fly immediately to Saxony, that he might overlook the execution of his work. Being in want of money, he sold the poem of "The Phantom Vessel" to the directors of the opera, for five hundred francs, reserving to himself the proprietorship in Germany.

The representation of "Rienzi" in Dresden in 1842, thanks to the splendid performance and singing of Mme. Schrœder-Devrient, was a success which fully repaid the composer for his disappointments whilst in France. This success was followed by his nomination as chapel-master

[1] The composer, who had met with no encouragement in Paris, determined to try elsewhere : he therefore sent the score of "Rienzi" to the director of the theatre in Dresden, who put it upon the stage.

to the King of Saxony, so that he at once became one of the most popular men in Dresden.　Under such flattering circumstances, he had no difficulty in bringing out his "Phantom Vessel" at the theatre in Dresden, under the name of "Fliegende Holländer."　This opera, given Jan. 2, 1843, but increased his fame.

Although innovators in general seem to despise those who have preceded them, few can resist the temptation of boasting of their predecessors.　Wagner is no exception, when he puts what he considers his musical reforms under the patronage of some revered names, some sincere friends of art.　Gluck and Beethoven are the two men whose doctrine he intends to develop.

His position in the Dresden theatre permitted him to put the "Alceste" of Gluck upon the stage.　But not satisfied with showing up the master-pieces of this composer in their pristine beauty, he must retouch them after his own ideas, — he must surpress certain airs and phrases that do not just accord with his own views ; and thus, under the pretext of refining and ennobling, he has despoiled it of many of its delicate inspirations.

"Tannhäuser" was finished and brought out at Dresden in 1845, with brilliant success.　The composer then commenced "Lohengrin," which was ready for the stage just as the revolution of 1848 broke out in Germany. Wagner, who was a republican, took an active part in the political events of the period, and was consequently one of the victims of the re-action that followed.　He fled to Zurich ; and there, reflecting upon the cruelties of fate, he gave himself up to the study of Schopenhauer.[1]

In 1850 the devoted and indefatigable Liszt, succeeded in having "Lohengrin" played at Weimar at the inaugu-

---

[1] Schopenhauer has been called a pessimist and an atheist.

ration of the statue of Herder, September, 1850. The celebrated pianist led the orchestra himself, and was presented with a silver baton by the artists. The perfect success of this opera insured that of other works by the same composer.

"Tannhäuser" was performed at the opera in Paris, March 13, 1861, interpreted by Niemann, the German tenor, and other first-class artists; but it failed to please the French, and did not succeed. Wagner then went to St. Petersburg, but his glory profited him nothing. New tribulations awaited him, when, on his return to Germany, he thought of bringing out his "Tristan and Iseult." The artists of all theatres refused to try to sing it, saying that it was badly written for the voice, and therefore could not be well executed. Annoyed and disgusted, the unhappy composer would in all probability have bidden adieu to an art from which he had received little else than vexation and disquiet, when his fortune suddenly changed.

The royal prince of Bavaria had been for some time one of the fanatic admirers of Wagner. He was scarcely seated upon the throne, under the title of Louis II., when he despatched a courier to his favorite musician, with a pressing invitation for him to appear at court. Soon after Wagner arrived at Munich, where the young king received him in princely style, made him leader of his chapel, and lodged him in the palace. The next year, 1865, "Tristan" was put upon the stage at Munich. In this opera the master affects more freedom from classic habits than he does in any of his previous compositions.

The royal favor placed at Wagner's disposition the means of realizing his views of dramatic art.

Munich soon promised to be the sainted city of musical heresy; but it seems that the artist had not the tact to

restrain himself from mixing in politics. His meddle
someness raised enemies ; and he was again obliged to
seek refuge in Switzerland, notwithstanding the affection
of the young king, who was forced to sacrifice his favorite to the necessities of the state.

In 1870 Wagner married for the second time, a daughter of his friend and admirer Liszt.

With the assistance of the music-loving King of
Bavaria, and the Wagner societies of different countries,
the composer has erected a theatre at Bayreuth, where he
proposes to bring out his operas on a grand and magnificent scale.

In a letter to a friend, Wagner says, "In spite of a
serious and scientific education, I had been from my earliest youth in constant and intimate association with the
theatre. This early youth of mine was passed during the
last years of the life of Carl Maria von Weber, who peri-
odically brought out his operas in the city where I lived, —
Dresden. I received my earliest impressions of music
from this master, whose melodies filled me with dreamy
seriousness, and whose personality fascinated me even to
enthusiasm. His death in a foreign land filled my childish heart with dismay. I first learned of Beethoven when
I was told of his death also, which occurred not long
after Weber's ; and I learned his music too, attracted to
it, as it were, by the enigmatical news that he was dead.
Excited by such sad impressions, a love for music developed more and more strongly within me. But it was
only later, and especially after my other studies had
introduced me to the knowledge of classical antiquity, and
had aroused in me the impulse to poetic efforts, that I
attained to the deepest musical study. I proposed to
compose the music for a tragedy I had written."

Friends of Wagner in Mannheim founded a society for the promotion of his enterprise, under the name of "The Richard Wagner Society." The example was soon followed by his friends in Vienna, where a second society was formed. Soon Pesth, Brussels, London, and finally New York, had their "Wagner Societies."

Mr. Hullah says, "The new theory propounded by Wagner is, that the world has not yet seen a work of art in the production of which the poet and the painter and the musician and the *corps dramatique* have worked with equal energy and success ; that such a work is possible ; and that, being achieved, it would at once restore poetry to its ancient influence on the feelings and the actions of mankind, turn painting to a thoroughly practical account, and transform music from the mere amusement of an idle hour into a vehicle for communicating the noblest impulses and exciting to the noblest deeds."

VERDI.

1814-.

GIUSEPPE (JOSEPH) VERDI was born Nov. 9, 1814, at Bassetto, in the dukedom of Parma. He was early initiated into a knowledge of music, and obtained some notions of harmony from an organist in his native town. This kind of teaching did not lead the young artist very far, and he seriously felt the necessity of more thorough instruction ; but he belonged to a poor family, who could ill afford to maintain him away from home. Fortunately he became acquainted with a generous man, Signor Barezzi, who offered to be at the expense of his musical education until his talent should secure for him the means of support. Verdi was about nineteen, so there was no time to lose ; and he accepted the proposition of his kind benefactor with a thankful heart.

In the summer of 1833 he went to Milan, with the intention of entering the Conservatory of that city ; but the director refused to admit him among his pupils. Whether it was because he looked like a statesman rather than an artist, as some say, we know not ; but we do know that the unhappy candidate of 1833 was in a few years avenged by the brilliant success he everywhere met. Instead of being a pupil at the Conservatory, Verdi placed himself under the direction of a musician attached to the theatre of La Scala. During three years he studied hard ; then he commenced composing marches, serenades, &c.

This dramatic *début* took place Nov. 17, 1839, at Milan, by the representation of "Oberto di San Bonifacio," which was favorably received by the public. The same may be said of "Nabuchodonosor," which was represented in 1842. With this opera the reputation of Verdi commenced. "Lombardi" and "Ernani" followed. These also being successful, it was natural that the master should feel sanguine of success ; but he soon learned, to his cost, that the theatre is a field of battle, where one has to fight continually. The public began to grow tired of the master's violent manner,[1] which, however, they had enjoyed in his preceding works. Therefore the six operas that he gave from 1845 to 1847 were so many failures. That was enough to discourage a less energetic man ; but Verdi, who possessed a character of unchangeable firmness, was not thus to be discouraged. He went to Paris, made some changes in one of his operas, and brought it out successfully. But his good fortune did not last long. Of the four

[1] In some of his works force seemed to be a prominent feature.

operas that he gave in Italy in 1850, one only, "Louisa Miller," written for Naples, succeeded.

"Rigoletto" is the first work by which the composer gained renown in Europe. This opera was performed for the first time at Venice, March 11, 1851. The description of the storm, the gusts of wind, obtained by means of chromatic thirds vocalized behind the scenes, *a bocca chiusa* (with closed mouths), was entirely new. One advantage that Verdi has over other masters, who do not spare means to produce effects, is, that he never fatigues an audience. Always short and rapid, when he has attained the end sought for he insists no longer, but passes on to something else.

The conception of this opera is bold, and the effect admirable. The melody is very pleasing, and each personage preserves his own characteristic very distinctly.

Before the performance of "Rigoletto," it was a question whether a successor of Donizetti was found. But after this master-piece there was no longer any doubt on the subject; and Verdi, in giving "Il Trovatore," an opera in four acts, performed at Rome, Jan. 17, 1853, gained the entire suffrage of the people. There was tragic enough in the poem of this opera to furnish the composer with means for the expression of violent emotions. The interrupted phrases of Leonora may be considered as an effect properly belonging to Verdi. The appogiaturas, broken by rests of short duration, well express the beatings of a heart under the influence of strong emotion, either of grief or joy. We observe the same thing in "Rigoletto."

"La Traviata," an opera in three acts, brought out at Venice in March, 1853, shows the master's liking for sad and painful subjects. "La Traviata" is Alexander Du-

mas' "Dame aux Camélias." Those who are familiar
with this opera must know what a painful impression is
caused by the sight of a young woman in consumption,
whose cough is heard in every scene, even amid the laughter of drunkards and gay companions. Verdi's music
accepts such subjects. Many parts of this opera merit a
place among the best this composer has written. The
fault of the instrumental performance is, that it frequently
drowns the voice instead of sustaining it.

Verdi's " Vêpres Siciliennes," an opera in five acts, was
composed for the French theatre, and represented at Paris,
June 13, 1855. Notwithstanding that this work is more
carefully written than some others, it has never been
accepted as one of his best. "Un Ballo in Maschera,"
written for Naples in 1858, was forbidden by King Ferdinand, but performed the next year at Rome. In 1862 the
composer was invited to St. Petersburg, to bring out " La
Forza del Destino," taken from a romantic Spanish drama.
At the end of the play there is not a person left : they are
all dead ; and not only that, but one of them died several
times. What, then, must have been the force of destiny ?
"Don Carlos," an opera in five acts, was performed in
Paris, 1867. It is the work of a great musician, but has
little variety and less melody than the other works of the
same master. Besides, the piece, though taken from the
magnificent drama of Schiller, is not pleasing to the
generality of listeners.

Fortune comes with fame. Verdi is more than a prophet
in his own country. He is a wealthy landholder, possessing an immense property near Basseto, his birthplace,
where he has built a splendid villa. Ask any peasant for
leagues around, and he will direct you to the fine villa,
besides informing whether you will be likely to meet the

professor or not. Here the composer goes to seek rest from the fatigues and annoyances to which he is subject in large cities. Here, with his gun upon his shoulder, he walks from farm to farm, making a conscientious study of agriculture. The country people all love and respect him. In the evening, when he goes out to walk with Signora Verdi,[1] the laborers unite in singing some of the finest choruses of his operas.

The cry, " Viva Verdi ! " has often resounded in Lombardy, and even in Piedmont. At the time of the war against Austria, it was the rallying cry. The word of the popular enigma is well known. The five letters of the name of Verdi are the initials of those of Vittorio Emmanuele Rè d'Italia. The composer was known to be very liberal withal, so that nothing was more natural than that he should have a seat in parliament.

Verdi has been reproached by distinguished critics for acting upon the nerves rather than upon the feelings, and addressing the senses rather than the heart. This, to a certain extent, cannot be denied ; but are not the public in fault that they allow the senses to be acted upon, rather than the mind and the heart?

Finally the Leonora of Verdi, in the " Trovatore," does not make us forget the Leonora of Donizetti in the " Favorita ; " neither does the interesting Gilda of " Rigoletto " eclipse the unfortunate but charming Lucia. However, it is none the less true, that, since the death of Bellini and Donizetti, his superiors in art, Verdi is the only Italian composer who has given us inspired works.

Aside from his ability as a composer, we respect Verdi for the gratitude he ever and openly manifested towards

[1] Signora Verdi was the daughter of Barezzi, married in 1839.

Barezzi, the friend of his youth, and without whom his musical talent would, in all probability, never have been known to the world.

WALLACE.

1815-1865.

ACCORDING to Clément, William Vincent Wallace was born at Waterford, Ireland, 1815. His father, leader of the military music in that place, gave him instruction, and then sent him to Dublin, where the young artist studied, and soon became a skilful performer on the piano, violin, and clarinet. At the age of fifteen he was nominated organist of the Cathedral of Thurles, and soon after leader of the orchestra of the theatre and concerts of Dublin. He directed the first representation in Ireland of the oratorio of Beethoven, " Christ on the Mount of Olives."

At the age of eighteen he had a severe fit of sickness, which endangered his life, and the physicians advised him to make a very long voyage. The rest of Wallace's life was spent in wandering and odd adventures. Following the doctor's advice, he went to Australia, where he gave concerts, and reaped a rich harvest. Thence he went to Van Dieman's Land and New Zealand.

The inhabitants of this last island were accused of having devoured some English seamen, and a frigate was preparing to go and chastise the anthropophagi. Wallace joined the crew ; and, after witnessing the cannonading of the Zealanders, he took it into his head to live among them for a while. The project was a very bold one ; but the artist, filled with the spirit of adventure, knew no fear. The surgeon of the frigate, who wished to botanize in the

Bay of Pounamon, gladly accompanied him. Both these young men, with no other security than the promise of two chiefs who had sworn friendship and protection to them, passed several weeks among the savages, living the same life as their hosts, generally speaking. A young girl named Tetea became very much in love with the artist, who, like Orpheus among the women of Thrace, could not reciprocate her affection, and thus came near being a victim to the fury of this Oceanic beauty. Just as he was about to quit the island, Tetea gave him a striking proof of her love, by piercing him in the breast, and drinking his blood as it gushed from the wound. Of course Wallace was but too happy to escape such savage tenderness.

The composer continued his wanderings, however, going to the East Indies, the West Indies; to Mexico, where he directed the Italian Theatre ; to New York, where he was well paid for his concerts, and where he remained a long time for him. In 1846 he again went to Europe, where he wrote the romantic opera of " Maritana," which is much liked by amateurs of delicate and refined taste.

His " Matilda of Hungary," brought out the following year, was well received. After a long silence Wallace returned to the stage in 1860 with "Luzinne," an opera in three acts, which was performed in London to admiring audiences.[1] This work was soon followed by the " Triumph of Love."

The style of Wallace shows that he had a good musical education, combined with originality and boldness. His instrumental performances are well managed, and in many respects he is much superior to other English composers. The overture of " Lorely," heard in all popular concerts of classical music, proves our assertion.

[1] In 1861 he wrote the " Amber Witch."

Independently of his dramatic works, this artist has written a great number of light works, such as nocturnes, waltzes, studies, &c. The health of Wallace was in a very bad state when he went to Paris, where he attempted to bring out some of his works. Still suffering, he retired to Passy. While there he composed the first act of an opera for the theatre of London; but, too unwell to finish the opera, he again went South. He died at Château de Bayen, Oct. 12, 1865.

FRANZ.

1815–.

Robert Franz, a highly esteemed song-composer, was born June 28, 1815, at Halle. There was nothing in his father's house calculated to incite a love of art in the boy: on the contrary, all that did not belong to daily life, in the common sense of the last century, was cast aside as useless and pernicious, so that his early youth passed without any manifestation of the talent he afterwards displayed. At the age of fourteen he tried to acquire the elements of music, without assistance from his relatives, who, however, when they were convinced of his ability, procured him the desired instruction.

Franz decided upon music as a profession, and studied diligently at the Gymnasium of the Waisenhaus. In 1835 he went to Fred. Dessau, then to Schneider, with whom he studied composition.

After his return to his father's house, in 1837, he was in great trouble. He was not sufficiently advanced in music to make his music profitable, and his relations and friends were not sparing in unkind remarks as to the negative results of his studies. At this period of contest, anxiety, and doubt, he might have succumbed, had not his mother, with a woman's perception and a loving heart, encouraged him to follow his bent.

He studied Bach, and made himself acquainted with some of the more modern composers. Finally he attained honor and success in the career of a composer. He lived in Halle, where he was an organist and director of the singing academy and concerts.

BENNETT.

1816–.

WILLIAM STERNDALE BENNETT was born at Sheffield, Eng., in 1816. He lost his parents when quite young, and was educated by his grandfather in Cambridge, who sent him to King's College Chapel, where he sang in the choir. A few years after he was sent to the Royal Academy of Music in London, and studied under Crotch, Holmes, and Potter. He was a good pianist, and had written some excellent compositions when he went to the musical festival at Dusseldorf. Mendelssohn was much pleased with his performance, and signified his approbation, which proved very advantageous to the youth. The newspapers prepared the way for a favorable reception on his return to London.

In 1835 Bennett played one of his own compositions at the concert of the Philharmonic Society with good success.

" In 1836 he brought out his overture of ' The Naïades,' the most popular of his works." In February, 1838, he was admitted as a member of the Royal Society of Music. In 1843 he commenced a series of chamber concerts, which were given annually for twelve years.

Besides a considerable number of compositions for

pianoforte alone, as well as in connection with stringed instruments, he also composed overtures for poems in the Mendelssohn style, and arranged some exercises for his pupils under the name of "Classical Practice for Pianoforte Students." A lecture of Bennett's on harmony, delivered in 1848 at Queen's College, London, was published in the introductory lectures of the college. In 1856 the University of Cambridge appointed him professor of music, and at the same time he succeeded Richard Wagner as leader of the Philharmonic Concerts in London. He brought out his cantata, "The May Queen," in 1858, at the musical festival in Leeds. His composition for the opening of the International Exhibition of 1862 was less favorably received.

GADE.

1817-.

WILLIAM NEILS GADE, a distinguished composer of modern times, was born at Copenhagen, 1817. His inclination to music was manifested while he was yet a child, but his musical education was for a time very limited: however, when he did receive first-class instruction, he improved rapidly, and it was not long before he was able to enter the Royal Chapel as violinist. He turned his attention to composition, which he studied zealously. His first overture, "Nachklänge von Ossian," received a prize from the Musical Society of Copenhagen in 1848. This distinction not only gained for him a name, but also a travelling stipend from the king. It is said that Gade wrote to Mendelssohn about this time, and sent him a copy of his best symphony. Mendelssohn, charmed with Gade's music, said, in answer to the letter, "You begin where I leave off."

The Danish musician accepted the invitation of the musical director of Leipzig, and passed the winter of 1843 in that city, where his symphony received the prolonged applause of musical connoisseurs. The news of Gade's success created a sensation in Copenhagen, and from that time forth the Danes proclaimed their fellow-countryman a great master.

In the spring of 1844 our composer went to Italy, but returned to Leipzig and took charge of the direction of the Gewandhaus Concerts in Mendelssohn's absence. During the seasons of 1845–6, he directed the concerts in turn with Mendelssohn; and after the death of the latter he directed alone, until he went back to his native city in 1848. In 1850 he took the leadership of the Musical Society's concerts, received the title of professor of music, and was chosen leader of the music of the Royal Theatre.

Though less masterly in some respects than Mendelssohn or Schumann, he is their equal in delicacy of expression. His earlier compositions have a peculiar charm in the tinge of Northern romance which he knows so well how to give them. In his more modern works he has freed himself somewhat from this local coloring.

He has written seven symphonies, five overtures; "Comala," for solo, chorus, and orchestra; "Erlkönigs Tochter," likewise for solo, chorus, and orchestra; the opera "Marietta," besides a great number of songs, quartets, &c.

The story of Comala runs thus: Comala, daughter of a king of green Erin, smitten with a violent passion for Fingal, abandons her paternal roof for the Scandinavian hero, whom she follows, disguised in manly attire. King Fingal, affected by the devotion of the young princess, whose irresistible beauty had at first seduced him, prepares to marry her, when war breaks out with the Romans, under the Emperor Caracalla. Fingal goes forth to meet the enemy. Finding that Comala was determined to follow him in the midst of dangers, he ordered her to stop at a certain distance from the field of battle, promising that if he escaped death he would come to meet her that very night. Sad and silent the royal maiden waits; her two dogs lay crouched at her feet, her noble face leans upon her arm, her loose hair waves with the breeze of the mountain, she turns her blue eyes to the field of battle.

Meanwhile, Hidallan, son of Lemor, is sent by the king to announce to Comala his victory and his return. Like Jago, Hidallan has loved, and his disdained love is changed into a sentiment of ferocious jealousy. A messenger of joy and happiness, he perfidiously relates the false news of the defeat and death of the hero.

A flourish of trumpets interrupts the lamentations of Comala : it is Fingal who comes, surrounded by his bards and his warriors. They salute him, they proclaim him triumphant : all recognize Fingal except the pale young girl, whose grief has broken her heart. Prey to a melancholy allusion, she sees only the ghost of her well-beloved. "Oh, take me to thy dwelling, and let me partake of thy repose, dear child of Death!" It is in vain that Fingal tries to reason with her. The fatal idea has taken possession of her, and when she recognizes the truth it is too late. The death which she invoked has answered her appeal. "It is him, it is Fingal! He comes in his glory! his victorious hand presses mine ! Ah! let me sit upon this rock until calmness enters my troubled soul. My harp ! give me my harp ! Sing your songs, daughters of Morna !" This delicate and tender soul could not overcome so many emotions : joy finished what despair had commenced.

GOUNOD.

1818-.

GOUNOD possesses a good knowledge of his art; but passionate for innovations, he has introduced a singular element, which belongs rather to literature and philosophy than to the science of sound. Thence arises the obscurity complained of in his works. Very classic in form, very faithful to the traditions of the masters in the disposition of his orchestra, he is nevertheless romantic in his tendencies and in the choice of his librettos.

Charles Francis Gounod, one of the most prominent French composers of the present time, was born in Paris, June 17, 1818. He studied music at the Conservatory of his native city, under Halévy, Reicha, and Lesueur. In 1839 he obtained the prize for composition, and was sent to Rome as stipendiary of the government. Here he busied himself with the study of old Italian church-music, and became so much attracted to the beauties of this branch of his art, that for a long time he entertained serious thoughts of consecrating himself to the priesthood. One of his masses for voices alone was sung at Vienna in 1843.

On his return to Paris he was made chapel-master of the Church of Foreign Missions, and devoted himself to sacred music with a zeal that showed the tendency of his mind. He even wore the ecclesiastical habit for a time. Certain it is that many years passed before the name of Gounod was familiarly heard in public. Since that time, however, he has well proved that he does not despise the trumpet of fame, or yield to any one in legitimate ambition. If, then, he suffered himself to be forgotten for a while, it was, it seems, that he was preparing for a contest, and did not wish to enter the lists until fully armed.

Suddenly, in the beginning of 1851, it was reported that the ex-aspirant to priestly orders was about to bring before the public four compositions in a concert given at Saint-Martin Hall, London. The article in " The Atheneum " which announced this news signalized it as a musical event, and produced much sensation. Gounod was no longer unknown. All eyes were turned upon him, when in April, 1861, he brought out " Sappho," an opera in three acts, upon the first lyric stage in France. The public did not appreciate this opera, but the musicians prophesied well for the young musician. The choruses of " Ulysses," sang soon after, met with a similar fate. The composer, who seemed ambitious to put his stamp on all kinds of music, tried comic opera in " Le Médecin malgré lui," Jan. 15, 1858. But this work of Molière did not yield to the transformation Gounod desired to make, and remained much less a comic opera than a comedy, of which the music did not appear to make an integral part. However, no one will dispute that it abounds in pleasant details, and displays great musical knowledge.

But the work to which Gounod owes his renown, and the immense popularity he enjoys, is " Faust," an opera in five acts, performed March 19, 1859. This immortal conception of Goethe, has had the privilege of a crowd of imitations or emanations, more or less direct.

Two works, given by Gounod soon after, did not succeed ; but " Mireille," taken from the charming poem " Mireio " of Mistral (an author admired in the South of France before Lamartine praised him in his " Entretiens littéraires,") was received with unbounded applause.

Some people may reproach Gounod, saying, What ! he

who has borne the habiliments of a priest, and who ought to have some respect for religion, — how could he borrow the "Lauda," "Sion," "Salvatorem," from the Catholic liturgy, for the theatre? We do not venture to call it profanity; but there are pious people who see in it an impropriety to be regretted. The *chef-d'œuvre* of the liturgy belongs to the Church, and should not be heard elsewhere. The ear and the heart of the pious auditor are pained to hear it given by the artist of a theatre. Christianity has not become mythology, where one has a right to take what he chooses in order to produce dramatic effect. In general, composers have been careful not to infringe upon songs consecrated to public worship: they have taken pains to write special music to express effects they needed. Gounod would have done better had he followed their good example.

If Gounod had given himself freely to his natural faculties; if he could have been satisfied with being a good musician, a thorough artist, — in all probability he would have produced works still more remarkable, superior works, that would have defied all criticism. Instead of which, he troubled himself with the imaginary theories of able musicians, and tried to bring together the different elements of the past and those of the so-called music of the future.

Gounod has written a great deal of music of all kinds, — operas, comic operas, sacred music, symphonies, choruses, &c.; among which "La Sérénade" is always sung with pleasure. Every one must acknowledge that he is an able and skilful musician of great talent.

OFFENBACH.

1819–.

Music has the power of ennobling all that to which it is united. The simplest words become important ; the most common thoughts lose their grossness ; sound and rhythm give harmony to the movements of the body, which deprived of this accompaniment would be mere contortions. Can any thing more clownish be imagined than dancing without music ? Unfortunately, however, our greatest gifts are sometimes profaned by being transformed into mere parodies, dangerous to the public taste, and degrading to those who invent and profit by them.

The opera bouffe, for instance, which amuses us by its light and pleasant melodies, loses its charm when carried to excess.

Jacob Offenbach, composer of burlesque comic operettes, was born at Cologne, July 20, 1819, of an Israelitish family, one of the members of which, a chorister in the synagogue of that city, published songs commemorative of the exodus from Egypt, with a German translation, and ancient traditional melodies, in 1838. Jacob's musical talent displayed itself at a very early age ; and his father, a distinguished chapel-master, taught him until he was thirteen, when he sent him to the Conservatory of Paris, then under the direction of Cherubini, where he remained until 1837, after which he played the violoncello in the orchestras of different theatres, and finally in that of the comic opera. In 1841 he brought out some of his own compositions, and became known as concert-violoncellist. At this time the young musician manifested his originality and taste for parody and eccentricities. Thinking, doubtless, that the sound of the violoncello was insufficient in itself, he imitated the violin and other instruments. He imitated the bagpipe so well that he misled his hearers, and excited the enthusiasm of the uneducated class, who formed the majority in the concerts of that time. In 1848 he went to Germany, but returned to Paris in 1850, when he was engaged as leader of the orchestra in the French Theatre through the influence of Mlle. Brohan.

The deplorable state into which the orchestra had fallen was proverbial. Offenbach wished to make this the starting-point of his fortune. He got up the characters, composed pretty little airs, preluded parodies of La Fontaine's Fables, the publication of which obtained for him considerable success. The manner in which he made his orchestra execute Gounod's beautiful music for the choruses of " Ulysses " did him great honor. Meanwhile his talent for jesting, drollery, and buffoonery was becoming more and more known in his circle of acquaintances. Artists and writers pressed him to take advantage of it in the music he wrote for theatres. But while he found no difficulty in getting texts, he for a while could find no theatre willing to bring out such works as he was desired to write.

Finally, in June, 1855, Offenbach's wishes were fully realized : he had a theatre for himself. He obtained a privilege for the Bouffes-Parisiens, which he installed in the Champs-Elysées. The new theatre was inaugurated by the performance of " Les Deux Aveugles." His success was so great, that hardly had a year expired when he was obliged to exchange his theatre in the Champs-Elysées for the large Salle-Comte in the centre of the city.

Among the multitude of pieces given by this composer we will notice " La Rose de Saint Flour," an operette in one act. An agreeable romance and a duet are about all that is of any account in it.

"Orphée," played for the first time in 1858, is a grotesque and clownish parody, which commences by transforming Orpheus into a master of the violin giving private lessons, and finishes by a vulgar dance. This work obtained immense success. It was given over four hundred times in Paris alone. "Orphée" was in every way advantageous to its authors : it not only drew full houses, but even the honorary favors that government voluntarily bestowed to success, if not always to the beautiful, the good, and the useful. This work has served as a sort of signal for the fabrication of pieces of the same stamp ; so that all the French theatres have been inundated with them, to the great detriment of good taste, wit, and art. Before long it was perceived that they had entered upon a dangerous path ; but the impulse had been too strongly given, they could not bridle it. Such kind of buffoonery replaces the pleasures of the mind, the ear, and the emotions of the heart, by unhealthy sensations. Many of the melodies, however, are charming : we would willingly acknowledge their artistic merit ; but then we cannot forget that they are associated with the grossest scenes.

In "Daphnis et Chloé" there are fine melodies ; and the same may be said of the operette "Fortunio." Offenbach, who had the singular idea of competing and offering prizes, made a musical tour through England with his troup in 1857, and through Germany in 1858. In 1860 he tried a ballet with the opera, but did not succeed.

In 1861 the composer tried "Barkouf" upon the stage of the comic opera ; which had the reception it merited in this theatre, where it was out place. The failure of this piece was partly owing to Scribe, the author of the libretto, who had chosen a dog for the hero of the piece. The frequenters of the comic opera, though not very particular in their selections, protested against this novelty.

Offenbach resumed the direction of the theatre, which he had given up for a while, and brought out several pieces : one of the most amusing was " Lischen und Fritzchen." The latter, an Alsacian domestic, murders the French language so outrageously that his master turns him out of doors. Just at the moment he is venting his grief in comic complaints, he meets Lischen, also a young Alsacian ; and the two speak so extravagant a language that they astonish each other. This little work is filled with pleasing melodies, and is very comical.

" La Belle Hélène, a burlesque composition, put upon the stage in 1864, has had unparalleled success in France, which nothing can justify, and which is not particularly creditable to the French taste of these times. Except the introduction, in which is a fine hautboy solo, there is nothing but dance-music and drolleries.

" La Grande-Duchesse de Gérolstein " has also attracted a crowd, although the music is less interesting than that of the preceding works of the composer. Such is the infatuation which this piece has caused, that at the time of the *Exposition universelle*, in 1867, many of the sovereigns of Europe, who were then in Paris, visited " La Grande-Duchesse."

To do Offenbach justice, it must be said that his talent as violoncellist is indisputable : he was a remarkable virtuoso before he became a composer ; he has great facility for composition, as his numerous works prove. Besides, he possesses originality, drollery, and good-humor. With such natural gifts, it is a great pity that Offenbach had not set a higher standard, so that he might have produced works

that would have placed him in the rank of the great masters.

This composer received the Grand Cross of the Legion
of Honor, Aug. 15, 1861.

RUBENSTEIN.

1829–.

ANTON RUBENSTEIN, the well-known pianoforte player
and gifted composer, was born at Wechwotynetz, Nov. 30,
1829.   He received his first musical instruction from his
mother, then studied with Alex. Willoing at Moscow.   At
eight years of age he played in public.   At eleven he
went with Willoing to Paris, where Liszt aided in unfold-
ing his talents.   He remained a year and a half in Paris,
then made a great artistic tour of three years, through
England, Germany, Holland, Sweden, &c. ; after which he
returned to his parents for a time.   Then his mother and
brother Nikolaus accompanied him to Berlin.   Whilst in
this city he took lessons in composition of Dehn, and frequently played at court.   His mother and brother being
recalled to Russia by the death of his father, Rubenstein
was now thrown upon his own resources.   In 1846 he
went to Vienna, where he busied himself in giving and
taking lessons.   He did the same for a while in Presburg.

In 1848 he went to St. Petersburg, and was appointed
chamber-virtuoso by the Princess Hélène.   In this situation he had leisure to pursue his studies in composition.
In 1854 he made another tour through Germany, France,
and England, in order to make his music more generally
known.   Afterwards he became director of the concerts of
the so-called Russian Musical Society, and leader at the
newly erected Conservatory in St. Petersburg.   As a piano-

forte player, Rubenstein takes a place among the virtuosi
of the first rank. As a composer, he must be reckoned
among the most gifted of this generation.

His principal works are the Russian operas, " Dimitri
Donskoi," " Die Sibir Jäger," "Die Rache," "Toms der
Narr ;" and the German operas " Die Kinder der Heide,"
and " Feramors " (" Lalla Rookh ") ; besides the oratorio
" Das verlorene Paradies ;" symphonies, overtures, songs,
&c.

His younger brother Nikolaus, born at Moscow, 1838,
studied with Willoing and Kullak in Berlin. He is an
excellent piano-player, and has published his composition
for that instrument.

ALPHABETICAL INDEX.